FROM THE TEXAS PRAIRIE TO THE MOUNTAIN TOP

A Journey from Rags to Riches

To Steve
Conquer Your mountains
Love
Stacy

Sidney Randolph Bonvallet

From the Texas Prairie to the Mountain Top
A Journey from Rags to Riches
All Rights Reserved.
Copyright © 2024 Sidney Randolph Bonvallet
v4.0 r1.0

ISBN: 979-8-218-97612-5

Extraordinary Measures Publishing

PRINTED IN THE UNITED STATES OF AMERICA

For my beloved children

Table of Contents

Introduction

When I talk about "rags to riches," I use it as a metaphor to describe the levels of enlightenment my life has taken me through. But it also refers to literally climbing up from the dark pit of poverty to prosperity, and the reality of climbing several mountain tops.

I do not believe in coincidences or accidents; I believe things happen for a reason. My life taught me so many valuable lessons. Some very hard or painful and some surprising and joyful. Each one had a part in shaping the person I became. I feel as if I am still "becoming," even as an octogenarian. Ever since I was old enough to understand the concept of God, He has been my constant companion, navigating the journey that was meant for me. I know I have a reason to be on this planet.

I have been blessed with an extraordinary life, and this is my story. Each chapter is a vignette that makes up the larger story. Before I grew and matured a little, I would have said I had been cursed and blessed. But in hindsight, one step after another, over time, the puzzle pieces came together to teach me I had a God-blessed destiny. To fulfill it, I had to have the many experiences that made up the fragments of my life. Some experiences that appeared at first to be curses ultimately became diamonds in my jewel chest of adventures that led to the mountain top.

The characters in my story are me, my momma, and my daddy, my four precious siblings, Wayne, my three children, an occasional villain or bully, and many mentors, earth angels, heroes and guides. I needed them all, and they came. I have had a life of incredible joy, love, magic, and enlightenment foreshadowed with trauma, abandonment, violence, and poverty. These various conditions revealed a broad spectrum of confusion, pain, and a passionate search for psychological and wellness healing to discover normalcy and balance.

In my various careers, which started with chopping and picking cotton, babysitting, ironing, and various retail jobs. Finally, I hired into General Motors as the lowest level clerk and resigned as an executive in the auto industry. My husband and I became business owners; I became a public speaker, life coach, Value Engineering Problem Solver, and we were leaders of personal growth seminars. One of the keys to leading a meaningful life is to learn from our experiences, both the positive and negative lessons. How did we respond to them? How did they impact that moment and our future? I saturated my healing journey with getting certified in amazing therapies like EMDR (Eye Movement Desensitization and Reprocessing), Integrated Breath Work, Theater, Role Playing, Reenactment, and many others. Each one I applied to my own life.

At the end of each chapter, I have included the lessons I learned from the featured experience and ask you to contemplate two questions that allow you to reflect on similar experiences in your life. We are humans and have many experiences in common. Such reflection gives you the opportunity to use your current wisdom in the present time to exchange pain for peace you may have experienced in the past. Or to see how you might take that experience out of the negative column and legitimately redefine the experience as positive given what you see in it now. You may have a similar experience to mine of gaining some very interesting insights as you consider your life in this way.

Let's get on the trail to discovery, shall we?

Momma's Remembrance of My Birth

Just as Momma wrote it in her journal in the year of 1998

Precious Sidney Flynn, you came to us October 15, 1940. We lived in Hermaleigh, Scurry County, Texas in the China Grove community, on a farm. Your Daddy paid for your birth with a wagon load of maize. He brought me a little tin tray that had 2 bars of soap on it. I gave that tray to you, and you still have it today.

Granny was at the house with us and stayed with us about two weeks. As you know, we had a hard time getting you born. You decided you would come out feet first, you were purple, and we thought we were losing you. When I heard that smack and you cried out, I was so happy. We were scared to death.

Well, back in my room when the nurse put you in my arms, I thought you were so beautiful, and I didn't want to let you go. I can still feel your sweet warm body cuddled up to me! The nurses would hold you and rock you every day. Granny took real good care of us. She would give us our malt-o-meal every morning and rock you and love you! And she cooked such good food for me. and of course, Ginger, Troy, Jo Katheryn and your Daddy.

My Daddy came and got us after about two weeks. He was tired of eating his own cooking, and he wasn't much on staying by himself. Well, so much for family. Your Daddy, Elvin, didn't care

(L – R) Jo Kathryn, Sidney Flynn and Troy Alvis Randolph. Ginger was in the house and Kayo wasn't born yet. We were living with Momma's parents.

for that too much. So, we landed at his folks outside of Midland.

We were back and forth to my mother and daddy's, and we ended up with my mother and daddy and he took off to work at Toya, Texas for a while. He got hurt there and came to Daddy's to work. That didn't last long. Then we lived in Lamesa two weeks in his aunt's house. Then he took us back to Mother and Daddy's. And

4

off for Dallas to Uncle Cecil's. We stayed there a while and then took off to Houston. We stayed with Uncle Matt and after a while, he took us to his mother and daddy's. We stayed with my in-laws, Mr. and Mrs. Randolph for a few weeks, and this was where we were when he came to get us.

He had been gone three or four months and you wouldn't go to him. You had forgotten him. You were about six months old at the time. That hurt him pretty bad.

Well next, it was to Houston. Elvin and a friend, in a one seat car, came for us and, to say the least, we were very crowded. We lived in a one-room apartment, out in Foster Place.

Mrs. Reynolds was our Landlady, a great big redheaded woman. She had had polio and walked with a cane. She did not care for Elvin at all, but she liked us and was good to us. She had three children Tony, Thelma and Bubba. They really loved you babies and played with you all the time.

Thelma carried you on her hip everywhere and loved you very much! She babysat for me some for 25 cents an hour.

<u>LESSONS</u>

- I learned about the difficulty of providing for a family at that time in history.
- I discovered with whom and how we lived. And that we were homeless in these times.
- I discovered kindness in other families trying to help us.
- I learned to be quiet, not to be a bother, and don't eat much. Because Daddy would drop us off at various relative's homes, Mother taught us these things, so we weren't such a burden. I learned the many times we were dumped is why I have a difficult time allowing anyone to help me. It became a misguided sense of pride thing. However, when we figure these things out, we have more mastery over our mysterious behavior. This pride showed up many times as I grew into adulthood. It will vividly show up in the chapter about my adventures.

<u>TWO QUESTIONS</u>

1.   What is your story of origin in your family?

2. Have parts of your life helped you understand more about that time in history? In thinking about your life, what has it taught you about your family?

My Destiny Born to Live God's Seeds of Greatness

For years, my mother told me the story that when I was being born, the doctor was so convinced that I wouldn't make it, he had "born" crossed-out, and "stillborn" typed in its place. Apparently, I had been what they called a "blue baby."

It was unheard of at the time, but the doctor had my Daddy come in the birthing

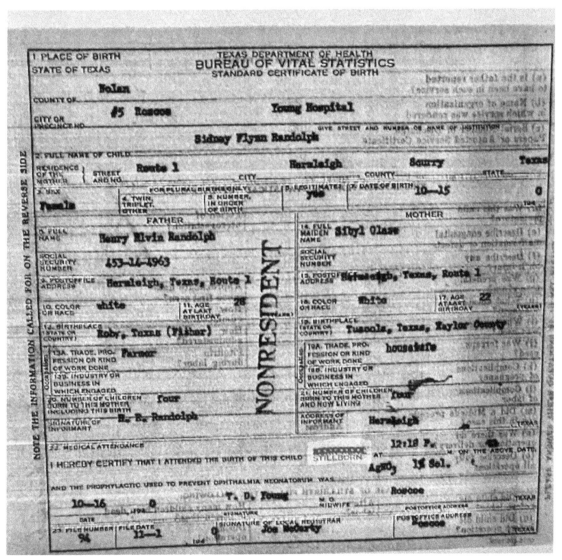

My original birth certificate where I was marked stillborn because of the assurance of my death.

room because he thought if I did live, it would only be for a few minutes. So, Daddy did.

Until I was 60 years old, no one, not even me, ever looked at the details on my birth certificate. That is, not until our business, empowerment, was hired by MGM Casino in Detroit to train people in team building, leadership, and confidence. Because it was a casino, we had to get bonded and go through FBI clearance. Being a new casino in town, MGM wanted us to train 4,000 people. This meant all our credentials had to be in order and impeccable. They told us to carefully read each document to make sure everything was correct so we could get the contract. I was doing the dull job of reading each document, word for word, and was stunned to read "stillborn," on my birth certificate. What a dilemma! This just would not do at all.

A chill ran up and down my body. I had not been born alive! Knowing this error would stop us in our tracks, I flew down to Texas, collected my little 81-year-old mother, loaded her up to drive her to the Sweet Water, Texas courthouse so she could validate that I was indeed born alive. We had to file the change we wished to make and then go to the Midland County Court House for the publication of a revised birth certificate.

Somehow, a date was wrong on the revision, and we had to get that certificate revised again and reissued. I ended up with three birth certificates. At the time, I was like a robot, getting all the documents in order, but not really thinking about the impact this has had on my life.

Slowly, the realization dawned on me. Being a parent now, I imagined what Momma and Daddy must have felt. Thinking I could die in their arms, yet seeing me live, would have been like a miracle, and they might have had such gratitude that they would have touched me in awe. Being a baby and babies are all feelings, I probably felt that energy. It answered one of the huge questions I have had for years. I have had the feeling from a very young age I was supposed to do something very important with my life.

I had to make a difference. After all, I was supposed to die but didn't, so I must have thought I was alive because God had a plan for me. My life has been confusing, full of obstacles and extreme poverty. This caused a lot of pain, enlightenment, overcoming, and touching lives.

The revision that changed "stillborn" to "born alive."

In 2008, when I was 68, my daughter, Cindy Christopher, my husband, Wayne, and I formed a 501(c)(3) charity to give back for all God and others, who I call my "earth angels," had given to me. If God had not walked the valleys with me in my life, and people had not helped me, my life would have turned out much differently. I feel everyone needs someone at different points in their life.

God's guidance in my life, and help from others, had a profound impact on me. Was I living the destiny for which I was spared? I had been brought back from the threshold of death. Was I living my greatness with passion? Was I following my star and shining to light the way for others?

These were deep and serious questions for me. I was supposed to be dead, but I am not. I'm alive, and I am here. How am I repaying that gift of life?

Momma told me that she and Daddy responded to me differently than they did to the older children. My daddy never punished me. Momma did that. But he could be very harsh in punishing Ginger and Troy, my two oldest siblings. They said Daddy never spanked Jo, Kayo, or me.

LESSONS

- I discovered the circumstances of my birth, which influenced the rest of my life.
- From my earliest memory, I felt I had a destiny. I was supposed to do something significant with my life. I had known for most of my adult existence, that I had to make a difference in our world to be fulfilled.
- There was a deep emotional connection between me and my parents, particularly with my mother. Despite the dysfunction in our family, I always felt the deep rootedness of my parents' love.

TWO QUESTIONS

1. Have you ever had a deep conviction or drive to "be" or "do" something significant with your life?

2. What life experience or thought process caused this? Where did it come from?

A Demon Lived in that Wind

Her name was Sibyl. No Southern nickname, or fancy middle name. Just plain Sibyl Randolph. She was young, smart, creative, and pretty. She had long, raven hair, bright, shiny blue eyes, and creamy delicate skin. She was the best storyteller in the whole world. And she was my Momma, a fact I appreciated. She married my Daddy, Henry Elvin Randolph, when she was only 16.

When he came riding up on a palomino horse to their one-room schoolhouse looking dashing as a movie star, what was she to do? She was smitten. But that is a whole other story. Momma could weave magic with her storytelling. When she uttered those sacred words, "Let me tell you a story," we gathered around her, and a hush fell over us as we anticipated her magic. When I was about six years old, she said she wanted to tell me a story about when I was a baby and a West Texas

The shanty house we lived in at the time. Momma tried to make whatever house we landed in a home.

11

sandstorm raged out of nowhere. Unless you've been to West Texas, or the Sahara Desert, you haven't experienced a real McCoy, sandstorm.

I was born in Roscoe, Texas, in Nolan County. Momma and Daddy moved to Tuscola, not far away, and share cropped a farm just out of town. We lived in a house she called a shanty house. It was old and rickety. The sad walls with peeling wallpaper, drooped, tired from all the years it clung to that fragile wall which didn't offer much protection from the weather. Farmers around these parts usually grew cotton, sorghum, and a garden of vegetables for their own table. One hot July day, Momma and Daddy were working in their garden, and some distance away, they saw a fierce wall of dirt, looming up to the sky, brawling in from the east. It was a sight to see. She said there is a difference between a dust storm and a sandstorm. A dust storm, with its small puffs of sand, is just a little whippersnapper next to a raging

I was a baby, and my parents had me near them in the garden.

12

sandstorm, the kind that has been known to suffocate babies and small animals. Texas sandstorms were something to be reckoned with.

When Momma and Daddy saw that great wall of dirt charging ahead of the sun toward us, blotting out daylight as it came, they sprang into action. Daddy ran to put the horse away, who was already spooked. The horse sensed danger and looked wild eyed at that ominous brown cloud. Fear griped the horse as he bucked at Daddy who desperately clutched the reins, grabbed their tools and got horse and tools into the shed. He then hauled thunder for the house. Momma had already grabbed me and ran ahead of Daddy to where my three older siblings were playing in the eerie silence. They knew they didn't have long before all heck broke loose. Momma frantically built a small tent out of a sheet and pillows, while Daddy secured the door and urgently started closing all the windows. Momma put me into the little tent, then pulled Ginger, Troy, and Jo under the bed clutching them to the safety of her bosom. The sand whacked that shanty so hard, it just shuddered, and whipped us around something fierce.

The sand blocked out the light of the sun, and the doom of night settled over us. The angry, howling wind sounded like a monster, bent on destroying everything, showing no mercy. Momma said there was a demon who lived in the wind, and it was shaking that whole house, rattling all the windowpanes as if they would explode out and be carried off into the dark abyss.

Inside, a heavy fog of sand swirled around, slapping up against the walls, engulfing us in an open tomb. It seemed like it would never let up, but it did. The storm eventually allowed the shanty to slip out of its clutches and passed on over, leaving a thick layer of dirt on everything. Which was disheartening to Momma since she liked to keep us and her house clean and orderly.

Momma and Daddy rushed over to the tent on the bed and gingerly lifted the sheet off. She said there I was, pristine in my little white dress. There wasn't a speck of dirt on me nor in the spot where the tent had been.

LESSONS

- We choose how we look at things. We can look at a situation, keep our spirits up, and start anew (which is what Momma did), or we can sit on the curb, cry, and say what bad luck we have, and the mess still doesn't get cleaned up.
- *Never give up.* I learned to keep strength in reserve for what happens after a disaster.
- Some parts of our life were rough, but Momma always just got up and kept on going.
- Even the unbearable seemed bearable because of her example of not giving up. And the hope in her stories.
- In all our challenges, I never saw Momma lose heart, except this one time on the prairie. I share this story with you now so later when you read the other story, "Cyclone," you can more clearly understand what happened when we lived on the prairie.

TWO QUESTIONS

1. Tell about a time you were discouraged, but you went ahead and did what needed to be done.

2. When were you faced with the choice of either being a victim or an overcomer? What did you choose?

A Dollar for My Tears

Back in the 1940s, one dollar was a lot of money. And that is how much my daddy offered me if I'd stop crying.

Despite the financially disadvantaged position we were in most of the years we were growing up, Momma was still able to capture more photographs of us kids than I thought would have been possible. We didn't have a lot, but we had enough to chronicle our lives. Relatives would take photos at events and give them to my dear momma. Ginger received a Brownie camera for a Christmas present from her boyfriend Miley Ed at the time. She took many of our photos that became treasures.

Momma's sister, whom we called Aunt Sissy, or Aunt Queenie, (but Aunt Sissy most often) was several years older than Momma. Aunt Sissy loved Momma with all her heart. She was often busy crocheting, knitting, or making ceramics. And when she wasn't, Aunt Sissy was doing something to help Momma, or to make her happy. On one occasion, she had crocheted me a soft, seafoam green, little over-jacket and sent it from Ackerly, Texas to Houston in the mail—which was a big deal. Momma had had to wait until I was nearly a year old before it fit me.

When I was a little less than one year old, Momma had her heart set on getting a professional photo of me. And she wanted Daddy to come along with us to the studio. Momma said we took a bus to downtown Houston and disembarked close to a professional photography studio. So, when this delicate little jacket came of size, Momma dressed me up real pretty and put Aunt Sissy's creation over my little white dress.

Upon arrival, the photographer set me up on a high table, and I started crying. He tried everything to get me to stop, but I was inconsolable, and cried even harder. Finally, not knowing what else to do, Momma *was not* going anywhere until she had a proper photo of me in Aunt Sissy's crocheted jacket, Daddy in desperation, pulled out a green dollar bill and said, "Mickey (my nickname), if you will stop crying, I'll give you this pretty one-dollar bill."

Well, what would you do for a dollar bill in the 1940s? Since I obviously didn't know the value of the dollar bill, maybe I liked the color, or maybe I just liked the idea of getting something. I quit crying. Momma wiped away my tears.

Right then and there a pattern was created. "Crying is bad, or at least, crying was not good. It is not allowed." As an adult, I would not have wanted to be a crybaby and cry at the drop of a hat, instead of being able to do what had to be done to correct the situation. By the same token, I didn't want to be an empty shell. So, in essence, I was rewarded *not* to cry and would have been punished (by not getting the prize) if I *did* cry. This was the first incident that began shaping my do-not-cry dilemma.

My green seafoam jacket and my dollar.

Unfortunately, I witnessed my older sister being beaten by Daddy and heard him say, "Stop that crying right now! You've got two minutes to shut that crying off, or I'll give you something to really cry about!" It scared me and reinforced the lie I already believed that it was not good to cry.

I find it very hard to cry, even now. There have been enough experiences in which I could not cry, thus unintentionally training myself to become stoic and not cry even when it would have been the appropriate thing to do. Even when something very painful happened, like when my sweet Granny died, I couldn't cry.

All that pain and sadness just went deep inside me, forming a hard, cold knot, and just got stuck there. I can't get the relief crying gives most people.

My momma told me this story about the dollar often enough that I began to believe I was able to remember this occasion. But I surely was too young to have remembered it on my own. Yet, what has intrigued me is that I have held onto this memory, and I still experience an emotional reaction when writing about it. My heart is saddened that as a child so young, I intuitively knew I wasn't allowed to have a normal feeling. This incident held one of the keys to my inability to grieve appropriately in the face of loss. I felt odd, that my behavior wasn't normal. Now I know that I was not heartless or unfeeling. My heart just did not have the permission to cry over losses as a normal person would do.

I lost my beloved husband Wayne, after 41 beautiful years of marriage. He was my soulmate, the love of my life. I not only allowed myself to cry and grieve, but I took wise advice and no matter when or where the tears came, I would give myself permission to experience the pain of this biggest loss of my life. I fought the fear of getting lost in the tears and encouraged myself to let the pain drain out with the rivulet of tears. It was actually a new experience for me, and it was so critical for me to discover I could live through it and come out better on the other side. I have said countless prayers to encourage myself to openly grieve this terrible loss, experience my emotions, and to allow myself to live through the pain. By openly giving myself permission to cry, I can feel that cold, hard ball of pain from the years of "uncried" tears beginning to soften and thaw.

<u>LESSONS</u>

- I was rewarded not to cry and would have suffered disapproval if I did cry. I liked to please people.
- When we acknowledge our experiences and what they caused us to do, we can see our life making more sense and make small changes to free ourselves from these emotional traps.

<u>TWO QUESTIONS</u>

1. How do you react to stressful situations?

2. Do you cry to relieve the pressure or stuff the urge to cry down

The Giant Drank Dr. Pepper

My granddaddy's name was Tom Glaze, and he was 6'5" tall. He was a giant! My granny's name was Lova Glaze, and she was less than 5'6" tall. Most people called her Lovie.

My statuesque granddaddy with Pud, his youngest child and my older
sister Ginger at Three Rivers, Texas

19

Granny was a Bible-reading, church-going woman, and sweet to the core. These were my momma's parents, and they were down-to-earth farm folks.

After his farming days, Granddaddy travelled around selling mules and eventually bought a gas station and general store in Tarzan, Texas, the home of about 350 souls. There was not a proper town of Tarzan. There were two churches in town: the Church of Christ—which the Glazes attended—and the Baptist church. There

Tom and Lovie Glaze. Proud Owners of the only general store in this spot in the road between Tarzan and Stanton, Texas.

was a small post office, a cotton gin, and that was it. There, in that little one room church, Granny and Momma taught me the sweet love and comfort of Jesus.

A fact that touched me deeply was Granddaddy and Granny's lifelong love story. They wrote each other love letters most of the years they were married. We still have those precious declarations of devotion written in a tender language from a bygone time. It was a beautiful thing to read their genteel and powerful words of love. I dreamed of that same kind of love and tenderness for my life someday.

The gas station and general store were where I remember seeing Granddaddy the most. Their house, wherever it happened to be, was one of the places our daddy dropped us when he went off on some of his wanderings. By this time, I was used to Daddy being gone. Once, he was gone so long I forgot. Him. I guess that hurt his feelings really bad, but that seemed strange to me that he'd be hurt since he was the one who left. Once Daddy dropped us off, he'd either come back by and get us himself eventually or send his brother Cecil to come get us and bring us to him.

As I said earlier, we learned not to eat too much, to never ask for seconds at whosever's house we might be staying. Momma also taught us to be quiet, don't be a bother and do chores to help out.

The Glaze Gas Station had two hand pumps outside where people could gas up their car or truck. He also had an air pump so folks could fill up their tires, and a water hose for overheated radiators. Many bottle caps had been crushed in the driveway by vehicles rolling over them and flattening them out.

The Glaze gas station and general store was magical with the nostalgic smells undulating in the air around the outside and inside of the store. The spilled oil and splashed gas from the gravity fed gasoline pumps leaked and clung to the crushed rock driveway below. There was the earthy smell in the air that gave proof to the war between West Texas and the unconquerable wild prairie.

The store was a wonderland. The welcoming screen door was wood and when it fell shut, it made a soft wood to wood sound as it bounced to a standstill. Sweet candy promised to melt in your mouth and an ice-cold soda pop to refresh the traveler after riding through this parched expanse of prairie. Travelers were welcomed to this oasis replete with new merchandise. Granddaddy carried milk, bread, lunch meat cheese, candy, and other food for travelers. He also sold work clothes, gloves, and straw hats for people working in the fields. The smell of new clothing mingled with the presence of Mrs. Baird's Bread and oily metal tools.

I especially remember the big soda pop cooler where the bottles of pop were held up in the cooler, so they hung by the neck into the icy water below. It kept that

Momma holding me in Granny's garden.

soda pop frosty cold. Just right on a hot Texas day.

One day, Momma carried me over to the store. I was about three years old. She stood me next to Granddaddy and my gaze kept going up, and up, and up to every 6'5" of him. I was awestruck because it was like his head reached the sky, just like the giant in "Jack and the Beanstalk." He held a Dr. Pepper in his hand, tipped it up and took a long, ice-cold swig.

This giant, Tom Glaze, looked down at me and asked, "You want some Mickey?" I vigorously nodded my head yes. Granddaddy gave me my very first drink of Dr. Pepper. A flavor bomb burst in my head with an unbelievably delicious taste. I had never tasted anything like it. It was lightning fast. I was hooked from the very first sip.

That Dr. Pepper changed my life because it was tied to a precious memory which made it all the more desirable.

Since that very first tender moment Dr. Pepper has been my drink of choice. I craved Dr. Pepper from that day forward. My most favorite thing is to eat a Hostess chocolate cupcake and wash it down with Dr. Pepper.

I do not know what made this safe and tender Dr. Pepper experience such a vivid memory, but it was a bright and shiny moment in my life. It might have been the magnificent stature of Granddaddy, Granny's and Granddaddy's love story, the store with all the mystery it contained, how happy Momma was while we were there, or just the blast of taste of the Dr. Pepper, but it was most likely a mixture of all those factors and certainly a joyful and pleasant memory.

LESSONS
- One big lesson was about true love between a husband and wife. I did not realize that it became my standard for the kind of relationship I would yearn to have.
- Seemingly small experiences can be so important and pleasant, that they can leave a lifelong impact, like the love of my grandparents, or my Momma's happiness being a safe and loving place, and the overwhelming taste of Dr. Pepper.

TWO QUESTIONS
1. When have you experienced a bright and shining moment in your life?

2. Describe what it was and who the moment was with?

Dark Secrets on the Bus

Was it true or was it made up? All my life I heard stories about what happened on the bus that Daddy drove in Houston. Ginger often said she was on the bus and

Momma and Daddy in Galveston at the beach. Kayo on the right.

saw the whole thing. But Momma said Ginger wasn't on the bus. I never knew Momma to fabricate a story. She had an ironclad rule about telling the truth and she told this story.

Ginger's version of the story: One day one of the other bus drivers, Stonewall Jackson told Daddy a man was looking for him. Stonewall said the man told him that

Daddy cheated him, so he was coming after him with a knife and going to cut him up. Daddy owned a gun but had lent it to a friend. The man got on Daddy's bus and rode to the end of the line. Ginger said she was on the bus and witnessed the whole thing. Daddy walked to the back of the bus. Ginger was sitting next to a kindly woman. Then the man lunged at Daddy with his knife. They scuffled. The man managed to cut Daddy several times. Ginger said blood got all over the bus and on her. Daddy finally wrestled the knife from the guy, and in the struggle the man was killed.

Because Daddy was defending his life, he was not charged with a crime. But the damage to Daddy was like that of someone having had to kill someone in a war. He didn't really want to, but the alternative was to lose his own life. Momma said the story appeared in the Houston newspaper. He had already been a drinker, and this incident drove him deeper into alcoholism.

Momma's version was identical to Ginger's except she said Ginger was not on the bus during the incident. Ginger said that because Daddy often told her his problems (she was the oldest), she could no longer discern whether she was part of the experience, or she just heard about it later. But the truth is, whether she was on the bus or not, our daddy was changed after that. The story always hung like a dark cloud over our family history but wasn't talked about. I was probably five years old at the time and these kinds of things were not discussed with children around. Ginger would have been nine. Her being on the buss is still a mystery and there is no one living now who would be able to tell the truth. I don't spend a lot of time thinking about such things, but still I wonder.

LESSONS
- Family secrets create doubts and confusion. What we don't know does have the ability to hurt us. I believe it created a trauma in Daddy making him drink to try to forget and his drinking put us into extreme poverty.

- Don't judge when you don't know all the circumstances that cause a person to act as they do. Daddy was judged by us and not discussing the problem made it hard to deal with.
- You can't heal from what you don't acknowledge.
- People fill in the blanks with their imaginations when they don't know the facts. Knowing the truth is healthier, and less confusing.

TWO QUESTIONS

1. Recall a family secret and write it down.

2. Why was it kept a secret?

Ashtrays Flew at Our House

I was playing in our girl's bedroom in the Courts in Houston. Things were getting heated up in the kitchen. What Momma was yelling at Daddy about I don't know. I usually liked to get outside of the house when they fought, because it scared me, but I couldn't get past without them seeing me. So, I quietly closed the door.

My sister Jo in front of our apartment

The bedroom Ginger, Jo, and I slept in was at the head of the stairs and next to the bathroom. The three of us had to sleep in the same bed because we did not have enough beds. Ginger slept on the right side, Jo in the middle, and I slept on the left side. I couldn't sleep in the middle because doing so made me feel I would be suffocated. Jo, a peacemaker, said she would sleep in the middle, but we suffered the consequences. Jo would shake her left foot rhythmically back and forth until she hypnotized herself to sleep.

She said if we didn't like it, she'd trade places with us. It nearly drove me crazy to hear her foot swishing back and forth, back and forth, moving the covers with each move of her foot.

This day, I was home alone with Momma and Daddy because I was too young to go to school. We didn't have kindergarten but went right into first grade at six years old.

The commotion quieted down downstairs, and Daddy called me to come down—which I did. He told me to go to the little neighborhood store and get myself an ice cream cone. I couldn't believe my luck because today there wasn't any kind of special occasion going on.

Daddy dug a nickel out of his pocket and gave it to me. He sent me off to the little store. It was a real hot day, and the sidewalks were like a griddle heated up for pancakes. The hot Concrete scorched my feet causing me to skip along at a pretty good clip. I made my way to the store and opened the screen door.

Daddy Our back porch was telling me my bloomers were showing.

Stepping inside onto the wood floors was a relief, they soothed my feet after the blistering of the hot sidewalk.

The ice cream case held three divine flavors: chocolate, vanilla, and strawberry. I studied which flavor might be the best and reckoned on strawberry. Whoo-wee, it was delicious. A most heavenly taste! I happily stepped back outside on that sweltering hot sidewalk, licking my strawberry ice cream with vigorous enthusiasm. It was already melting down the side of the cone. I licked that ice cream so hard; I licked it right out of the cone. It tumbled down and splatted on the sidewalk, and limp from the heat and licking, the ice cream started melting at lightning speed.

I burst into tears and was sobbing big-body boo-hoo's for my loss. Between the Texas sun and the hot sidewalks my ice cream was disappearing like magic. I knew it wasn't any use to go back and tell the store people what happened, they would not have had any sympathy for my plight.

Tears were flooding down my cheeks. I raced back to our apartment, jumped on the porch, burst through the door, and catapulted myself over to Daddy. He was sitting next to a kitchen wall, and just as I got to him, a big green, glass ash tray came flying through the air and crashed on the wall near his head. It fell on the concrete floor below and exploded into hundreds of pieces.

Daddy just turned his head toward me, and as if nothing had happened, said, "What's the matter baby?" I sobbed out my sad story about how my ice cream melted into a puddle before I even got a chance to get a whole lick! He pulled out another nickel, and said, "Please don't cry baby. Run back to the store and get yourself another one, okay?"

I went back to that store and got me another strawberry ice cream cone, determined to be more careful. I licked that ice cream cone real gentle as I could, so as not to lick it out of the cone again. Then I got to pondering what had just happened. It occurred to me that Momma must have thrown that big, green ash tray, sailing it through the air and barely missing Daddy's head. It stopped me in my tracks, and I thought for sure, had her aim been better, had she hit him, it would have kilt him for sure. But there was no reaction from my daddy or my momma. They never explained it nor even acknowledged that it had happened. Of course, as a child, I was most interested in getting my ice cream, and nothing else really mattered, at least in that moment.

However. this was crazy making. Something did happen, and there were probably other "ash trays flying through the air" that were not talked about either. Apparently, Daddy had been flirting with a woman on his bus. Mother was a very jealous and fiery woman, and when she found out about the incident, she went into what Daddy called one of her "fits."

Daddy had learned to ride the storm out. But his passive-aggressive behavior was maddening to Momma. Instead of working issues out as they came up, each such incident stacked up on top of the others that had come before till one day the whole stack would come tumbling down.

LESSONS

- Violence is dangerous and can lead to trouble.
- Wounding each other chips away at the foundation of a relationship and eventually the people in it can no longer stay together.
- Acting in inappropriate ways toward each other is destructive.
- Examining our own behavior and daring to make the necessary changes is hard, but it pays off in lasting love and respect for each other.
- My daddy knew flirting with other women was inappropriate.
- My momma knew her rage was a large problem.
- Self-examination is healthy and nurturing to a relationship and is a much more loving choice.

TWO QUESTIONS

1. Have you ever witnessed something in your family you thought was odd, but no one ever explained to you?

2. What do you imagine it was about?

"Stuff of the Universe"

I was sitting in a high-powered 1:00 pm GM meeting deeply focused on the business at hand. I suddenly, experienced a vivid, technicolored slide popping into my head. A wrinkled old man's face loomed up from the dark, and behind his head a bright, psychedelic light pulsated in the glow rocks of a fish tank. Then, just as suddenly, it disappeared. The image felt disturbingly familiar to me, but I didn't consciously recognize it, and it didn't make any sense, so I shook it off and refocused on the meeting. I was 38 at the time and worked in a responsible position in the auto industry. I forgot about the image and went about my life.

But a couple of years later, I was at home deeply concentrating on what I was sewing, I had the same experience. Again, the time was about 1:00 p.m. This time it disturbed me more, but after a while, I forgot about it.

The apparition did not appear again for another two and a half years, and when it did it was the same. But this time something else appeared. I saw a little girl in the scene about four or five, wearing a pretty pink dress. It looked like me as a child. I'm getting a little freaked out. I felt it was me when we lived in Houston.

When I was that age, we lived in the housing project, called San Filipe Courts, which was housing for the poor. Daddy was a bus driver and Momma worked part time for Levy's department store in downtown Houston. She rode to work on Daddy's bus because his route went right by where we lived. Momma was Hollywood-beautiful, so it wasn't long before Levy's had her modeling clothes for them. Levy's gave her the clothes she modeled, and that suited her just fine. They even gave her a glamorous fur coat she had modeled. Momma loved getting those pretty clothes because she would not have been able to buy them for herself.

Life in the Courts was precarious. Because there were gangs, policeman patrolled our neighborhood daily. We had a 9:00 p.m. curfew, and that's when the police ran us all into our apartments before dark. Life seemed fairly safe, but one can

31

get used to whatever conditions one finds themselves in. We may have become oblivious to what's really going on.

The apartment complex was huge, with rows and rows of two-story apartments. There was an office next to our roller-skating rink where everyone went to pay their rent. Ms. Aster ran that.

Something happened in those Courts that left a lasting scar on me, though I did not recall it until I was in my forties. Then it came to me in bits and pieces.

I had left the auto industry for our own consulting business run by me, my husband Wayne, and my daughter Cindy Christopher. We conducted public, high-intensity seminars that helped people discover the behavior that was keeping them from being as successful as they desired. I often hired my older sister Ginger to come and help with these three-day seminars. We addressed people's negative memories, taking them through some healing processes that increased their self-esteem.

While I was conducting the seminar, the apparition appeared for the final time. This time the old man, the fish tank, and me with one more added feature—another little girl. I finally realized it was my little friend who had lived in the apartments across from us, not too far away, but still a bit of a walk. Little by little, a memory was trying to emerge in my conscious mind.

One day, Ginger asked me how I had dealt with the old man in Houston. I was shocked, I didn't know what she was talking about and said, "What old man?" She said, "You need to call Mother and ask her." Something must have warned me I was approaching danger, and I actually forgot about it again. Our safety defenses rear up to protect us from anything our brains aren't ready to accept. But something had broken loose the memory and every once in a while, another part of the puzzle would fall into place. As the memory made itself known in bits and pieces, it made my heart ached at the realization of the truth. Shame appeared.

Momma, me, Jo and Troy in a common play area. The old man lived down the divider on the left.

My little friend was Susie. We were between four and five years old, and we often played together. We especially liked to play outside. I had gone over to her house to get her one spring day after lunch, about 1:00 p.m. The apartments were separated by a grassy median where we liked to play outdoor games. We could roller skate all over the neighborhood on the sidewalks which separated the apartments further. We were walking hand-in-hand on the sidewalk, and this really old man came out of his door and started being friendly. Talking with us, he invited us in, but something in my tummy lurched and scared me. I said "No," but he kept trying to pressuring us, and then told us he had lots of candy in there to give us. We succumbed to the temptation of candy and went in. The contrast between the bright light of the sun, and the darkness of his living room was stark and heavy. We were blinded for a few seconds. The only light was from his fish tank where the light and bounced off the psychedelic glow rocks in the tank. He suddenly got real mean and commanded us to be quiet and be still. Susie and I were both so frightened, we froze in place and couldn't move. I was so terrified, my eyes fixated on the colorful rocks. I think Susie was still by the door for a while, but my fear caused me to leave my body. It's like I could see myself standing there in that pink dress, and I believe he molested us both, but I don't remember that. I could still see the awful look in his ugly eyes and him leering at me as he pulled out his pocketknife. Slowly opening it up, he viciously rasped, "If you say anything to anybody, I will cut your ears off." I didn't think I ever told anyone, but after I talked to Momma, I found out the other missing parts. This memory had been buried for over 35 years, yet it finally bubbled to the top.

It had taken me almost a year to remember to call Momma, but I eventually did call her. When I asked her why she never told me about it, she said. "Well, honey, because of all the commotion you were causing, I thought you knew this had happened." I asked her how she knew about it, and she told me, "Why, you came home a-squalling and a-bawling and told me this old man did something bad and threatened to cut off your ears. You were in hysterics. When your Daddy got home, I told him, and he took care of it. He was going to beat up the old man, but the man was very old and fragile. Your Daddy went straight to Ms. Aster, and they forced the man to move out of the Courts. The next day, his daughter, with whom he lived came over and threatened to beat me up. The whole ordeal was a mess for a while, but it finally calmed down."

My strange realization after this conversation was if Momma knew about the molesting and I had myself told her about it, then it must have happened. Up till now, when someone would relate a very traumatic incident and say they hadn't remembered it for years, I didn't really believe them. But there I stood, faced with the fact that this memory did not exist in my mind. Somewhere, early on, I let it slip into obscurity and forgot it.

When I researched this topic, many sources said forgetting is more often the case than remembering. And even then, the victim still has periods where they don't believe it really did happen. Well, both my momma and my big sister knew about it, even when I didn't.

Another thing that can happen is that the victim may never recall all of the incident because of the trauma and fear. When the predator achieves their objective, the victim often does not remember that part of the violation. I have, to date, never had the complete memory at this point. Often, a victim will not remember things until the predator is too old to hurt them anymore or dies. Then something releases in them that tells them it is safe to remember it now, and their healing work can begin. This time period in my childhood is when my great fears began. I was terrified of the dark, being alone, and many other things scared me.

Prior to these discoveries and my healing work, if I was in a group of two or more and someone asked me a question, with the attention or the group focused on me, when I responded my face would burn with unexplained shame. I felt dirty and unworthy. The shame was not my shame, it was that old man's shame, and I had been carrying it for him all those years. It is our challenge to give the shame back to the rightful owner, the predator.

There have been many occasions I asked, "why?" Why did this happen to me? I truly believe that God takes the tattered experiences of our lives and graces us with their meanings. He helps us to use them for a greater good. My journey took me through the pits of darkness, to a time of breaking the chains for freedom and discovering courage. And ultimately to finding out I was worthy, loved and had a great purpose for my life.

It became clear to me that my journey was not only to heal and free myself, but I was supposed to help others through this painful but liberating transformation. Had I not suffered this confusion and pain, and found healing for my soul, I would not have been able to help so many others. I created the concept of the Healing Circle from Shame. Our destiny takes us through many strange and wondrous places. These are tough situations, but the painful journey is one towards enlightenment and fulfillment.

My childhood experience had consequences. For instance, I was always puzzled by the fact that I loved spontaneity in almost everything—except sex. To engage sex, I had to climb over a huge barrier of fear and impending doom. If Wayne reached for me, and I didn't expect it, I froze, became fearful and had to engage in a silent struggle in my mind to overcome the fear. But fear and struggle came back every time.

When I finally understood, Wayne and I discussed it and came up with a plan that worked, and which allowed us to return to spontaneity. I would ask him to let me know during the day before nighttime what his desires were. I would say to him, "I will cook you a nice dinner if you will make love to me tonight." He would agree, and it worked. We made a game out of it. My fears eventually melted away. He would not take out a knife and cut my ears off, and we had conquered the demon. Such is the "stuff of the universe."

The experiences we have in life are molding and preparing us for our destiny. Even the worst of things can have a positive outcome, a higher purpose and meaning. *I am the summation of every experience I've had in my life.* The universe is not wasteful. All the bits and pieces of our past can be used to design our future. This is hopeful. Our character is refined and matured as we gain wisdom and compassion. The televangelist Robert Schuller proclaimed, "We can turn our *scars* into *stars*, so we can shine and add our light to the darkness, illuminating the path for others to follow."

I was privileged to help hundreds of women and men overcome the tyranny and hopelessness of sexual or physical abuse. They were able to break free from the prison that had kept their secret shrouded in a heavy cloak of shame and humiliation. They were able to break their chains, walk out into the sunshine, and choose a new life.

Some of my greatest lessons came from some of my worst and most painful experiences. What seemed a tragedy at the time, transformed into a wonderful gift.

srb

LESSONS

- There is evil in the world.
- Some of my greatest victories came from what seemed like my greatest despair.
- God uses what happens and who we become to turn evil into good.
- There is healing for all wounds.
- Our lives are refined by the fire of overcoming trauma.
- We have a choice to either wallow in the defeat or turn the seeming defeat into a diamond to help ourselves and others.
- It has everything to do with our attitude. Do I allow myself to use it to be a victim, or work to turn it into a triumph?
- I am not saying I am glad or that what happened is okay. It happened. Life is what it is—take that and make something good with what you have instead of wasting time in regret.
- When experiences scar our life with fear, that fear is a trigger that something needs to be healed. You don't have to remain in fear.

TWO QUESTIONS

1. Write about a time you suffered a traumatic event that created fear or shame? (The most debilitating thing is to harbor the secret. We are as sick and as hurt as our secrets. We deserve to let the secret out in a safe venue to be free).

2. In what way have you sought healing?

Healing Circle Process to Heal from Shame

Because we discovered so many people had suffered sexual and physical abuse, I created this process to help people overcome shame.

1. The shamed person must break the silence.

2. They must speak the secret out loud to safe people.

3. The leader must stay in contact with the shamed person, so they do not feel so vulnerable, keeping their head up and eyes open while making eye contact with a safe person(s) and telling the story of abuse...

4. Give the blame to whom it belongs—the perpetrator. Give them back their shame. It does not belong to you.

5. Allow shamed person to receive the proper response that they never experienced at the time of the abuse. Speak words of comfort, tell them that they did not deserve to carry this burden of shame. That they were now free, and that this negative experience can eventually just be a bad memory that cannot harm them. The shame belongs to the perpetrator. Have them relax with soft, healing music.

The Big Fat Plastic Jewelry Must Have Given Me Away

I broke two of the Ten Commandments in less than an hour. The sting of the consequences realigned my sense of right and wrong in a split second.

We were still living in San Filipe Courts in Houston. It was a beautiful day and seemed like no one was getting into trouble at the time. I was about 5 years old, and I was about to learn a big lesson in my life. Jo and I were drawing and coloring in the living room. When we were through, Jo meandered upstairs to our room.

Then I saw the mail flap in the door open and letters dropped through ending up inside on the floor. Momma had already told us to gather the mail up when it came and put it on the table. We were not to mess with her mail. I was more curious this day than usual due to boredom, and I looked through the envelopes. A couple of them looked really important. I recognized our name, but not much else, but I felt around on the envelope. There was something hard inside. I got to wondering what could be inside that envelope.

Finally, I couldn't stand it anymore. I just had to open it up. When the contents poured out on the table, I found a metal plate with Momma's name and address embossed on it. Glory be, there was a nice crisp one-dollar bill lying there! My goodness, what all that dollar bill could buy! I was getting in deeper and deeper, and so fast that my conscience couldn't keep up with my possibilities.

I immediately did the next wrong thing. I grabbed that dollar bill and threw the envelope, metal I.D. tag and letter in the garbage and took off for the little store at the end of the Courts. I walked in through the screen-door and started searching for just the right treasure to buy. There were all kinds of neat things in that little store. It was like I was in a trance, not thinking about any trouble that would be brewing for me ahead. That's when I spotted all the bright sparkly plastic jewelry. I had hit the jackpot! I was mesmerized by its beauty. I looked at that jewelry, piece by piece, and

39

settled on a necklace and bracelet. Putting them on transformed me into a movie star. Whirling and dancing around, I suddenly saw my image glide across the cheap, foggy mirror hanging on the wall.

The two pieces of jewelry were constructed of interlocking plastic circles, which made them stand out and appear really big, which pleased me even more. Oblivious to my crime, I skipped home happy as a lark.

When I walked into the living room, I felt like I had just stepped into the raging fires of hell and damnation. Momma was waiting there for me, and she asked me straight out if I had opened any of her mail. I should have known it was a trick question and I did not give the right answer. I instantly denied that I had opened her mail. Her anger ratcheted up another big notch. I had forgotten the evidence was hanging around my neck and wrist. I was stunned into silence. She asked me again, "Are you sure? Are you telling me the truth?" I found my voice, and grasping for straws, searching for a safe way out, I adamantly blurted out, "I am telling the truth!" Momma marched right up to me, got eye level, and spit out the venom. "Then what is this around your neck and wrist?" She had caught me in my own web of lies. Momma valued honesty and wanted to be able to trust us kids. I had betrayed her, and I could see a changed look in her eyes. So, there are the two offences, really three. I stole her money, I bald faced lied to her, and I broke her trust in me. This was not going to turn out well at all.

Momma told me that she had been counting on that money, and now it was gone. I was growing smaller and smaller, shrinking down into my dress. But she wasn't through. "Young lady, you march yourself outside to the little tree in the yard and choose a switch." I had to choose my own weapon of destruction. Momma switched me hard, and I thought she would never stop. I was jumping around from the sting of each lash. It was amazing how accurate her aim was through the whole execution.

40

I know a lot of parents don't believe in spanking their child. But when I endured that painful consequence of lying and stealing, it altered my whole perspective. I no longer had any desire to steal or lie to Momma again.

The sting of that switch deterred my actions. Nothing else could have sent home that message so thoroughly as feeling that I could not get away with that kind of behavior. Worse than stealing and lying was realizing that I had lost Momma's trust. It broke my heart. I had traded honesty, trust, and respect for cheap, jewelry. And it was a sorry trade.

Here is where remorse entered my life. I never wore that plastic jewelry again. The blessing that came out of this is I never wanted to act this way again. The penalty of her loss of trust was not worth it.

LESSONS

- I lost my Momma's trust.
- The little I gained temporarily was not worth the depth of trust I lost.
- For every action there is a consequence, negative or positive.
- Do not steal. Do not lie—those are unholy actions. Be trustworthy.
- Once we have lost someone's trust, it is very hard to win it back.
- And worst of all I demeaned myself.

TWO QUESTIONS

1. When was a time you did something that was wrong for you?

2. What was the consequence? How did it make you feel?

A Prank that Wasn't Funny

Momma never learned to swim. She grew up in the part of Texas that was more desert than lush green anything. She was very afraid of going in the water.

We were all visiting Uncle Joe's and Aunt Jack's farm in Tarzan, Texas. We came in from Houston. Aunt Pud had picked us up from the train station in Midland and brought us out to Tarzan. The adults right away sent us kids outside to play, so they could cook and visit, which suited us just fine, I was five going on six years old

The comic character my brother Kayo was named after.

and Kayo, my little brother was about one year old or less. I adored him and thought he was a precious novelty.

Let me stop here and deal with some of our nicknames, in particular mine and Kayo's. In the South, it was usual to be called by a nickname. Mine was Mickey because my favorite toy was a plastic Mickey Mouse toy. You could stretch out Mickey's arms and legs, and when you'd let go, they'd pop right back into place.

When Momma and Daddy brought Kayo home from the hospital, they didn't have a baby bed for him yet. Daddy went and got a drawer from a dresser, put a pillow in it, and laid Kayo down on the pillow. He had to sleep there until they could get him a proper baby bed. Daddy announced the baby's name was Kayo, after the comic strip character, Kayo, who was Moon Mullin's Street urchin kid brother who slept in an open dresser drawer. He was a boxer and wore a derby hat and most of the time, polka dot pants. His name, Kayo, which was a play on K.O., the sportswriter's shorthand for the knockout punch. The name stuck to this very day.

Kayo was a sweet, sweet baby. Very pleasing and cute to the max who had a happy countenance that made you want to laugh with him.

It was a huge treat to visit Tarzan because there was always so much interesting stuff on Uncle Joe's farm. A gutted-out Model T car, a swing hanging in a tree, animals of all sorts, a watering hole, things growing, especially watermelons, corn, and other vegetables. I don't know where the other kids went off to, but Kayo was left with me.

Pretty soon, I ran out of things to do. I got to looking at the old windmill that delivered water to Aunt Jack's house. There was a wooden water storage tank (like the photo below). But on Uncle Joe's windmill, the water storage tank stood on a wood platform right next to the windmill. The water was gravity-fed to their house.

This photo was Granddaddy's windmill. It was very similar to Uncles Joe's windmill, except his storage tank was on a platform that you could climb onto and walk around the tank.

I saw the water tank and the ladder and thought it would be great fun to climb up to the platform. I was a wild child, and an adventurist at heart, so this seemed like a natural thing to want to do. Then I remembered Momma couldn't swim and thought, wouldn't it be funny to make her think Kayo had fallen in the tank of water? What would her reaction look like? I lugged Kayo up to the platform, put him behind the water tank and told him not to move. Then I shimmied back down the ladder, preparing my best-Oscar winning performance and ran in the house shrieking that

Kayo had fallen in the water tank. Momma jumped up, frantically ran outside, and started to climb up to the platform. Aunt Jack and Aunt Pud were running after her because they knew she couldn't swim. All three of them were terrified, and everything started to get out of control. Aunt Pud ran around the windmill looking up, Aunt Jack ran after Momma. My laughter turned to tears when Momma started screaming, "My baby, my baby! Kayo! Oh, my God, my baby!" I got really scared because Momma was hurting real bad. She truly thought Kayo was drowning! This is not how I visualized this in my head. My vision was more like the Keystone Cops, bumping into each other, and getting all flustered and running off in all directions. That wasn't what was happening at all. There was palpable fear looming like death in the air. What had I done? I was choking from fear and dread.

Aunt Pud had seen Kayo up on the platform behind the water tank, and she quickly climbed up and rescued him. She was crying when she handed him over to Momma, who was crying broken-hearted tears. Momma cried and cried as she frantically hugged and kissed Kayo. I got so sick to my stomach. I thought I would surely die. This windmill prank wasn't funny after all. I caused everyone to be alarmed and caused Momma to be badly hurt. I couldn't stop shaking. My heart was breaking for the pain I had caused in Momma.

I can't remember many of the details, but I can remember Momma talking to me and I couldn't stop crying. She said she wouldn't spank me because she was so overwrought with fear and anger at me for putting Kayo in danger, that she was afraid she'd lose control and hurt me. I was sobbing now. I loved Momma with all my heart, and I had hurt her. She then told me how dangerous the prank was. That I had put Kayo up there on that platform, and if he had crawled close to the edge, he could have fallen off and gotten killed. I loved Kayo so much and the fact that I could have killed him started up body racking sobs. I hadn't thought of any of these things. I was shaking with what I could have caused with such a senseless act.

Momma didn't have to spank me. I understood every word she said and was so remorseful, I couldn't stop crying. She let me go and I ran over to a tree and cried until I couldn't cry any more. I swore not to do such a thing like that ever again. Momma let me finish crying, then came over with Kayo, sat down by me and just held me. She let me hold Kayo and love on him. It took a long time for the bad feelings and fright to go away. This memory was burned into my heart and memory.

I finally felt peaceful about it because I knew I would never pull such a dangerous prank like that again. There was no fun in seeing people I so dearly loved being so deeply hurt. This memory still scares me when I think about what could have happened and has brought tears of gratitude because the worst didn't happen.

LESSONS

- An innocent plan can really backfire on us if we haven't thought it through before implementing it.
- Harmful pranks are not funny. They are dangerous.
- It is not an option to put someone in danger so I can get a laugh. This is non-negotiable.
- Boundaries are in place for safety reasons. Scaring someone or putting someone in danger is unacceptable.

TWO QUESTIONS

1. Describe a time you played a prank on someone, and it did not go well.

2. What Happened? How did it make you feel?

Digging to China

It was a sultry, humid dripping Houston summer day, and Troy, my oldest brother, the great teaser, was telling me he had just read that China was directly below Houston. And if I dug straight down, before too long, I would hit it and come out in China.

I was six years old and in the first grade at Cleveland elementary school.

WOW! That was a revelation to me. What an adventure that would be, and I wouldn't even have to travel by boat or trains around the world since I didn't have money to pay for a ticket anyway. So, I began to hatch my plan on how to dig to China. I was probably about six or seven years old at the time. And I craved having a daring adventure for my own life.

I went outside to survey the situation. There was grass in most places on the lawn except under our back porch. It was mostly sand under there. I didn't have a shovel. One wouldn't fit under the porch anyway. I was small, so I'd be able to get under the porch.

Undeterred, I ran to Momma and asked her for a big spoon. She asked what I needed it for, and I told her I was digging to China. She said, "Okay, but don't lose it, and bring it back to me." I grabbed the spoon and ran out back, ready to get started. I crawled under the porch, which was a little harder than I imagined. In the 1940s, girls didn't wear pants, we wore dresses, which was a lucky thing. As I dug the loose sand out, I'd put the dirt in the skirt of my dress and then scoot out from under the porch. When my makeshift pouch got full, I dumped it out on our tiny yard. Digging with that spoon was easy when it was loose sand, but when it turned to hard dirt, that spoon was a little puny to work with.

I was mighty enthusiastic about my adventure, and my enthusiasm propelled me on for the whole afternoon. I kept visualizing myself stepping out of my hole and greeting people in China.

By the time Momma called us in for supper, I was exhausted and had made only a small dent in the earth with my hole to China. Momma never discouraged me from any of my many endeavors, instead, letting me self-discover in the midst of it all. I returned the spoon to Momma as she asked, telling her I wouldn't be needing it again until tomorrow. The sun rose, and I jumped out of bed, ready to tackle the dig. Momma gave me her spoon again with the same agreement, to give it back to her by the end of the day.

The day was heating up. There were many little piles of dirt lining our back yard. Under the porch, was musty-damp, hot, dark, and I crawled out and dumped my skirt-loads on the lawn. My hands were dirty and sore from yesterday's blisters from digging so vigorously with that metal spoon, and I was rubbing my legs raw from scooting in and out from under the porch. By noon, I could hardly move. Whoo-wee, this was hard work! I began to wonder if I had maybe bitten off more than I could chew.

Momma called me in for lunch. I was mulling over my whole situation. I was beginning to doubt my mission, Chinese or no Chinese.

Our Houston apartment. The courts were new when we moved in. You can see the stairs led to two apartments, the small space on the left of steps is where I crawled in and out on my China Mission

I needed more intelligence, more information and went looking for Troy. He was nowhere to be found, so I went back home, put on my roller skates, the kind you needed to use a key to tighten onto your leather shoes. I skated over to the outside rink that was next to the Court's offices. And sure enough, Troy and Ginger were there skating in the outside rink. They were good skaters and decided to play "pop the whip" with a few other skaters. They called me over and said I could skate with them if I would be the end of the whip. I didn't really know what that meant, but I felt like a big girl, exhilarated to be chosen to play anything with the older kids.

Ginger and Troy often used me as their "test pilot" when they had a good idea, at least a good idea according to them, because they could talk me into anything.

They told me to go to the end of the line of kids and hold onto that person 'with all my might.' (a key piece of instruction). We started skating in a large circle. So far so good. But before long, I realized I was going faster than all the other skaters. I clamped down onto the skater next to me for dear life.

In this game, the whip got "popped" when the end skater, me, could no longer hold on, letting go and crashing into something to stop themselves. As I was detached from the line, I crashed into a lot of empty cardboard boxes, scattering them asunder. The force of my body hitting all those boxes crushed a lot of the boxes and hurt me like "blue blazes."

My dear siblings ran over, all concerned and worried-like. "Are you OK? Did you get hurt?" Well, I couldn't give them the satisfaction of thinking I got hurt, so I hollered out from beneath the boxes, "No, I didn't get hurt!" When I crawled out from all that stuff, I told Troy he needed to come home and talk to me about my China project. Then I gingerly skated to our house, sore all over my body from both the digging and being popped from the end of that whip.

Going home, I did have to admit to myself that it had been exhilarating to zoom around that rink at lightning speed, being "popped" and going sailing towards those boxes. It didn't hurt until I hit them. But I didn't especially need to do it again either.

Troy, *dreckly*, taking his good, sweet time, got home and came out to the back porch. He crawled under the porch and surveyed my hole and my progress. He crawled back out, put his hands on his hips and gave me a detailed report: "Because you don't have a shovel, and because you're running out of lawn to put the dirt on that you get from making the hole, I hate to tell you this, little sister, but you've only dug about 10 inches down. You've got more than a mile to go. I don't think you'll be able to make it." I could tell he was trying to let me down easy, and he suggested I choose something else that was more possible. I was feeling the pain of defeat. But I had to be practical.

It sorely disappointed me for a while. It was hard to give up the glory I would have felt climbing out of my Houston hole and stepping onto China. Secretly, I was glad not to have to dig any more though. It was really back breaking work. I pacified myself by saying, "I didn't quit, I just dreamed a new dream to do something better."

I took Momma's spoon back to her and said I wouldn't be needing it anymore. She hugged me and said, "I'm sorry you didn't make it all the way to China, Mickey, but you gave it your whole effort. I know you will find another adventure really quick."

It didn't take too long to rally my older siblings to help me get a blanket from Momma. We built a tent by throwing that blanket over the clothesline and pegging it down, so we could sleep outside. We couldn't stay out at night because of our police induced 9:00 p.m. curfew. But we could play like we had a campfire and take a nap in our tent during the day. Which is what we did.

As I think about this, I realized Momma would let me try all the hair brain, crazy ideas I could dream up. She figured I could find out by myself what would or would not work. She was a very creative person herself and she didn't have it in her heart to discourage our creativity. I learned a whole lot from this China adventure.

LESSONS

I learned to figure out what I was capable of and not capable of doing, when I could or could not be successful, and not waste my time and energy on what couldn't be done, at that moment anyway.

- I was able to admit when it is prudent to stop and redirect myself.
- Always encourage creativity in myself and others.
- Size up what I want to accomplish and get sound advice.
- I learned to become a risk taker.
- Use my energy to figure out how to make ideas work, rather than make excuses why something couldn't work.

- I learned the delight of allowing myself to be in the magical mind of a child, and how it opens surprising worlds for me.

TWO QUESTIONS

1. As a child, what big dream did you have that wasn't achievable?

2. What did you do about it??

The Biggest Fight of All

Momma and Daddy faced off against each other in the kitchen. They still had on their party clothes. It was late at night and their fighting woke most of us up. The scene seemed like a dream. They fought a lot, but I could tell this time was different. The fear, frustration, and viciousness coupled with a hopelessness hung like a cloud of impending doom in the night.

Their emotions seemed to be ratcheting up to yet another unexplored level. They were standing about six feet apart, hurling terrible insults, accusations, and

My parents at the time this terrible fight took place. Momma was 26 and Daddy was 33.

names at each other, yelling at *the top of* their lungs. I was getting scared because the tension seemed to be escalating toward violence. I was running from one to the other, frantically begging them, "Stop, please stop. Please don't hurt each other. Please, you are scaring me!" I even grabbed them around their legs and pleaded with them, "Please stop, please stop, please stop! I'm scared. Momma, Daddy, please stop!" But, in their rage I felt invisible to both of them.

They were so caught up in their own pain, they could not see or hear the awful terror it was causing us kids.

As if from a far-away place, I saw Momma, dressed in a delicate blue sequenced dress and her luxurious fur coat from Levy's. She spun around and hurled her arm back to hit Daddy. The movement appeared to shift as if it were in slow motion. Her forceful swing made her coat fan out in a perfect arc that gently brushed my face as she completed the full circle.

Daddy wrestled with her to keep her from hitting him, but it only made her spin out of control. All the time, she was screaming , "I hate you! I hate you! I hate you!" That's when I knew things had reached a new low. We were not allowed to utter the word 'hate" out loud in our house. Yet she was screaming it over and over. It sounded so awful. Momma was sobbing, and Daddy was yelling. It was so horrible, my ears were roaring, everything sounded muffled and far away. We were present but non-existant to them. My pleas for comfort and reassurance fell to the floor and were trampled under their dance of anger. My last tiny shred of hope snapped and disappeared.

I didn't even realize I had had that hope until it was gone I just felt, no matter what was happening to us kids, whatever we wanted, they were so deeply entangled in their own desperate situation, they were blind to ours. They were screaming eye to eye at each other.

I don't remember going to bed, but Ido remember huddling under the covers, wondering what was going to happen to us kids. Who was going to take care of us? Who was going to take care of me?

The next thing I knew, Daddy was gone and didn't come back. I later found out he hadn't left at that time. It was several years later. But in my mind, Momma and

Daddy had that really bad fight and then he left. Our family was broken. I only remember him coming back a few times on the prairie. Strange how trauma causes a faulty memory. This affected me so deeply that I became very afraid and anxious when people fought. In my heart if people fought, one partner was going to leave and it would break up the family. I couldn't tolerate fights with my first husband, and he was a screamer. We were never able to work out our differences.

Years later, when I married Wayne, I reverted to the same behavior of trying to get Wayne to not ever act angry because I thought that would end everything just like it had with Momma and Daddy. Wayne was older, mostly mild tempered and a very reasonable man. One day he sat me down and said, "Sidney, I know you don't ever want me to show anger because it really frightens you. But as a man, and your protector, there will be times when we will need to have heated exchanges while we work things out. So, I will not agree to never being allowed to show my frustration and anger. That is an issue you have, and need to work on. We need to be able to have our honest emotions."

Wayne usually explained things that were real important in a loving but firm way. He told me he was going to make us a hot cup of cocoa, and we would not stop talking until we solved this for both of us. On a few occasions it took a good five hours of conversation and exploration before we could resolve an issue.

One thing I knew, I needed to figure this out. It was true, I didn't like people to show anger around me. I had figured out that my fear of anger took me back to that violent night of my parent's fight and also some of it was a result of Ginger's bipolar outbursts of rage and abuse.

On Wayne's side, we discovered that his parents never allowed him or his brothers to show their honest emotions. The brothers were expected to act as if there was never anything wrong. They could not question their parents' behavior.

We learned that a reoccurring frustration usually triggers a hot issue for both spouses. I didn't want anger displayed in front of me, and he wasn' tsupposed have his authentic emotions. When we finally understood this, the next step was to alter our behavior and how we responded to each other. I would discipline myself to try not to stop another person's anger, expecially Wayne's. I would pay attention to how it made me feel until I could respond without shutting Wayne down. As I noticed my reaction to anger, I realized it took me

right back to that horrible scene when our family fell apart. And Wayne would go back, emotionally, to his parents not permtting him and his two brothers to express theit emotions. We would remind ourselves, we were not our parents. We had the choice to create a different outcome for ourselves. We avoided the trap of getting stuck in the ways our parents had limited our lives. Just reminding ourselves of this helped.

LESSONS

- Trauma in our own childhood leaves an unhealed wound that affects our lives with our relationships in adulthood until we examine what is happening and write our own new ending.

- Parents can be in so much pain, they can't see or feel the pain and confusion they may be causing their children. It then can become multi-generational.

- When we are triggered by our mates reoccuring behavior, the amygdala takes us right back to the the pain and fear of the original experience. It doesn't get healed without intention and a new outcome.

- Usually, when one mate is triggered by the other's behavior, the other spouse is also dealing with an unresolved issue. I didn't want anger displayed because my family might be broken assunder. As a child, Wayne never got to have his true emotions, so he didn't want to hold his emotions inside and deny anything was wrong.

TWO QUESTIONS

1. When did you experience an upsetting event between your Mother and Father?

2. How did it affect you?

Billy Goat Gruff

Who says fairytales are harmless fantasies? At least no who studies them! They are almost like a horror show! For instance, take the Brothers Grimm. They scared us to death with "Hansel and Gretel" when they had them run away from home and almost get eaten by a witch. How scary, how ghastly! Seems like multiple generations of parents wanted to strike terror in the hearts of their children so they could control them better. And these fairytales certainly did that.

No better example of this can be found than "The Three Billy Goats Gruff and the sadistic troll under the bridge (the Norwegian *De Tre bukkene Bruse*" first published between 1841 and 1844, but originating from a story around 1315). That's centuries of parents horrifying their kids? I particularly remember this one because it terrified me as a child. Proceed at your own risk. Read the story that can curdle the blood in any young child's heart.

The three Billy goat Gruff brothers wanted to go to higher pastures where the grass was most luscious, just waiting to fatten any animal. On the way, they had to pass over a bridge under which the giant, ugly, hungry troll lived. His appetite was ferocious, and insatiable. He had yellow bulging eyes with slimy green pupils, his tangled hair matted to his huge head, with the remains of other unfortunate animals who tried to cross the bridge still mangled in his gross beard. The smelly troll's booming voice

The troll hid under the bridge ready to pounce on any prey who dared to cross his territory.

58

shook the surrounding mountains. Listen to the story that introduced terror to me and allowed this barbaric tale to stir my memory. The first Billy Goat Gruff was such a young and tender thing, and he inched onto the bridge and started (tiptoeing (trip trap, trip, trap).

The horrible Troll roared out, "Who is that crossing my bridge? I am going to gobble you up!" "Oh please," the little Gruff whined, "don't eat me. I am too small and puny. Wait for the second Billy Goat Gruff brother, for he is Much bigger and fatter than I am!" The nasty troll grumbled and growled, "Be off, then!"

Later, the second Billy Goat Gruff came to cross the bridge, (trip, trap, trip, trap). "Who is that trying to cross my bridge?" yelled the evil troll. He was getting really hungry, and hunger put him in an even worse bad mood.

"It is I, the second Billy Goat Gruff brother. I am going to the hillside to fatten up," said the second Gruff Brother, whose voice was not so quiet. "You're not going anywhere," screamed the ravenous Troll. "I am going to gobble you up!"

"Oh no, don't eat me. Wait till the *Big Billy Goat Gruff brother* comes. He is bigger, fatter, and much more tasty," promised the second Gruff Brother. "Then get out of here," growled the foul-smelling, ugly troll.

Suddenly, "trip, trap, trip, trap" as the bridge shook under thunderous hooves, for the third Billy Goat Gruff Brother was so *big*, the bridge groaned and creaked under his powerful hooves. "Who is that tramping over my bridge?" roared the angry troll. "It is I!" thundered the Biggest Billy Goat Gruff, who had an ugly, hoarser voice of his own. "Come on out! I have two spears; I will poke out your yellow eyeballs at your ears. I've got besides two curling-stones, and I will crush you to bits, body and bones," threatened the third Billy Goat Gruff.

Big Billy Goat Gruff brother charged at the troll like a raging stallion. He poked his jaundiced eyes out with his horns, and crushed that nasty troll to bits, body and bones, and threw him out into the cascading stream where he promptly drowned.

The story of Billy Goats Gruff was the backdrop for one of the most terrifying circumstances of my whole life. The Billy goat for the migrant workers was my second Billy Goat Gruff. #3 My most horrible nightmare was just about to come true, in vivid living color, right before my very eyes.

My Uncle Joe hired migrant workers to work the fields and bring his crops to market. He wanted to reward their efforts for the good job they had done, so he bought them the goat they requested. They were planning a Fiesta to celebrate the harvest. He asked me and my cousin Linda, if we wanted to go with him to buy the goat. A chance to get off the farm and out of the fields! Without having found out any of the details of what this "purchase" would entail, we enthusiastically responded in unison, "Yes!" After he bought them a big, fat goat. We noticed, he didn't have a trailer to load it into, he just had the pickup truck we'd come in. It had a cap cover on the bed of the truck with no windows. It was ominous and pitch dark in that cavern space.

He and a couple of workers flopped that goat on the ground, tied his hooves together like they did when they roped calves on Friday nights. That goat was bellowing and tossing his body around something fierce. His eyes were bloodshot and huge, crazy and wild, he was thrashing for his life to get loose, his nostrils flared out in rage. When he was hog tied, the workers threw him in the back of our pickup truck.

Suddenly he loomed before me, and he looked just like Big Billy Goat Gruff #3 must have looked. That fairytale had always put the fear of the devil in me, now it was real! It wasn't just a story. Now, he was aggressively pawing the air and screeching in the back of that pickup truck. And Linda and I were going to have to ride in the back of that dark truck with that enraged Billy Goat Gruff, who, by the way was so mean and powerful, *he* had killed the big, fat, ugly troll.

It was too late, and Linda and I couldn't back out now. With trembling hands and quaking legs, we climbed into the dark torture chamber. We backed up as far we could and as close to each other as possible. The brightness of the sun was blocked out, and I couldn't see anything in that black dungeon, we were suffocating. Big Billy Goat Gruff flopped and pounded around, kicking the sides of the truck, snorting through his nose.

Each time he flopped around, he actually moved a little closer to us. The hair on the back of my neck tingled and stood straight out. I was sweating, thinking, Billy Goat Gruff killed that troll. How much worse could he do to two scrawny little girls? I was completely consumed with the fear of this monster.

I knew we were "goners" for sure. There was no way Linda, and I could survive this ride. The experience was made worse by being in total darkness. Occasionally, we'd get little glimpses of Gruff and all we could see was a face of pure hatred and unabated rage. By now it seemed like we rode for more than two hours in sheer terror, scared for our very lives. I was soaking wet from sweat and riddled with the fear of my doomed fate. In reality, the ride was only about 20 minutes, but it was the most awful 20 minutes of my whole life.

When we finally pulled into Uncle Joe's farm, I was exhausted and shakily crawled out of the truck and wobbled up to the front porch. I was thinking, I should find out more stuff about an adventure before I say "Yes" to volunteering to get that involved again. And I made a mental note not to read anymore fairytales for a while

LESSONS

- Fear has great power to squeeze the life out of us, weakening us and rendering us helpless.
- My fear kept me stuck in a picture of what I thought it was and couldn't get myself out of that preconceived point of reference to paint a more realistic picture so I could tame my fear. Opportunities pass.

- We can make a choice. I can choose to live in fear, going through life limited to a small and anxious world, or,
- I can choose to conquer fear and paint a new picture that is more expansive and liberating.
- -Facing our fears is the only way out. They are never as big as we think. Get the facts!
- -This is when I firmly decided, "I will not live my life in fear and languish in a small, safe corner leading to dull mediocracy

TWO QUESTIONS

1. Have you ever felt a debilitating fear? Of what were you afraid?

2. How did you handle it?

Sampson the Bull

My cousin, Larry Kenser Taylor, was the same age as me.   He was always a source of fun and adventure, which is also my character. We were both equally curious about the world and were prone to trying just about anything. So, together we could get into some real good mischief. What one of us didn't think of the other one

Paula, Joe Riley, Aunt Sissy and Uncle Chester. Larry is in front of Paula. He was a lot older when we out fought Sampson.

did. Most of our daring experiences didn't cause any trouble. But sometimes trouble comes calling.

Let me tell you the story of one of those times when our scheme was questionable, and you decide for yourself.

I had gone to spend the summer at Aunt Sissy and Uncle Chester's farm in Ackerly, Texas, so I could earn some money hoeing cotton. Doing so would allow me to buy some school clothes. Uncle Chester did what was called "dry dirt farming," which meant they didn't irrigate their cotton like Uncle Joe did. It showed too, because Uncle Chester's cotton was short, stubby, and anemic while Uncle Joe's cotton was tall, plush, and green.

It was another one of those hot Texas days, and we needed something to while away the afternoon. Larry and I had plenty of time to figure out something that would suit us. We were out playing near the bullpen where Uncle Chester kept his big old bull—I called him Sampson. He was huge and meaner than a cougar with a thorn in his butt. We looked at that sullen bull and Larry figured it would be good fun to out trick Sampson, because he didn't look too smart. He had the bright idea to climb up on the low barn where Sampson stood, lulled into a stupor by the heat. Shoot, he wasn't paying us any attention at all.

Larry went on describing his plan. We could get to the edge of the barn and jump down into the bullpen, before the bull could figure out what was going on, then swiftly make our escape.

So, we did that. After all, we had the element of surprise on our side. One at a time, we got on the barn and jumped down into the bullpen. Of course, the bull didn't like that too much, so he would come after us and we'd go running liceity-split for the fence. The fence was wood, with barbed wire on the top rail.

We each ran fast and beat that old bull to the fence. We were getting pretty cocky and decided to do it one more time. We couldn't just celebrate our victory and let it go. No, we had to show old Sampson who was boss. It was my turn again, so I climbed on that barn, got a running start, and jumped off. The bull was really mad by then and getting faster too.

What happened next could probably not be repeated in a thousand years, but when I hit the ground with my right foot, my elbow hit on my knee, and drove my arm and hand up my jaw and I bit down real hard on my tongue. My tongue was hanging way out and bleeding. Sampson was snorting at me in an angry state of mind, pawing the ground. Our eyes locked and he came a-running! He snorted fire and brimstone out his nostrils.

Two thousand pounds of bull muscle and sinew with a small brain thundered toward me. It was like an earthquake churning up the dirt under his hooves, coming after me dead on. I jumped up and ran for the fence like I was being chased by the devil. My tongue was hanging out and you remember that barbed wire on top of the wood fence? My tongue got caught on one of the barbs—it was awful! I was bleeding really bad by then, and Sampson actually looked like he was laughing at me. I know Larry sure was.

I managed to get out alive, but Aunt Sissy had to take me in to see the country doctor. I couldn't believe my ears. He was telling Aunt Sissy there wasn't much that could be done for my tongue, but it was going to be real sore for a few days. I could only eat soups, gravy, and ice cream. Ice cream! My flavorist thing in the world. The other kids were real jealous of my treatment plan, but I got their respect for bravery. Larry wasn't too happy that he didn't get any ice cream since the escapade was his idea.

Ever since that day, I have had a huge scar where I bit my tongue, but I was the hero and still like ice cream to this day.

LESSONS
- Don't think you can get away with doing something stupid over and over, because your *bull* will catch up with you sooner or later. And you ought not to mess around with something that is that big, that mean and that stupid. It just might not end well.

- The insights Forrest Gump's Momma always told him. "Stupid is as stupid does." Be smart in what risks you take.
- When there is such an obviously dangerous situation, maybe one should think the consequences through a little better.
- Some caution is prudent.

<u>TWO QUESTIONS</u>

1. Consider a time in your immortal youth, when you wanted to do something that presented high risk. What was it?

2. How did it turn out?

Torn Apart for a Year

Daddy was a drinker, and his drinking worsened with time. I knew Daddy loved us, but the addiction possessed him. His love for the alcohol won out. He wasn't a mean kind of drunk. But he would go off on binges for a weekend or a week or even months at a time. He would sometimes take us to some of his relatives "for dinner," then he would just leave us there.

Momma cringed in shame. She had to keep all five of us quiet and taught us not to eat too much of their food. She would do whatever work they would let her do and taught us how to do chores so we could be useful. She finally convinced Daddy to get help, and he was put into rehabilitation.

Daddy had other issues we didn't know about because in those days no one told children such things. At the time the ages of my siblings were Ginger, ten, Troy, nine, Jo Katheryn, seven, I was six, and Kayo was two years old. Momma had to go to work in another town, and no one relative in her family could keep all of us. So, they got together and split us up between them.

This is not a story of cruel, mean aunts and uncles, for they loved us dearly. They were all good farm folks and ranchers. Ginger and Troy went to Aunt Pud and Uncle Bud's; Jo and Kayo went to Aunt Sissy and Uncle Chester's. I was left at Aunt Jack and Uncle Joe's. We worked on their farms hoeing cotton in the summer and picking cotton in the fall and winter. I lived with my four girl cousins, Georgia, Nancy, Linda, and Janice. We had a lot of fun. I went to their small one-room school building in Tarzan, where the population was about 350 souls.

This was quite a change from life in the Courts in Houston and the big city life. I was a Momma's girl and missed her so much my heart physically ached. And us kids missed each other badly. Even though we lived fairly close, people on farms didn't leave very often. We did get to see each other at the little church we attended every Sunday morning, Sunday night, and Wednesday evening. It was very comforting, and we knew people cared for us.

Every night I prayed Momma would come get me. I prayed to be with my brothers and sisters. I cried tearless tears till I fell sleep—deep, silent dry tears that choked my heart.

People didn't tell kids much back in those days, so our living arrangements confused me. The separation hurt all of us badly. We had learned to grind and trudge our way through the pain, whatever the circumstances. I felt cut off from my life source, like I was floating without an anchor to hold me stable. The loneliness was almost unbearable. Aunt Jack and Uncle Joe would console me from time to time, but I kept my feelings buried and made myself appear happy.

Christmas was just around the corner. And Aunt Jack had us all write Santa letters to be hung in their peach trees out front. Momma had always made holidays very special even in the leanest of times. So, my spirit tentatively lifted. Then Aunt Jack told me Momma and Daddy would be there for our family Christmas and I couldn't believe my ears! I was ecstatic and danced around the house. All I could think about was what I could get them for Christmas. Uncle Joe paid us for our labor in the fields, so I had a little money. I dreamed of what I would get Momma, how she would look surprised and say it was exactly what she'd hoped for, and how Daddy would laugh, swinging me up in the air, and hug me close.

Finally, the day came! I sat on the porch in a dither, watching for cars to come down that long, dusty road alongside the cotton fields of Uncle Joe's farm. You could see for a long way off. Uncle Darrell and Aunt Duder had gone to Midland to get Momma and Daddy, and I finally saw the dust boiling up behind their car. My heart jumped, and I ran to the edge of the yard waiting the eternity it took them to get to the house.

When Momma and Daddy got out of the car, I was overwhelmed with love and joy. The ache in my heart melted because I thought we would all get to go home together. We had a wonderful Christmas. Our family was back together, and I floated back down to earth again and felt grounded in the love that had always sustained me.

The whole Glaze family, my Momma's people, were there. Now it was time for the music! Granny played the banjo, Uncle Joe played the fiddle, Uncle Jay played the mandolin, Aunt Sissy played the accordion, and Momma and Aunt Pud played the piano. The house rang with joy as we all sang together and ate the finest food this side of Dallas. We five kids were practically vibrating as we assembled around the tree. We were holding onto each other and often looked back to make sure it was true that Momma and Daddy were really there with us.

It had been five months since we had last seen them. The excitement was thrilling. Granny had handmade all the girls' dresses for the dolls that we each got for Christmas. We cousins had exchanged names and bought each other gifts. Momma and Daddy got us each something special. I watched intently as Momma opened the bottle of Midnight in Paris cologne I had gotten her. I had looked at every single bottle of cologne in the variety store and mulled over which I could afford and which she might like. She slowly opened the package, and with a great intake of breath she held it up and said those magical words, "This is exactly what I wanted!" And Daddy was just as pleased with his Old Spice shaving cream. I was so happy, I thought I would burst from it all.

And, burst I did when it was time to leave. I was waiting for Momma and Daddy to say, "Come on now. Let's load up and go." But they didn't. Something was bad wrong. They were already hugging Ginger and Troy and saying *goodbye!* I couldn't believe it! Apparently, I was the only one who thought we were going to get to be together as a family again.

I ran and threw myself in my momma's arms and clung to her for dear life. Waves of sobs shook my body. Momma and Daddy were crying. So were all my siblings. I remember how desperately I was clinging to Momma and felt big pieces of my heart rip, break off and fall to the ground. I felt others trying to pull me off and heard myself screaming "No! I want my Momma! I want my Momma!" as though I was dying, and I was dying of hurt.

I was too young to know that Daddy was still drinking, they had no money, we were homeless, and Mother had to go to work. Momma had gotten a job in Midland, Texas and there was no place for us yet. Relatives pulled me off her, and I just let go. Then they were gone. I walked quietly back to the room where I slept, laid on the bed and closed my eyes. If I closed my eyes, I didn't have to feel this awful loneliness deep in my soul.

Everyone that meant anything to me was gone. A fearful calm came over my heart. I kissed Aunt Jack and Uncle Joe goodnight because that is what we were supposed to do. Then walked quietly to bed as if nothing had happened. Nobody ever mentioned it again.

The moon was shining, and I watched the shadows of the trees moving across the ceiling. Something broke inside of me, but I didn't know what it was. Everything went silent and I felt a deep emptiness. A void came over me that I got lost in and didn't know my way out.

I now know that the pain was so unbearable, I detached. Many years later, I discussed how this experience affected me and asked my siblings how it affected them. They all agreed that it was the most painful experience we had suffered up to that time. We got used to these kinds of experiences. And there would be others.

I had already felt and somewhat accepted abandonment by my daddy, but now Momma had abandoned me too—not by choice, but a little six-year-old doesn't know

70

such things. My world was shaken to the core. Who could I trust? Somehow, I had to learn to cope with this awful hole in my heart on my own.

I would have to build a world of pretend. Pretend that things weren't broken, pretend everything was okay, and pretend life would get better. I remember walking around as if everything were far away. That way, I couldn't be hurt I could hear everyone, but it all sounded hollow and detached. I responded alright but I didn't feel connected to anything. I immersed myself in school and whatever tasks were required. My tears were still dried up. Why cry? And I didn't. My tears stayed dried for many, many years.

I poured my heart and energy into activities, like getting straight A's in school, playing all the sports girls were allowed to play in, my art, winning contests and just being the best. This is when I became an achieve-a-holic. I could not be good enough. I could not achieve enough to make myself be satisfied to accept that I was good enough as I was.

I felt empty. I just didn't know the empty hole in my soul could not be filled this way. I never celebrated my victories but went directly to the next challenge. This would follow me well into later years, hounding me to always do better, be better.

I learned in the rawest way that this dramatic experience with abandonment leaves a scar—a spiritual wound—a gaping hole we try to fill with work, drugs, all kinds of things but nothing can fill it. Fortunately, I never turned to drugs or alcohol. We must take the time to heal our wound. When I reflected back on this time during my own healing journey, it can be difficult to find a positive outcome for such a truly painful experience. But blessings do come. I was motivated to earn a great education, attain an excellent career, and eventually marry my one true love. It also taught me that hope does return, and we can create a future we choose that is a lot better than our past.

As a psychologist and life coach, I know it is vital to understand the painful experiences others have gone through. None of us have escaped with our self-esteem fully intact. What are the hurts locked behind the brick walls we have erected around our hearts? What would liberate us? I can understand, at the deepest level, what such traumatic experiences can do to a child's heart and how they have to build defense mechanisms to stay safe as they survive these hurts, and ultimately make it. Our hearts have to be "broken' open before we can let the pain out. We must cry those years of tears we've dared not to cry.

I know that the same defense mechanisms that helped me cope as a child can become the very thing that has the power to ruin my adult life. We can open that horrible door behind which we have kept our secret and find a hurt little child who longs to be whole again.

LESSONS

- My parents and siblings were more important to me than anything else.
- Sometimes you can hurt so bad, it becomes a trauma.
- Traumatic experiences leave a scar that we try to fill, but the hole cannot be filled. It must be healed. We build defense mechanisms for dramatic experiences to stay sane.
- Our hearts can truly be broken by a single incident that impacts how we see life.
- None of us made it through childhood without some degree of damage to our self-esteem. If not from parents, from other childhood experiences at school, or other people of influence in our life.
- God was walking this lonely journey with me in the form of family members, and other compassionate people. He said He would never forsake me. He sends

people to us when we need them. We have to know how to recognize His messengers.

TWO QUESTIONS

1. Describe a time when you hurt so badly you didn't know if you could get through it.

2. How did you cope?

The Black Angel of Doom and the Exuberant Angel of Light

There was a tornado brewing, and an ominous dark cloud hung over our house no matter where we lived. We had all been alerted. My sister was working up a head of steam. Her gathering clouds brought either crashing thunder and lightning, or a sweet, mellow rain followed by a breathtaking rainbow, exquisite in its array of brilliant colors. The trick was, we never knew which it might be. As for this one, it was going to be a horrific storm. No one yet knew the consequences.

My age when the curling iron incident tangled up
my life.

I have had Ginger in my life from my birth until January 2022 when she died at 85 years old. I was 81 when Ginger passed from this world. The storm passed with her.

When I look back on our lives, some of my first memories were of being hit by Ginger. It was worse if she started her count down game. 1–2–3…*Bam!* The hits were hard enough to make you not to want to experience them again. We had already learned not to tell on her to Momma or Daddy. If we did, the next time she had us alone, she would terrorize us even more.

Daddy worked at the bus station all day. Mother worked part-time at Levy's department store. When their schedules overlapped, Ginger had to baby sit us three younger kids Jo, me, and Kayo. She was almost four years older than Jo, five years older than me and eight years older than Kayo, who was just a baby, but she was only nine years old herself. She was like another parent, only meaner. I was very afraid of her.

Ginger Gay Randolph in 1939

Ginger went from being a happy and carefree child to a
disturbed girl of gloom and rage.

When I was about five, Ginger was trying to get us ready for church the next day. She heated a curling iron on the stove, and I was afraid she would accidently burn me as she curled my hair, so I was squirming all over the place. She yelled at me to sit still, or she would comb it out right then and there. Well, I must have squirmed around one time too many. When I saw her go for the comb, I seized the opportunity and ran out the door. Ginger grabbed the comb and didn't lose a beat running out the door after me. I ran for dear life. To have curling iron curls combed out was a horrible torture. I was sprinting all over the Courts, screaming at the top of my lungs, trying to get away from her, but her legs were longer than mine and she was stronger.

I ran upon Ms. Stingler's front porch screaming for my life. Ginger's storm cloud picked up a head wind. She pounced on me in the corner of the porch. She held my body down with her knee and grabbed my hair, crudely raking the comb, yanking it as she forced it through my tangled hair.

I feared my hair was being yanked right out of my skull. The pain was excruciating. She wasn't satisfied until I had completely lost control, crying my heart out. When I was too exhausted to cry or feel the pain anymore, she got up and just left me there. I was too traumatized to get up for quite some time. When I finally stumbled home, her mood reversed and she was treating me real sweet, as if nothing had happened.

Ginger in her Angel of Light personality.

This went on for years. I lived with her and her husband, Lewis, for a while when I was in high school. Their house was in a better part of town and more convenient for me. Her behavior ranged from out-of-control rage to tender, loving behavior like an innocent angel of Light. In one moment, she'd be beating on me. In the next, she'd be beating someone up who was trying to hurt me.

One morning during the time I lived with her, I got up for school and still had on my shortie pajamas. Ginger was already in the danger zone. When I didn't move fast enough to suit her, she started screaming at me. Rattled by her roaring voice, I went to get a glass out of the cupboard and didn't shut the cupboard door all the way. That's when she lost it. She grabbed me and started throwing me around with the incredible, terrifying strength she had during her episodes.

I kept telling her I wanted to go home to Mother. She stopped dead in her tracks. "You want to go home to Mother?" she asked in a deadly, wicked voice, "then you are going home to Mother right now!" She didn't even let me get dressed. Instead, she pushed me with both hands out the front door and threw me in her car.

She drove like a maniac from Ruby St. all the way over to 1210 S. Colorado St. She grabbed me, pulled me out of the car, and dragged me up on our little front porch, while screaming the whole way. She threw me up against the screen door and got right in my face, her spittle flying all over, the look of fury contorting her face. In a disgusted, icy voice, she blustered out, "You wanted to go home to Mother. Well, you're home and *nobody wants you! Nobody! Not Mother, not Daddy, and not me!*" I was shaking with terror. She pushed me into the house and stormed off to work.

I was shattered. Broken. Like a China doll dashed to the ground with her head broken into pieces. I truly felt that nobody wanted me. Daddy had abandoned me for years, and now Ginger said Mother didn't want me either. Ginger's words cut to my soul. The jagged wound gapped open with indescribable pain.

It took me some time to rationalize that Mother did love me. I felt it in her touch, the sound of her voice, and the look in her eyes. I also knew, at the level he was able, Daddy also loved me, but alcohol had turned his life upside down.

Ginger's storm of physical violence and the cruelty in her vicious words struck me to the core of my being. She had found my jugular vein. There was no easy way back to normalcy after these attacks. When she was through being enraged, and she was no longer in the eye of the storm, she transformed back into the other version of herself: the sweet, exuberant Angel of Light. She acted as if nothing had happened. She was alright so we were supposed to be alright.

We grew accustomed to her moods that set the tone for our whole family, but we never understood them because they were over the top in intensity. No one said anything, and we were trained to wait till the storm blew over.

As younger siblings, we made certain decisions to try to protect ourselves. We either appeased her or apologized to her, as if it were our fault. As adults, Jo, Kayo, and I would not get in a car alone with her at the wheel. We tried to always have a plan for a way home if we needed to get away from her. We pretended that a bad episode had not happened, just like she did, just to keep the peace. Until I left home, married, and moved to Michigan, I was terrified of Ginger. I just wish Mother had discovered that there was also a medical issue which caused this heartache that plagued her. She always wished she could have been closer to Ginger and felt guilty and like a failure with her.

There were countless other outbursts, but they seemed to have the same pattern. Ginger became abusive and violent, then cruel and emotionally dangerous to the point of damaging the very soul of her victim. Then she would run out of steam and just stop or become exuberant. The anger I felt for her in her dark side turned to guilt when she morphed into the angel of light because the poles of her personality were so diametrically opposed to each other. When Ginger expended all that rageful energy, I felt like the field was littered with blood-soaked bodies and awe.

As I grew into adulthood and had my own children, I began to understand some of what happened to Ginger. Mother and Daddy had her babysitting three younger children when she was only nine. She was scared most of the time because we lived in the San Filipe Courts, where there were armed gangs.

Ginger felt totally responsible to keep us safe from the real prospect of violence. In truth, she had her childhood stolen from her. Mother and Daddy had so much pain in their lives individually and between them that they could not see the pain and need in us kids. Ginger and Troy were beaten, but we three younger ones were not. When I considered what it must have been like for Ginger, my anger changed to compassion. She and I built a very close relationship in adulthood. All of us siblings were intensely loyal to each other because we survived poverty and living on the prairie together.

Yet, there was something that made Ginger swing from rage to joy. The rest of us tolerated these outbursts because Mother wanted, more than anything, to keep us together since all of us had suffered so badly the year we had been separated. She vowed she would never let that happen again. Still, Ginger's behavior was truly dysfunctional.

At one point when Ginger could not conceive a child, she asked me if I would have a baby for her. I was astonished and repelled. I knew I would never do that because of her and Lewis's abusive behavior. Even though I loved them both dearly, I knew how they treated children. I refused, of course.

How could I birth a child for her and watch them abuse him or her, knowing the child was really my child, and I would not be able to save it? The thought made chills course through my body. I could not believe she had asked for such a thing.

In the summer of 1966, when my daughter Cindy was eight years old and my oldest son, Bo was six, we went to Texas for a visit, as we did each year. At the end of our vacation, Ginger asked if Cindy and Bo could stay.

Cindy and Bo begged me and their dad to let them stay. There were horses on Lewis and Ginger's ranch and lots of cousins to play with. I was uncomfortable with this but thought she would surely not hurt them. I finally gave in and let them stay.

My husband, Jack, Brett, my younger son, and I drove down Illinois St. in Midland, headed for Fenton, Michigan.

After about two weeks, on one of my calls to check on my babies, they sounded really strange and stilted. I didn't know until much later that Ginger always stood right with them when I would call. A few days later, Mother called and said I needed to get my children home right away. Without even questioning her, I immediately got them airline tickets and told Ginger to take them to the airport and send them home. When they got home, they hugged us like they'd never let us go, but they still didn't say anything. I thought they had just been really homesick, and things went back to normal. Perhaps subconsciously I did not want to

Our young children Brett, Toby, Cindy with Auburn, Bo when they stayed at Ginger's, and she abused Toby and Bo.

know that I had not been there to protect them, or to have even prevented it, because the damage had already been done.

In 2018, Cindy and I were visiting, and she asked me if I remembered when she and Bo were supposed to stay at Aunt Ginger's house for the summer. I said I did. She told me that when we pulled away from Ginger's house, and as soon as our car was out of sight, Ginger got a switch from a tree in her yard and switched Bo and their cousin Toby (who Ginger was raising) until their legs bled.

It scared them so badly that they were afraid to talk about it. Anytime they were on the phone with me, Ginger would not let them talk without being there. A sickness rose in my stomach, and seething rage burst in my heart and mind. My children were subjected to her terror, something I had sworn I would never let happen to them. Never had I been so absolutely furious. Even though I saved them, it was not before Ginger had already done that terrible thing.

I confronted Ginger. She denied it and tried to make excuses, but both my daughter of eight remembered it and Mother had called me to tell me I needed to get my children home. I told Ginger her denial did not take her actions away. She tried her last trick. "If I did do that, I am very sorry."

I exploded with even more anger. She could never take responsibility for her actions. "I don't know if I can forgive you for this terrible thing you have done," I told her. "You had no right to touch my children in such a violent way." I hung up the phone. It took a long time for me to consider talking to her again. It took talking to my pastor over a long period of time for me to forgive her. I didn't want to be vengeful. I wanted to keep a relationship with her, just not the kind it had always been. I was very upset and just as soon not talk to her another day in my life. Yet I knew this unforgiving state of mind would not be healthy.

It occurred to me that Ginger was probably bi-polar. I searched for and attended a day-long seminar at the University of Michigan where two professors presented about living in a family with a bi-polar member. Since I had a Master's in Clinical Behavioral Psychology I was familiar with the disorder. It was amazing that Ginger's behavior was right under our family's noses, but it had become normal, so we didn't question it. We tolerated it and we shouldn't have.

At the end of the seminar, I spoke to the professors about Ginger's behavior throughout my life and asked them many questions. They said that from what I shared, it definitely sounded like it could be bi-polar or a personality disorder. About her violet and abusive behavior, they said no one should put up with or allow a bi-polar person to be abusive. They have enough discernment to know when they cannot get away with their abuse.

Since I learned about bi-polar disorder, much of our family life and the useless pain we had endured became clear. A lot of questions were answered. Ginger's odd and horrible moods followed by euphoric highs started to make sense.

One Christmas, Mother and all five of us kids were at Ginger and Lewis' house. Ginger had bread baking in her new bread maker machine. She had asked for it, and Mother got it for her Christmas present. The aromas of turkey, dressing, mashed potatoes, and pumpkin pie wafted through the house with a pleasant nostalgia. We congregated around the brightly lit Christmas tree to open our presents before we ate. Two of the older children passed out the gifts. Then we all joyfully tore into our treasures.

I opened mine from Mother and it was a pretty, soft white sweater with sparkles on the front. It was beautiful. Ginger looked over at it, and sneered at Mother in a nasty voice, "You always get Sidney the pretty things." The Black Angel of Doom instantly appeared as she went into her hostile doom and gloom, building up to another spoiled Christmas. I reminded her she had asked Mother for the bread machine, which at that time cost $200. My sweater cost about $50, but she was already in destruction mode. I said I would be glad to trade gifts with her, but she was already past being appeased. She started slamming cupboard doors, yanking pans from drawers, and pounding them on counter tops, with the look I had come to know so well on her distorted face.

Wayne had been taking videos and inadvertently captured some of Ginger's hostile display. I felt my stomach getting nervous, like it was being tied in knots. I went into high-alert posture to try to smooth everything over. Something was different this time though for me to notice *my* reaction. What if I didn't do anything? I just paid attention to what I was doing and feeling.

82

In the past, I would immediately try to settle her down. It occurred to me that some time, long ago, I subconsciously made the decision to take responsibility for Ginger's moods. As I watched her brewing into disaster, I realized she had never asked me to be responsible. So why was I doing this? In that lightening flash of insight, I fired myself from that job to let her take care of her own emotional moods. Just as quickly, my stomach and shoulders relaxed. It was a miracle.

Two huge things happened in that moment. A short time earlier, I had realized Ginger probably had a bi-polar disorder. I also understood that I was feeling responsible for taking care of her moods. This explained so many of the dynamics in our family. It was like discovering a treasure chest of answers to so many puzzling questions! Mother felt guilty, as if birthing Ginger made her the culpable party. Troy and Kayo just avoided her with disgust during these episodes, and Jo hated her. We all reacted to Ginger without knowing what was really going on.

We siblings had not done ourselves or Ginger any favors by allowing these patterns to persist since she herself was responsible for the abuse. This led to some healthier, exciting, fearful and peaceful feelings about a new way of being together. There were wonderful possibilities, yet not without pain and consequences. The family balancing act was busted wide open. Relationships needed to be redefined. This was the time for truth telling. But that is another story for another time.

LESSONS

- We were tolerating abuse to keep the peace at any price. The price was too high.
- Repeated behavior, even if dysfunctional, will be normalized in a family or society, making it hard to change.
- I discovered that I had taken responsibility for changing Ginger's moods. She didn't ask me to, so why did I? Families seek balance. Members take on different roles to keep the family together.

83

- You cannot solve a problem that you do not acknowledge. Someone has to step up and say, *"We have an elephant in the room."* By saying it out loud, we can begin to do something about it.
- We cannot create normal, healthy dynamics if we hang onto the dysfunctional behavioral roles.

Two Questions

1. Has anyone ever crossed a boundary and done something hurtful to you or your children? What did they do?

2. How did you deal with it?

Prelude to the Prairie

We were living with Aunt Fannie and Uncle Frank. Aunt Fannie was Daddy's older sister, and I remember she was kind to us kids, but she didn't like Momma. When we left Houston, we landed in Dallas for an insignificant amount of time and then moved in with Daddy's folks on N. Terrel St. on the northside of the tracks in Midland, Texas. This was a memorable move because our destiny was being built right there in Aunt Fannie's backyard where our future little house on the prairie was being constructed board by board. Little did we know the impact this prairie house would play in our lives.

L – R Troy, Ginger, Kayo, me, and Jo. Our first day on the prairie.
Momma dressed us in in crisp, clean clothes so we looked nice,
and not poor or unkept.

Uncle Frank knew carpentry and showed Daddy how to help him build our prairie home.

Momma was working for the Southwestern Bell Telephone Company. She walked about two miles each day to get back and forth to work. A lot of mysterious things were happening this particular day. A big flatbed truck came to Aunt Fannie's house and loaded that little house up on that truck and carried it away. When Momma came home from work the little house was gone and it wasn't even finished yet. It just had the inside sheet rock and 2 X 4's but no outside walls. Aunt Fannie came out and told Momma that our Uncle Joe and Uncle Chester had come and had the house moved to S. Carter Street, south of the railroad tracks where they had bought us a small lot. Momma took a cab to find it. There it sat, a lonely forlorn structure in the middle of nowhere, the last stop for shattered lives and hopeless dreams. Momma said she looked at this sad state of affairs and determined we had hit the low mark. And that was as far down as she was going to go! She vowed we would get off that prairie.

The conditions were so cruel and raw, our relatives didn't come around.

Momma did what she had to do to get our life started back up again, and that was to get us hooked up to electricity. But we had no water, so she asked our new neighbors if we could get water from them. and they let us.

Momma had us clean up and put freshly starched and ironed clothes to take the picture on the first page.

Momma had taught us kids to help where we could. Troy became our water carrier, and that was no small task. Ginger had a job at a theater and helped Momma with expenses. Jo cooked and she and I cleaned the floors each day keeping the house clear of the relentless dirt that blew through every crack and cranny through our thin walls. Uncle Frank had told Uncle Joe and Uncle Chester they needed to get the house out of his yard because he didn't want to get into trouble with the city.

This was our new low level for living and life was not easy. We were dropped in the midst of forgotten humanity. Conditions were so poor our granny couldn't stand to come see us there. She couldn't bear to witness the brutal reality of our fate.

Momma said we were on the "bottom rung of the ladder." I don't remember seeing Daddy hardly at all during those prairie years, he was always gone. I just remember how hard Momma worked to make our life gracious. In spite of the poor conditions, she would always have an embroidered tablecloth on the table and set it real pretty for our beans and cornbread dinners. Momma said just because it was a meager meal did not mean it couldn't look pretty. Children are very resilient, so we did the only thing we could do, we adapted and carried on.

We had no idea how often our little souls would be called upon to adapt to the situations imposed upon us by adults. In less than a year Abilene would call us by name. We would only be there for part of a year. We never really knew why we were there. The prairie had a claim on us, and it did indeed reclaim us. We went back to that God forgotten place of lost souls and would not be free for some time.

<u>LESSONS</u>

- I learned that life was a moving target. Nothing stayed the same for very long. Whether it was a different town, different people, or different living conditions, we had to very quickly figure out what was going on and learn to live within those conditions.

- We all learned to be flexible in any situation and tried to be as happy as we could be within the circumstances.

- We also learned how to make the best of the circumstances we found ourselves in. We looked for the good in our surroundings. Very often Momma would ask us at supper, "What good did you find in your day today?"

- I learned to accept what I could not change for now.

<u>TWO QUESTIONS</u>:

1. Have you ever been in a move with your parents when you were young, in which you were surrounded with completely new circumstances beyond your control? Describe the situation.

2. What did you do? How did it make you feel?

Geraldine Shouldn't Have Messed with My Baby Doll

"*That is it!*" a voice roared from deep down inside me. And then I felt white lightening skyrocket inside my head. It sparkled and cracked like welding fire spraying the floor of my skull. All the while, I was rising like a samurai warrior and crouched ready to attack. In my life, I have only experienced this kind of rage four times. But wait a moment, I am getting ahead of myself. Let me go to the beginning of this story.

Aunt Blanche and Uncle Dean had come into Midland to shop and brought Geraldine by our house so we could play. The three adults went into town to take advantage of the after-Christmas sales. Well, they did. Momma went along just to window shop. I don't know where Daddy was. By this time, he was leaving us quite often. However, it had been a great Christmas.

Momma had gotten each one of us five kids one gift that we had painstakingly chosen from the little Christmas pamphlet Sears and Roebucks provided. We were ecstatically happy with what we got. I got a baby doll (probably my last), and she was beautiful beyond description. I thought I had died and gone to heaven and, as you can imagine, I treated that baby doll with tender, loving care.

When the adults left for downtown Midland, Geraldine and I got busy finding a box and a towel to make my doll a bed and set up a chair outside our prairie home. Because it was probably going to be my last year for a doll, since I was eleven years old by now, Baby Doll was important and precious to me. I don't know what it was with Geraldine and her brother, Tuffy, but they just couldn't stand for someone else to have something nice. Especially us, because we were the "poor cousins." When we did get something, we treated it with care because we had so little. After a while, she started handling Baby Doll very roughly.

I warned her real nice-like to be careful with my doll. But oh, no, she had destruction in her heart. And I saw her grab my brand-new Baby Doll, throw it on the ground, and rub her in the dirt real hard, getting her snow-white dress filthy dirty. We only got the one toy a year, so that toy was priceless to us, and I was seeing mine being ruined. The audacity of it turned me upside down.

That's when the lightning bolt took hold of me. I lost all reason and was driven by rage and her senseless meanness possessed me. I grabbed Geraldine like she was a limp rag doll, threw her to the ground, and rubbed her in the dirt just like she did my precious doll.

When I "woke up," I was standing over her, with my hands balled up beside me in hard fists, and through tight lips, I hoarsely whispered, "Geraldine, you should not have messed with my doll!" She could tell I was ready for battle if she dared anything else. There was a realization on her face that she shouldn't push it any further. She inched away from me and got into the house and laid down on one of the beds bawling and boo-hooing her eyes out.

I stayed outside and tried to clean my doll up, waiting for her to finish her show of being wounded. Though it wouldn't have bothered me at that point if I had hurt her some because it was such a mean-spirited thing for her to have done. Twenty minutes, thirty minutes passed while she carried on something fierce. Finally, she stopped. And it was just quiet. I thought maybe she had fallen asleep.

There was not a road or driveway to our little house. We were just in the middle of the prairie. I could hear the crunch of Uncle Dean's tires as he wheeled his car up to the house. Well, Geraldine heard it too. And that girl started bellowing and squawking like a pig being poked with a hot iron. She rose in a crescendo of wails, and short, jerky fake-cries. I was just plain amazed and disgusted. She hadn't cried for a good hour, and now here she was carrying on this way.

When Momma, Aunt Blanche and Uncle Dean came running through the door, Geraldine's version of what happened was quite a bit different than what took place. Supposedly, she was playing nice as could be, and I just grabbed her and threw her to the ground when she hadn't done anything! I was shocked.

My Mother bought me this doll when I was 60 years old to replace the one Geraldine had messed up.
I was deeply touched that she realized how much Geraldine's meanness hurt me and she wanted to
make it up to me. It was like getting to have a make- over and get the ending I wanted.

It was plain that Aunt Blanche wanted my mother to give me a whipping for hurting Geraldine. She was dirty, but not hurt. Momma turned to me and asked what I had done. And I told her, Geraldine had thrown Baby Doll on the ground and rubbed her in the dirt, so I had done the same thing to her.

Momma told them that it looked like everything was settled out even. So, Geraldine didn't get the satisfaction of getting me whipped. That marked the end of any friendship with Geraldine, for I had learned not to trust her and that she was not a kind or worthy friend for me.

LESSONS

- Prejudice exists towards people who are poor. We were deemed inferior just because we were living in poverty at the time.
- I learned that if a person is cruel, it comes to the surface when they think someone is inferior to them.
- It was a big lesson that there are people who have a mean nature. It is a very sad thing.
- I learned that Momma took the time to find out more and believed me. She stuck up for me and didn't let them intimidate her into whipping me.
- The world is not always fair. The guy with the white hat does not always necessarily win.
- I learned I did not have to subject myself to anyone's mean behavior.
- I learned to choose my friends for their character, not for what they had in material things.

TWO QUESTIONS

1. What experience have you suffered? What experience with a bully have you had?

2. How did you handle the situation?

Under the Shade of a Mesquite Tree

Dreams, truly *Big dreams* are a marvel. There are so many parts of my childhood that I loved, and I see now how important they were in shaping me. We didn't have as many toys as most kids did. We would get one toy at Christmas and depending on what we asked for, might get a toy for our birthday. We learned how to find joy from experiences that did not cost anything.

I remember about one day when Jo was ten and I was nine, that it was so stifling hot in that little prairie home, we thought we would die of suffocation. We had to get out of there! Heat waves were glimmering across the prairie, and we searched for the biggest mesquite tree we could find, which was the size of a big bush. I don't know why they were called it a tree maybe because people so desperately wanted to be around trees.

A mesquite "tree" is between and behind my brothers and me.

Finally, we spotted what the mesquite we were looking for, much bigger than the one in the photo. Mesquite shade is different than any other kind. The small leaves and

L – R Troy, Kayo, and me. Just prior to leaving for Abilene, Texas for less than a year.

93

the thorns created a lacy, feathery pattern, which created a hazy other worldly feeling, just right for pondering dreams.

We plopped down under that refreshing shade, careful to avoid the thorns, and looking up through the magic portal between the leaves, we could see a world of Texas blue sky. Immediately we were transported to another place, where all things are possible. Jo and I were surrounded by the soft drone of insects that were hypnotizing us into a detached, dream state.

Jo just started lazily rambling, about what, I don't remember, but then she started talking about her wishes and dreams. She said, "Do you know what I want most of all?" I heard the yearning in her voice as I replied "No, what?" Her biggest dream was to be able to lie under a monster vat that had a spigot on the end, and anytime she wanted to, she could reach up, open that spigot, and ice-cold Coca Cola would come out and fill her mouth. She could drink as much she wanted. When she got her fill, she could turn the spigot off knowing when she wanted more, all she had to do was open the spigot again. I thought this was an excellent dream. And on a hot day like we were having, cold Coca-Cola would be a mighty fine way to quench that awful cotton-dry thirst.

I thought about what my dream could be. I spent a lot of time in the Midland Library. It was thrilling to look through books that had lots of pictures of beautiful places in Europe and Africa. I was especially drawn to Italy and South Africa. The pictures were so inviting, it made me want to go to those faraway places. I told Jo my dream was to fly on an airplane (flying was a rarity in 1950) to Italy and see all the places I saw in those books... Trevi Fountain (I had seen the Movie, *Three Coins In A Fountain*), the Coliseum, and places Paul had walked in Rome. I could actually feel myself there.

It didn't cost anything to dream. It kept our minds off of the conditions we lived under for a while and for a while, life was desirable and beautiful. Though these were only daydreams, they were vivid and real in our minds and hearts.

We roused ourselves from this dream state and went back inside to get ready for Jo to cook supper and me to set the table. But those beautiful thoughts were with us for days.

It is ironic what happened in our real lives though. Jo married Clay, who eventually worked for the Coca-Cola Company, and they got all the Coca-Cola they wanted. I married Wayne Bonvallet, and he took me to Italy seven times.

Eventually, Wayne and I became world travelers. Along with my daughter, Cindy, we created a 501c3 Charity, and for the last 15 years, we have spent 2 - 3 months a year in South Africa doing charity work.

Be careful what you dream, you just might get it. Dreams are wonderful no matter what age we are. Dreams keep us alive, and Dreams are powerful. Dreams are a preview of a life you can create to invigorate your life. To have a playful, creative state of mind, keeps us young and full of hope.

LESSONS

- I believe in the power of my dreams.

- If you can dream it, you can achieve it.

- To have a child-like, creative state of mind, keeps us young and full of hope.

- All great plans start with a thought, a dream.

- Dreams are hopeful and give you something to strive for.

- To be able to think creatively and to dream of better things gave me an escape from the oppressiveness of poverty.

TWO QUESTIONS

1. What is a dream you have had? Describe it.

2. How much of it came true?

Ironing for a Blouse

I was about nine or ten years old when we found ourselves in Abilene, Texas. It was a sweltering July Texas day. The sun had heat waves of ringlets around it, and you could see flames leaping into the air and collapsing back to the surface of the scorching sun and I was ironing. Little drops of sweat trickled down my forehead.

My daddy had brought me to this pretty lady's house. She kept a cozy and tidy little house that had yellow wallpaper garnished with little pink flowers. The iron and ironing board was next to a rack that stood like a centurion warrior waiting to hold my beautifully ironed clothes as I completed each piece. The pretty lady said she would pay me if I could do her ironing. Well, I thought, I had been ushered first class right into "hog heaven!" Daddy and the pretty lady exchanged nice southern pleasantries, and he left after she showed him where everything was for me. A few minutes later she left too.

When my sister Jo and I had last gone to the Sears and Roebucks store, I spotted a white blouse. It was so beautiful; it took my breath away. It had a stand-up collar, real pretty little pearl-like buttons, and two rows of dainty ruffles halfway down the front. Only trouble was, it cost $1.95, and I didn't have $1.95. Almost two dollars was a lot of money in 1950 Abilene. But now this ironing opportunity had just dropped itself right into my lap, and I wasn't about to let it pass me by. Needless to say, that blouse became the goal of my intention for ironing all those clothes.

The first step was to sprinkle the clothes, which was done with a RC cola bottle whose lid I had poked holes into. This way, the clothes wouldn't get soaking wet. After sprinkling the clothes, I folded and rolled up the damp clothes, so the water spread out evenly, making them perfect for ironing. By the time I got through with the sprinkling, I had filled up a peach basketful of clothes to be ironed, but I thought, whoo-wee, that's a lot of ironing. I figured I could get it done by the end of the day. That blouse was certainly worth it.

My blouse was a sure thing now. I even imagined how beautiful it would look on me when I wore it. And I could wear it with just about anything because it was white.

Most people did not have air conditioners back in those days. A few people had old swamp coolers, a device by which a pump sucked water up to the top of the housing and poured it down the straw-like side panels cooling the water as it evaporated. They didn't really cool things down very well, but the lady didn't have one of those either.

Hour after hour, I ironed those clothes. The smothering day along with the heat of the iron, transported me into an inferno while rivulets of sweat collected under my hair and ran down my back. I could feel my face glowing red, and my damp clothes were sticking to my body. The thick humid air made it hard to breathe. But my special blouse was going to make it worth all this torment. I hung up each flawless garment on the rack, which I took great pleasure in counting the completed pieces. I was really proud of every single garment. My guess was I had ironed enough to earn $3.00, maybe $4.00, so I figured I could buy my blouse and then something else!

Finally, the lady came back all cheerful. A few minutes after she arrived, my daddy came to pick me up and take me home. I would ask him to take me by Sears and Roebuck so I could buy my blouse. It seemed an eternity since I had started ironing that morning. But now reward time was here!

Waiting for Daddy to get here, I could hardly contain myself for the thrill of anticipating that I would get my ruffled white blouse. I could see myself plain as day, putting that blouse on and seeing my reflection in the mirror.

The lady opened the door and my Daddy walked in. They greeted each other nicely and the lady asked Daddy how much she owed me. Back then, children did not do their own business dealings, adults settled it for them. I was holding my breath… and then my daddy did something unthinkable. He casually said to the lady, "You don't owe her anything, she was glad to do it for you!"

My heart fell to the ground and like fine crystal, broke into several pieces. She thanked him graciously as Daddy pushed me through the door. I walked out in stunned silence. I couldn't breathe. What had just happened? No $3.00 or $4.00… and *no* $1.95, *no* blouse, *nothing* for all of my efforts. I was empty handed after a full day's work. But my work wasn't worth anything.

How could I say anything? Children did not argue or talk back to their parents in those days. I don't think my momma ever knew my daddy had done that.

Over the years, I arrived at a very sad understanding of what may have transpired. This incident has kept coming up for many years in my life, and I didn't know why. I have had many painful memories, why did this one stand out so? I realized; it was because something was going on beneath the surface. I felt it but didn't really have it figured out until decades later. Daddy's drinking also led him to being a womanizer, or maybe he was one anyway with or without the alcohol. My older siblings told me that Daddy's disappearances for regular intervals, or the binges he went on when he would abandon us, was when he was with other women. The pretty lady had just been one of those women.

My daddy took me to this woman's house. He let me iron with the hope of getting something pretty when he actually had me iron for her just so he could please *her*, because they had something going on between them. *I had been used*! This was beyond humiliating.

LESSONS

- I struggled in my pre-teen years with a feeling of poor self-esteem and unworthiness. We get a lot of unspoken messages from the things we experience in our lives.

- I was not valuable. I was not worth anything. That sense of worthlessness was shameful to me.

- My own daddy didn't think I deserved to be compensated for my efforts. For so many years, I thought there was something wrong with my self-esteem when it was Daddy's self-esteem that was really wounded. It was a hurtful realization.

TWO QUESTIONS

1. When have you wanted something very badly, worked for it, dreamed about it? What was it?

2. What happened? Were you disappointed because you could not have it, or did you get it?

A Girl Named Shirley – For Two Weeks

How often had I heard, "Oh, you're a girl," and "Oh, you're so tall!" Zapped twice before the day even got off to a good start. That is how the first day of school had been for me each new school year. You'd think teachers would know better.

Kids are more fragile than they let on, and they don't yet have the sufficient confidence to be okay with who they are. At least I didn't, and I never got used to the "name game" happening. I dreaded that first day so. That is also the day a teacher can mess up your name.

With a name like Sidney Flynn Randolph, most people thought I was a boy. I always thought Momma and Daddy named me that because they had one boy and two girls and probably had wanted a second boy.

I was a little over nine years old.

When teachers called roll on that first day, they told us to stand up so they could see us and identify our name with our face. I was usually the tallest girl around at that age, and sometimes taller than many of the boys. That embarrassed me a lot, especially when an insensitive teacher reacted so radically about my height and my name. And if a teacher really pronounced someone's name wrong, they set that kid up for all kinds of merciless teasing.

So, I stood up, and when that teacher jerked her head back and shockingly blurted out that dreaded response, "Oh, you're a girl!" and "You are so tall," I cringed and wanted to shrink out of sight, or to crawl into the nearest closet and disappear. I also was horrified, not knowing what the teacher might say next out of his or her own discomfort. Which made a bad situation even worse.

Humiliation is one of our strongest emotions; we'll do anything to not get in the kind of situation that causes it again. Sometimes adults forget how painful being humiliated is. This first day of school routine humiliated me to the core. Suddenly, to be a girl, and tall, was bad.

Around this time, Daddy moved us again to Dallas and another new school. The way I handled this vexing experience outwardly was to laugh it off as if it didn't matter. It mattered. It hurt my feelings.

Even though we didn't have a lot of clothes, Momma kept us clean, and our clothes starched and ironed. That first morning, I got up and excitedly hoped that, in this new school, it would be different. It was a real ordeal just to get the role called. Miss Pearl, our teacher, sat us alphabetically. She was calling the roll real slow, going one by one, up one row and down another. I could see she was getting close to me. I wanted to run for the hills before it even started, but I was glued to the spot. My turn was next. I braced myself. Miss Pearl hesitated, struggled with my first name. She attempted to discern what it was, which came out as, "Si... Shi..." Finally, she blurted out, "Shirley Randolph?" I instantly seized my opportunity, took that name as my own and proudly answered, "Yes Ma'am, I am Shirley, and I am right here."

I had so learned to dislike my name that I thought Miss Pearl performed a miracle right then and there in that Dallas classroom. I was now Shirley! I usually made friends pretty easily and quickly got used to hearing the other kids call me Shirley. For two weeks this girl, Mary Sue, and I became best friends. We told each other our secrets, played together at recess, and really got along well.

I had the bright idea of inviting her over to my house to play, and she came. We were playing out back of our house, where there were lots of fruit trees, and all kinds of interesting old farm equipment to explore and make believe with. She yelled out my name, "Hey Shirley, come over here!" Momma was at the kitchen window and apparently heard Mary Sue and glided out the back door. By now I was used to kids calling me Shirley, so I didn't think anything about it. But Momma sure did. She was off that porch and up to Mary Sue, and sweet as syrup asked, "What did you just call her?" Mary Sue answered, "Why I called her by her name, Shirley." Momma glided back in the house all chipper smiley-like, as if she'd never come out the door at all. But I knew trouble was brewing in that sugary smile. When Mary Sue left, and I reluctantly went into the house, she took my arm and ask me what was going on with the "Shirley name." I made a full confession. That was it. We went to bed; nothing else was said.

Except the next day, Momma marched me down to that school and into my classroom right up to Miss Pearl's desk to straighten this all out. I had to tell that story of taking Shirley for my name all over again to Miss Pearl. It took a little doing to get it all straightened out, but within a hare's breath, my new identity was snatched away from me, and just like that, I was not Shirley anymore. I was "Sidney, the tall girl." At least I got to have my new name for 2 glorious weeks. On our walk back home, Momma looked at me and explained "I know you are disappointed right now, but when you are older you will be glad you have an unusual name and people will remember you. You see, I took a lot of effort and thought to all five of you

Alethea Flynn (Leta) and George Holmes in about 1908

My namesake, Momma's cousin.

'kids' names. Ginger Gay was named after a character in a play that your Daddy and I were in. That's how we met. Troy Alvis was named after your Daddy's best friend, Jo Katheryn was named after my brother, your Uncle Joe. You were named after my favorite cousin, Aletha Flynn. Kayo was named after your Daddy, Henry Elvin Randolph, Jr. but, of course, we called him Kayo. She wasn't going to put up with anyone messing with those chosen names.

I will never forget how great it felt to hear myself called Shirley. As I grew up, got educated and got a great job at General Motors, I was surely glad I had a unique name, just like Momma had said. And it became even more important when Wayne (my husband), Cindy (my daughter), and I had our own business.

<u>LESSONS</u>

- Children can be easily humiliated by adults' unconscious behavior; Humiliation is one of our strongest emotions. We will do anything not to experience that again.

- We don't need to try to be someone we are not. I am the best me I will ever know. Names are important. I didn't know what an asset it was to have an unusual name. It helped me in my career. People could easily remember my name since it is unique.

- Knowing why Momma named me a special name made me feel proud and special.

<u>TWO QUESTIONS</u>

1. Have you ever been humiliated by a teacher or other significant adult in a different setting? What happened?

2. How did it make you feel?

I Always Wanted to Be a Cowgirl

How Momma managed to get the money together to pay for the horse, I'll never know, but what a horse it was! The man came into the Courts with his horse that looked just like Hop-a long Cassidy's trusted Steed. Hop along was a movie star cowboy, and he was undefeated by the villains in the black hats.

The Hop-a-long horse look-alike. I was thrilled and
terrified at the same time.

For two dimes, the man with the horse would let kids sit on his horse dressed in full regalia of horse accessories and take a picture. Momma scraped together $.80, so she could get a photo of each one of us kids. Kayo wasn't born yet, so he didn't count in the $.80, which was a lot of money.

When it was my turn, I was a tangled mixture of awe and fear. For a four-year-old, that horse was as big as an elephant. Sitting on it was like sitting on a bolt of lightning. When that horse moved, the whole world moved because of him. The horse was a fierce thing to me, and, despite my fear I sat on him anyway. I was so thrillingly afraid, I told Momma not to let go of my arm, so I wouldn't feel left alone yet I could still fill the excitement of doing something so daring. It was so awesome I have remembered that experience my whole life.

When the old man came back to deliver Momma the photos of us four kids, we clamored around her like baby chicks wanting to see our photos.

Now, fast forward 8 years. I was staying the summer with Aunt Pud and Uncle Bud in Tarzan. It was the time of year on their ranch when they were making steers out of bulls, and Uncle Bud was going to take his cowboy crew out on the range, chuck wagon and all. They would be out a couple of days but wouldn't be too far from the ranch.

I had seen movie shows about cattle-drives and it looked exciting and romantic: riding a horse herding cattle, serenading them, and sleeping under the stars. I could just hear Roy Roger's gentle voice. I ran up to Uncle Bud and told him I wanted to go on the cattle drive. Uncle Bud said "No, it's too rough for someone who has never been on a cattle-drive before." Uncle Bud was usually an easy-going guy, so I dared to press him. I pleaded my case, "But I want to go, and I'll work hard. Please, please let me go, Uncle Bud." The cowboys standing around probably thought I was crazy because it really was hard work. But I got the picture in my head it would be a glamorous adventure and kept pestering Uncle Bud.

Finally, he said "Okay. You are going on a round-up, and even if you want to go back to the house, you will have to stay out here till nighttime because I can't spare someone to take you home before then." I was ecstatic. Me, a town girl, Sidney, was going on a real live cowboy round-up. We started out early, I was riding around on

107

old Croochie, a tame, older horse, but a little cantankerous. I didn't really know how to handle him, and he knew I was afraid of him, so he gave me a hard time.

I was getting exhausted; the shine on the glamor was rubbing off. It was hot, and all the commotion stirred up lots of prairie dirt all over the place from the cows being roped, thrown on the ground, and being castrated right then and there. The first time, my curiosity made me look at what they were doing, I violently threw up my breakfast. Things were going downhill. I didn't really know they were cutting off the poor bull's manhood without them even having a say in the matter. Oh, lordy, mercy, I got sicker than a dog, but by Uncles Bud's tone of voice, I knew I was going to have stay till nearly sundown.

Just riding Croochie to the campsite rubbed my legs raw. My hind end bounced up and down so much it jarred my teeth. Sweat dripped from every pore in my body, and I was stiffening up fast. We stopped long enough to have a lunch of beans, cornbread and BBQ, Texas style. It's hard to enjoy such luxury when you're so miserable you can hardly see straight.

After an eternity, the sun started to set. I didn't think I was going to make it, but somehow, I did. We weren't that far from the ranch house with a kerosene lamp in the window, so before it got pitch dark, Uncle Bud had one of the cowboys ride me

Six Glaze siblings. (L – R), Uncle Darrell, Aunt Sissy, Uncle Joe, Uncle Jay, Sibyl & Pud.

Aunt Pud was kind to me.

back. There are no words to express the relief and gratitude I felt when I saw that kerosene lamp welcoming us, and to get off old Croochie and go inside to a nice clean ranch house.

Aunt Pud was the quintessential cowboy rancher's wife. She had not only milked the cows that day, but she churned butter since Uncle Bud wouldn't be back until the next day. She suspected I'd be coming in that night, and she helped me with a hot bath, clean pajamas, and a nice bed. She was tender with me, and I sunk into heaven letting the pain drain out of my weary body.

My cowgirl days were over. Uncle Bud let me discover on my own that this was not a career path I would be pursuing. Sometimes, it is important to find out what you don't want to do. I resigned and looked for other opportunities that weren't so painful. It looked romantic and easy in the movies, and even the cowboys made it seem exciting, but that's because it was second nature to them. So many realities are hidden beneath what looks good and easy, and the dreams of what it might be, until you uncover the true picture of what it really is.

To Uncle Bud's and Aunt Pud's credit, they did not tease or torment me about this event. We all let it die a natural death and went forward from there.

LESSONS
- Be careful what you ask for because "all that glitters isn't gold."
- Not all that looks glamorous or romantic is. Some hard truths may be lurking below.
- I did find I could do what I had to. I stayed until Uncle Bud said I could go back. I had to be willing to chew what I bit off.

TWO QUESTIONS
1. When have you romanticized something until you believed only the fantasy in your mind?

2. What was your real experience like?

Life On the Prairie

Momma contemplating our return to the nothingness of the prairie.

I was about nine or ten years old, and life had its ebbs and flows. We had come back to our tiny house on the prairie'. This photo shows the unvarnished life we lived. It was a hard and unrelenting existence. Momma had fractured some of her ribs, falling on the pallet that served as our little porch. She bound her torso and continued to go to work with the fractured ribs because she couldn't afford to stay home. In the shack straight across from our house were the people who had a well and let us get water from them. Troy had to carry enough water every day for us to cook, bathe and clean house with. The perils of the environment were many. We had to dodge rattle snakes, tarantulas, red fire ants, and beds of stickers that hurt like "almighty get out" if you stepped in them barefooted. It was also a rough neighborhood to live in because we were all just hanging by a thread onto survival.

We walked a little over a mile to school, about one and a half miles to Church, and downtown Midland, was almost 2 miles. Momma walked that twice a day most days, and sometime 4 times a day if she had to work a split shift at the Southwestern Bell telephone company.

Momma did laundry at a launder mat in a winger type washing machine. Troy went with her to help her carry the wet clothes home. Jo Kathrine and I would hang them out on a barbed wire fence across from the front of our house. Then we ironed them. Momma was particular about keeping her children clean with clean clothes on.

The routine was the same for groceries. Troy went with Momma so he could help her carry them home. Ginger worked at the local Yucca movie theater selling concessions and gave her check to Momma to help feed us. Once in a while Momma gave me, Jo, Kayo and Troy $.25 each, and that would pay for the movie, a little bag of popcorn and a small coke. She knew the need to occasionally escape the dismal reality of poverty for all of us.

The house was divided in half. When you walked in, that room was all beds for us kids. The partition is where we all hung our clothes. The other half was the kitchen with a makeshift counter. Curtains hung in front of the cupboards that held our dishes, pots, and meager food supply. We had an actual ice box in which ice was delivered to us once a week, a small stove, table and chairs, and Momma and Daddy's roll-away bed. There was one light bulb on each end of the house. Our little butane heater was very small and hardly kept us warm; it doubled to toast our bread for breakfast. We ran out of butane often and just had to face the cold till Momma could afford to fill the tank.

We bathed in a #3 galvanized tub each night. Momma taught us to brush our teeth every night and every morning which we did outside, no matter what the weather.

We had a deck of cards and would play War, Gin Rummy, and Spoon. I made us a monopoly game and we'd play for hours, fighting like cats and dogs. We had a radio, and listened to shows like The Fat Man, Grand Ole Opry, Amos and Andy, and The Lone Ranger. We huddled around in a circle to share these radio adventures.

Momma bought us a ball about three quarters the size of a real basketball or volleyball. Troy hung a peach basket on the kitchen end of the house. There were 5 of us so we could play a pretty good game of basketball. Then he strung a rope so we could enlarge our sports repartee to play volleyball.

We would find a long stick and play like the stick was our horse and ride around on that prairie playing Cowboys and Indians. Our imaginations could take us anywhere.

The prairie was a stark reminder of where we were on the social scale. The railroad tracks were about a quarter of a mile from our house. At first, it sounded like the train would come right down the middle of our house, but we got used to it.

As you will see in our experience on the prairie, my Momma did not want us to think this was going to be our life forever. She did not want us to accept such a lowly station in life. She would look at each one of us, then in a level voice, she would say, "This is not us. This is only temporary. This does not define us. We will all get off of this prairie one day". In Momma's heart, she determined this prairie was the bottom rung of the social ladder and this was as far down as she was going to go.

Momma helped me to look beyond the moment, and not accept these miserable minimums for my life. There was something to hope for. Of course, I did wonder just how long temporary was. When I bring all this forward to today, it helped prepare me for the work we do for our charity. Having experienced poverty at the bottom level, I understand now how our little African children feel. The injury to their little souls is painful. I know how they live on the edge of survival, yet they can still smile. They figure out life "in the moment."

Life is always giving us clues and experiences that make us ready for that next great thing God wants us to ultimately do. His vision is bigger than our vision. He knows what we are capable of, we cling to safer harbors, but He gives us courage to go into the deeper water. There is more buoyancy there.

LESSONS

- I learned how to be responsible and take care of myself.
- A self-starter does a lot to get themselves ahead.
- I could adjust to extreme conditions.
- Never give up. Keep hope alive. If you have a goal, you have a chance.
- If you do not have your own goals, you will be used by someone who has their own goals.
- Rather than cry about your situation, find a way to change it. It is amazing what you can do if you set your mind to it.
- I learned a great lesson of gratitude for what God brought into my life.
- Most things really are temporary. Nothing is all bad or all good forever.
- Life offers striking changes.

TWO QUESTIONS

1.What have you had to overcome at some point in your life? What hardship have you had to face?

2. What did you do?

Where's the Gravy?

My stomach was growling again. I looked on the shelves, even though I had already looked, as if maybe this time some food would appear. No more food showed up. There was a can of evaporated milk, a little sugar, some salt, and pepper, two slices of bread, and a small amount of flour in the dilapidated bag. There was the usual container of grease drippings that is found in almost every kitchen of a southern

Momma working at Southwestern Bell training new employees.

home. Then the light flashed "gravy!" I could make gravy with what I had. I remember the lack of food being a real issue most of the time growing up.

As I mentioned earlier, Mother worked for the Southwestern Bell telephone company and her salary was $31.50 per week, not a lot even for the 1950s. That small amount did not always allow our supply of food to stretch all the way to Friday. We could have been some of the first practicing minimalists, but not by intention.

I loved gravy but I had heard it was hard to make without it being lumpy. I searched my memory for when I had seen Momma make a batch. I was hungry enough to convince myself I could do it. How hard could it be? Right? So, I put grease in the skillet, some flour, and some salt and pepper. It seemed right.

So far so good. I had poured the evaporated milk in a bowl with an equal amount of water. Good, that would make more gravy. I knew gravy had to be stirred constantly.

When the flour started turning brown, things started happening fast. I quickly poured the whole amount of milk and water into the flour concoction. It smelled right. I could see myself eating that gravy on the bread giblets. I cooked and cooked it, but it was really runny, so I figured it needed more flour. The gravy was getting runny *and* lumpy. I panicked and added the rest of the flour. To my horror, it started getting thicker and thicker! I was in trouble big time now. It was sacrilegious to waste food in our economic condition.

By this time my precious gravy had grown tall and seized up into a solid brick right there in my skillet. First, I tried tasting it but there was so much flour in it, the taste was chalky and putrid. I froze and panicked again. I can't let Momma see this mess. I can't let her see I wasted the last of our food.

I did what most anyone would do in this circumstance. The only thing to do was to hide the gravy disaster; get rid of the evidence. But where? I turned off the stove to let the brick cool down some, and I needed to think about where to hide it. There aren't many hiding places in a two-room house.

After the skillet cooled down and it could be handled, I took the solid brick of gravy outside. My searching eyes spotted some rather large rocks where Ginger had tried to create a division to mark off the prairie from our yard. It looked sort of odd, but she was trying whatever she could to make it less terrible. I ran over to the largest rock, set the skillet on the ground, dug a hole under the rock, dumped the skillet, and covered the lump with the rock.

Troy was witness to the whole bloody thing. He was sorry the scheme didn't pan out because he was counting on eating some of that gravy covered bread too.

Even though, Troy saw the whole sordid thing, he never squealed on me. Momma couldn't get to the bottom of the disappeared food, but she said she wanted to talk to all of us in the morning before we left for school. I was grateful to get through that one unscathed, but guilt stalked me mercilessly. I wondered what Momma wanted to talk to us about.

LESSONS

- Desperation led me to the boldness of trying something I didn't know how to do. I took a risk. When we feel desperate, we do desperate things.

- Desperation sharpened my creativity.

- Guilt from wasting food tried to eat me alive, so I confessed to Momma when she was in a good mood—like when she got her paycheck and was able to bring home some groceries.

TWO QUESTIONS

1. When have you made a mistake that resulted in you feeling you should cover up what you did?

2. Describe what happened?

Running for Cake

We were sitting on the bunkbeds. I was wringing my hands, Kayo was leaning up against me still sleepy, Jo had her hands in her lap, and Troy was whistling waiting for Momma to begin. She had told us the night before she wanted to talk to us. So here we were. She sat on a chair in front of us. Ginger sat next to her. Ginger was

Me at about eleven years old ready to run the
race of my life.

like Momma's partner in working. Troy carried all the water from our neighbors next door. My and Jo's jobs were to clean floors and cook. I was a survival cook. I could cook just enough to survive. As you might guess, Jo did the cooking. Kayo was to pick up things. He was too little for much else.

Momma said, "I want you to always remember, *this* is not us. We don't come from a background of such poor circumstances. *This* is not how we will always be. We will become better, all of us. *This* is only temporary. Can you remember that? We don't have any food for your lunches today, so I want you to please stay home. I don't want you going to school hungry and not be able to have lunch with your friends. As soon as I get my check and get off work today, I'll go to the grocery store and buy us groceries and we will eat real big tonight. Troy can meet me there at 4:30 p.m. and help me carry the groceries home. So please stay home, and I'll get home as soon as I can." She left to walk across the prairie to work.

We all sort of meandered around trying to take our minds off being hungry. I laid on the bottom bunk trying to be patient, but that wasn't working too well, so I said a little prayer for our food, then tried to sleep. A little thought bubbled up in my brain. I remembered we had races that day at my Southside Elementary School. The winners got cake and milk. I believed my team could win. Besides, I'd rather be around fed and full kids more than us hungry ones. I hatched a plan to sneak out and hot-foot it to school to the races. Upon arriving at school, I quickly rallied my relay race team. We were all excited and ready to scorch the grass running.

The starting whistle screeched out. We were off and running. I was on fire with excitement. I could win cake and milk. I ran like the wind and won all my individual race events. And now we were heading into the final relay race event. We huddled up, encouraged each other, and went to our positions. The whistle screeched one more time. The adrenalin was pumping through my body.

I was the one to run the last stretch in the relay race. The baton touched my hand and I burst into wide open throttle. My heart was pumping, and my legs seemed to pump faster and faster all on their own. I could see the finish line. I could see cake and milk in my head. I burst into a last push of energy. Dizziness was trying to slow me down, but I exploded over the finish line. We won!

I fell over on the grass from exhausting all my energy reserve, but I felt like a million bucks. Our team was yelling and crying, and people in the stands were jumping and cheering for us. Regaining my wind, I jumped up and ran to celebrate with our team.

Ribbons were given out, more cheering and jumping around. Then came the announcement I was waiting for. "A" Team, meet in the cafeteria for your cake and milk prize." We raced over to the cafeteria, and I kept telling myself not to eat too fast and appear too hungry. I can still remember closing my eyes and slowly tasting that first bite of cake. It was heavenly. When we were through, there was cake left, and I asked if I could take a couple of pieces home. The servers were happy to give it to me. I was able to share my triumph with my brothers and sisters. What a perfect day. God answered my simple prayer.

LESSONS

- With good motivation, I can be successful.
- God answered my prayers even as a little girl.
- We wouldn't always be poor. This state was only temporary. One of the most important pieces of advice I got from my wise Momma.
- Teamwork can get you what you might not be able to get alone.
- There is a prize for doing something well.

TWO QUESTIONS

1. When were you so motivated that you pushed yourself to extraordinary levels of performance?

2. How did you feel when you did it?

Stealing the S & H Green Stamp Books
from Our Dear, Sweet Momma

One day Momma gave me and Jo a whole drawer full of loose S & H Green Stamps she got from Whitman's Grocery Store. She told me and Jo to lick all the S & H stamps and stick them in the books before she came home from work. Well! It took us *all* afternoon to lick and stick, lick and stick.

Finally, exhausted, close to dehydration, we counted all those books. There were 13 full books! Jo figured since we had worked so hard filling those books, we ought to at least get one each for ourselves. We took our books and ran across the prairie. We crossed the railroad tracks, ran across Wall Street, dodged the cars, and opened the door to the redemption store, which was near the Piggly Wiggy grocery store.

We looked all over that store for something worth just one book of stamps. Finally, Jo ran up to me, all excited, with a Better Homes and Garden Cookbook. Course, Jo could cook, but me, not so well. (I remembered when I tried to cook that gravy!) Anyway, a cookbook wasn't exactly what eleven- to twelve-year-old girls would normally want, but it was still something that might come in handy. So, we took those Better Homes and Gardens Cookbooks and, hid them the best we could in our two-room house on the prairie. Somehow, Jo and I kept that secret from Momma until we were ready to get married. We had the books in a box we called our "hope chest."

Jo confessed our S & H Stamp book crime. Mother was happy for the story. *It became* a joyful prairie memory for her.

When we each got married, we took those Better Homes and Garden Cookbooks into our marriages. We felt guilty as sin the whole time. Over the years we both used our cookbooks and would talk of our life of crime and stealing from our dear sweet Momma. Every time we looked up how to make chicken and dumplings, or bake a pie, it brought all that guilt flooding right back in again.

Later in life, Momma ended up in Polo Park Retirement Living, which she loved. After a few years Momma was ready to be called to the Lord. Jo took it upon herself to perform that dreaded but soul cleansing moment of confession. Momma listened wide-eyed in disbelief. Jo's heart sank. We had shamed our sweet Momma and in turn, shamed ourselves. When Jo fell silent, Momma burst out laughing and eagerly asked if we still had those cookbooks after all these years!

Momma wanted to see Jo's book and she touched it with such tender love and reverence, as if it was sacred or something. We knew the cookbook from the S & H Green Stamps became one of her treasured memories.

I still had mine until recently. I gave it to my 63-year-old daughter. No telling how long that cookbook will get passed down from generation to generation. But, at least now, since the "confession," our cooking won't be stained with guilt. We are free at last.

LESSONS

- Don't steal from your Momma.
- The guilt of doing something wrong far outweighs having that ill gained thing.
- Ask first. Our Momma would have probably given the books to us because she was generous. We didn't have to steal them.
- Do the right thing.

TWO QUESTIONS

1. Recall a time you did an act you felt guilty about. Describe the incident.

2. Did you ever tell it to anyone? What was the outcome?

They Called It a Cyclone!

It was midafternoon, and usually the Texas sun would be blazing, but right now, the sun had given up and was turned off. It became as black as the pit of night. The wind turned into gale force. Mother and Ginger were working. Troy, Jo, Kayo, and I were playing outside at home alone. Just before Momma walked out the door, she reminded us to take our bath and to mind Troy because he was in charge. Troy, Jo, and I had bathed, and the next tub was ready for Kayo. That's when the wind started acting up, blowing harder than ever.

A neighbor took this photo of our Uncle Joe's Farm (on the right) in Tarzan., Texas. Our Cyclone was Similar but worse with the downpour of rain and dirt making it a mud storm with gale forces wind.

We all went outside. Once outside, Troy guided us toward the back of the house. The dirt was stirred up in a viscous dark brown wall of pure meanness and that meanness was headed straight for our house. The roaring dirt wind was picking up speed and the rain began to pour.

We felt like we were in a tornedo like Dorothy in *The Wizard of Oz*. The dirt and rain pelting our skin were like pellets from a BB gun.

Jo, me, and Kayo were terrified at how easy the storm destroyed our home. As if God was saying, "you will not live on the prairie anymore."

Debris from the prairie danced wildly in the wind. But then we saw large pieces of wood stabbing through the air. That was not good. We had no place to hide nor any shelter in which to take refuge. Typically, farmers have cellars they could go to. But on the prairie, we were without alternatives. Troy gathered us up and scooted us back into the house. Momma had left him in charge, so we minded him. And besides, Troy was our older brother. Once inside, he guided us toward the back of the house, through the kitchen where the galvanized #3 tub sat without a bather. Momma's cabinet sewing machine given to her by Granny, stood behind the tub. Because the machine was made of steel, it was very top-heavy.

The house started jigging' and a-wiggling like it had the St. Vida's Dance going on. The house was shimmying around on the cement blocks it was sitting on as if it were weightless and felt like it would take sail any minute. The sewing machine vibrated so badly; it fell over on the bathtub. Had Kayo been in in the tub, we probably wouldn't have our baby brother right now. We anxiously proceeded on to the back of the flimsy add-on section of the house.

We didn't have any safe place to hide. The wind sounded like many big jet engines attacking us and stirring up all the dirt on the prairie. Massive dirt clouds engulfed the whole area around Midland as far as one could see. We sat on one of the beds, trembling in terror. We had no idea what to do to save ourselves. Mud was spilling out of the heavens.

The weatherman on the radio said it was a cyclone. But I don't know how reliable weather forecasting was in 1950's I don't know what you would call this phenomenon, but it was big, and it was bad. Our original little house on the prairie was one long room, divided by a petition with siding only on one side. (Sheetrock and 2X4's were all that stood between us and the elements. One door, two windows. Toilet out back. No water. No indoor plumbing.)

I don't know where, but Daddy had found a part of another house about the same size as ours and had it brought up to our existing house to form a T-shaped building. There was no structure holding the two parts together, so he just used shingles to fill in the open gaps. The two partial houses were not anchored with a foundation. As the wind got stronger and the sand and rain were beating on this contraction of a house, the whole thing was trembling and being moved around on the bricks. Things got worse and the two-part house was beginning to pull apart.

Troy screamed above the electrified lightning and thunder crashes, "*Jump! Jump over the gap! Jump now!*" One at a time, as the two parts of the rickety house were tearing apart almost in slow motion, we all jumped, even Kayo. Once Troy was sure we all got over the gap, he jumped. As scared as we all were, we blindly followed Troy's desperate commands.

We all made it into the original house just as it was ripping apart. When the houses ripped apart, we really didn't know what to do. Troy said we had to get back out of the house. We inched ourselves back out into the black fury outside and leaned up against the house.

Time seemed to drag all the way to eternity. Troy made us stand together and hold on to each other as if our lives depended on it. We were all trembling crying and praying with all our hearts. We couldn't see a thing. The rain and sand were like a torrential downpour, only it was a mud storm. It seemed as if it would never end. Maybe God was determined to destroy everything so we **couldn't** live like this anymore. We would have to leave the prairie.

Our belongings were being blown out of the back side of the house. The other structure blew apart and collapsed a little way from where we were. How desperately we clung to each other crying such fearful tears against our merciless fate. It seemed like it took a long time to get through this nightmare, and yet, just as quickly as it started, it stopped. An eerie calm set in.

We ended up at my daddy's sister, Aunt Fanny's house for the night. Daddy was off again and wasn't there to help us. Once again, Momma had to handle this situation alone. Two of Mommas brothers, Uncle Joe, and Uncle Jay came over to help us pick our life up off the prairie floor.

We hesitantly looked at the extent of the damage. What was left? The add-on house had succumbed to the howling wind and had blown several feet away. It was a sorry mess, shattered pieces of a partial house and partial pile of useless lumber purged into a broken pile of hopelessness. The door between the two structures, along with some of the sheetrock, had blown off to God-knows-where, and left a jagged gaping hole.

A lot of our life was scattered around the prairie, covered with mud. It was a dismal sight except for the bathtub. It had blown outside and landed upside down.

Our tea kettle, which we used to heat water, had landed on top of the tub, looking pristine, as if it was ready to serve high tea. So that tub went from a death trap to a gracious teatime table.

Walking inside we caught sight the Singer sewing machine toppled off to the side. The tub had joined the rest of our meager world outside. The chilling truth, that had Kayo taken that bath, he would have been seriously hurt or worse, loomed before us.

When Momma saw this sight, she broke down into body-wrenching sobs. This was as far down as Momma was going to let herself be taken. Her youngest child could have been a causality of our desperate way of life.

Momma had gone to a counselor who told her, "If you want any changes in your life, it will have to be up to you. *You* will have to do that yourself. The way you have been living reveals to you a pattern of an alcoholic husband and father who abandons the family often. He simply isn't present for you or his family. You have moved from one broken-down house to another, none of which are fit for humans to live in. The children probably live in a state of shock. It is up to you to change this. It is up to you to say that enough is enough."

On the next page is Momma' Circle of Life. She created this during a three-day process of figuring out her life, how it has affected her, and how she wanted to design her future. The bottom-left quarter of the circle shows her drawing of our house being torn up by the cyclone. Mama's foot is beneath, dug in. She had hit the lowest bottom, and she took over.

Momma didn't cry very long because we had to move. I don't know how she bore all the trauma, but her fierce determination kept her going. She said it had never occurred to her that she couldn't do what she needed to do. She assured us that "things would get better now." Her grit got us through another horrific experience as if it were something normal.

Someone we knew had a truck, and we were able to retrieve most of our stuff and put it in the truck. Our uncles drove us to 1210 S. Colorado Street to a small house Uncle Jay owned and was going to let us live in. We put our scant belongings in it, cleaned them up and started our new chapter. It wasn't as terrible as the prairie because now we had an inside toilet, running water, but only cold, no hot water heater, and a small kitchen. We were still on the south (wrong) side of the tracks, but we had a roof over us and new hope. We thought we were lucky and certainly grateful to Uncle Jay.

So much damage to our souls in so short an amount of time. It revealed how resilient the human spirit really can be.

Momma took over the reins and filed for divorce.

"Walk In Strong Crawl Out Stronger" - Anonymous

LESSONS

- We are made stronger from our adversities.
- We siblings shared a common trauma, and like foxhole buddies, we became intensely loyal to each other for the rest of our lives.
- Triumph followed defeat and gave us courage to carry on.
- In crisis, if we don't focus on what we can't do, we will be able to do what we must for survival. Troy's action was a perfect example.
- We developed a high tolerance for emotional pain and physical hardship. We were not afraid of life.
- Getting through this tragedy taught me not to lose heart but build a tenacity from deep inside.

- We are not helpless. Don't give up.

- No one else can live life for you. With God's help, we are the captain of our fate.

TWO QUESTIONS

1. What traumatic event have you lived through? How did you respond to the emergency?

2. How did you get back to normalcy?

The Poodle Skirt Girl

There I was. Sitting in Principal Jones' office at Cowden Junior High School. I was trying to come up with an explanation for my behavior. It was certainly not the behavior one would expect from a refined Southern girl. And what would Momma think?

Cowden Junior High I attended in the '50's.

Let me answer the second question first. My Momma would not like it one bit seeing me act in an unfeminine way. Unbecoming behavior would be a black mark on my representation of our Southern heritage. *But*, if it was a matter of pride or standing up for myself, she would tell me to do the right thing. I had learned well from the bullies in Houston; you don't just let people run all over you. So, this was a dilemma.

Before you judge me, let me tell you the story of what happened. I was about13. I was in the 8th grade. I was smart, an excellent student, and made all A's. I was an artist, accomplished in sports, played "A"-string on the volleyball and track teams, and was a Student Representative for the 8th grade student council, acted in all our school plays, and sewed costumes for one of the plays. I loved school. It gave me a place to live out my intelligence and natural gifts. It provided me a positive venue in which to spend my energies and feel accomplished. Not what people in my social position are expected to do. I was, however, known to be rebellious if I sensed injustice.

It was January, just after the Christmas holidays. I had been nominated for "best-dressed girl," and wore my brand-new Christmas skirt and blouse to school. The skirt was made of an unusual material, had little black and gray ribbing that fit across my tummy, and flared out at the bottom. The blouse was a light lime color and felt silky.

On the day the students were to vote, Charlene Davis wore her beautiful pink and black poodle skirt with a crisp white blouse and a thin narrow black belt.

I didn't have a big wardrobe, but Momma had taught us very good hygiene habits, and our clothes were always clean, starched, and ironed. All of us, except Kayo, knew how to iron. The more affluent girls wore clothes that were the latest fads and, in 1953, pink and black poodle skirts were *it!* Charlene's mother made sure her daughter had the latest. When she couldn't find the pink poodle skirt Charlene wanted in Midland, she made her one, Charlene's mother was a really good seamstress.

Charlene worked really hard with her clothes and I'm guessing she had her eyes on winning "best-dressed girl." I hadn't thought about it too much, because with my limited wardrobe, I didn't figure there was any way I could win. Well, guess what? I won "best-dressed girl!" It was just as big a surprise to me as it was to Charlene Davis. The votes were all in

After the winners had been announced, we had health class, and we watched a movie that day. I'll never forget, it was about kids using heroin. We all filed in to sit in our desk chair. Charlene and her friend sat directly behind me and my friend. The movie was really scary, and I got absorbed in the fate of these kids. It showed a girl with her arms covered with pock marks where she had given herself shots of heroin. I was feeling real sorry for her, when I became aware that something was brushing against my backside. The desk chairs were open in the back. Again, something would lightly brush back and forth against my back, but then it would flicker away. It happened a few times, but finally stopped for the rest of the movie.

When the lights came on, I got up and started to leave. My friend gasped and said, "Your skirt has dirt all across the whole back of it!"

When Charlene gave a satisfying snicker, I figured out in a flash that it had been *her foot* brushing on my back!

This event was another time a lightning bolt exploded in my head, and I was blinded by the stars I saw. The reality flooded over me instantly. I had a limited amount of clothes. This outfit had been my one and only Christmas gift, compared to Charlene's probable extravagant Christmas and the many clothes in her wardrobe, and yet she had gotten my skirt filthy. I felt indescribable fury. Her uncalled-for meanness still brings tears to my eyes. I couldn't understand why someone with so much could destroy what someone else with so little had?

My anger, hurt, and humiliation smothered me. Unfortunately, Charlene had stayed around to enjoy my hurt and humiliation. Meanwhile, I grabbed her by both arms and did a "Geraldine" on her, right then and there. I swung her around, and then I let her go, which sent her sailing across the floor, getting her pink poodle skirt as dirty as she had gotten mine. That's when the teacher took us to see the principal.

Principal Jones went into another office to talk to Charlene, telling me to stay in his office. I thought for sure my goose was cooked. Why would he believe me after hearing her story? I wanted to run. Run home across that miserable prairie, but I just sat there in silence, waiting to face the music. Principal Jones finally returned.

He sat down, folded his hands out in front of him on his desk and just looked at me real closely. The roaring was so loud in my ears I didn't know if I'd be able to hear him when he spoke to me. He finally asked me what happened. He wanted to hear my side of the story. I told him the whole sordid thing.

He just sat there a few seconds before he spoke. Then he told me, "You know, Charlene expected to win "best dressed girl." And she was very angry because you won. You are from the wrong side of the tracks, and she thought it was unfair that you won because you don't have many clothes."

As he spoke, my heart was breaking, being told that because I was poor, I did not deserve to win. I was immersed in total shame.

He continued, "The kids voted you "best dressed girl" because, first of all, they really like you. Because you are friendly, fair, and so smart, many of them have asked you to help them. Which you have. Charlene is jealous that they like you because she isn't well liked. What concerns me is that your anger could keep you from getting the very things that you so badly want to have in your life. And you certainly deserve them. So please think about this because I believe in you and want you to succeed. I know you can. Winning would have been revenge enough. Please think about all these things." I felt transformed and utterly speechless. I couldn't imagine anyone would be jealous of me. It was an unimaginable concept to me.

When Principal Jones told me I could go, without punishing me, my eyes were as big as saucers. As I got up, he added, "It is not required, but it would be the bigger thing for you to apologize for hurting Charlene because she was hurt. She may not be able to apologize back, but it is more about you learning to do the more gracious thing. Bigger things in life will happen for you than will happen for Charlene."

I was awed by all that he said. I could never forget his words. Many of my teachers throughout my school years had told me how smart and creative I was, but this was Principal Jones!

Walking home, I went over and over what he had said to me in my mind. It was a life-changing revelation, and my heart was bursting with hope. He had given me advice that I could understand and act upon. I decided right then and there to learn to contain my anger, to look beyond the surface of things to find out the real thing that the other person, was experiencing, which might explain mean, or unpleasant behavior. Charlene was jealous of *me*! That changed my whole perspective. I actually felt compassion.

Much later, a wise friend once told me that if we really and truly understood a person, we could not dislike them because we understood them. That has been very helpful to remember.

The next day, I did approach Charlene. She was surprised, and I could see she was a little nervous. I apologized for losing my temper and hurting her. That what I had done was not a good thing for me to do because I really did not want to hurt her. Charlene did not apologize back as Principal Jones had predicted but that didn't matter, I had done what was right, and my heart felt more at peace.

Charlene and I never became friends because she couldn't cross the social barrier and I couldn't trust her. But after that our behavior became respectful to each other, and we didn't have any other unpleasant incidents. I treasure the gift of perspective Principal Jones gave me. I believe God sends us people to help us along in our life journey. If we will pay attention and make something good out of what we encounter, our perspective can remain positive and healthy.

LESSONS

- Understanding what was really going on allowed me to quickly change to a more positive perspective. It took away the feeling that I was shameful and undeserving.
- If I could get beyond the social divide, and truly understand others, I could change my perspective and thus change my behavior.
- There will be people who come into our life to help us when we need it most. Accept that gift.
- Give the gift of kindness to others you meet along life's path.

<u>TWO QUESTIONS</u>

1. Write about a time you suffered an injustice.

2. How did you handle it? Did anyone appear to help you?

We Drew Straws, and Guess What?

It was 1957, the beginning of my senior year. I was 16 going on 17 years old and was asked to serve on our yearbook staff as art editor for Midland High School.

I was nearly 17 with a lot of hopes

Our yearbook was called the Catoico because Midland was cattle, oil, and cotton country. Midland High School, like most, was a cliquish school. There was a social divide between those who had and those who had not.

Our whole staff was invited to a yearbook workshop at Columbia College in Columbia, Missouri, all expenses paid by the school. It was a lovely old college, built in 1851, and originally called Christian Female College. It was richly traditional with beautiful buildings and grounds. I had only been out of Texas once at that point. This was going to be quite an adventure.

Because of my situation, I did not join any clubs at school that cost money. We simply did not have it to spend in that way. So as to not stress our mother, we would not even ask.

When I heard each girl needed to bring $20 for spending money. That much money was out of my reach. I would have to back out. When I told Momma I'd have to back out, she wanted to know why. I told her I knew that was a huge amount of money, so I decided not to go. Momma just breathed out, "Hmmm... Just hold off on telling them so I can think about it." I listened to all the planning.

Finally, just before the deadline, Momma came to me with a $20 bill. I could not imagine where she might have gotten it. She and Ginger did it together. They did not want me to miss out on such a great opportunity. Instead of paying the butane bill, Momma called the owner, told him what she wanted to do, and he agreed to let her pay her bill in a few installments. I was overwhelmed that she wanted me to have this experience so badly that she made such a sacrifice. It was like a blessed miracle. I was amazed and grateful. I was really going on the trip!

The trip took two days, with one overnight stay. We stayed in a motel with four girls to a room: our teacher and chaperone staying in another room. When we got to Columbia, we stayed in the dormitory, two girls to a room. Meals were served in the dining hall over the two and a half days there. The workshop would be in a large, designated room. We rode in two cars driven by Ms. Brown, our lead teacher for the Catoico team, and a chaperone parent. Four girls rode in each car. We stopped at a Holiday Inn between Midland and Columbia; we would go the rest of the way the next day.

After we had eaten dinner and everyone was settled in, someone knocked on the door; I answered it, and there stood the other four girls giggling and chattering away. As soon as I shut the door, several girls pulled out cigarettes and started smoking. The room quickly filled up with a tobacco fog. I didn't want to smoke because I thought it was an ugly habit. When another knock came on the door, the girls ditched their cigarettes and pushed me to the door to answer it.

As soon as I opened the door, a huge cloud of smoke puffed out of the room right into Ms. Brown's face. She coughed that hacking sound, waving her hand in front of her face to disburse the smoke. She was red with anger. As you can imagine, we got the old shame-and-guilt lecture that lasted way too long. Having been properly chastised we agreed to no more mischief that night.

Our first night out and we were already in trouble! I knew that was not why Momma and Ginger gave me a $20 fortune. I vowed to myself to do better for the rest of the trip.

We drove the rest of way the next day. Wearily, we pulled up to the imposing entrance to Columbia College at dusk. We were met by a nice lady who was running the yearbook workshop. The halls were so drenched in history and tradition, we spoke in hushed tones. We were led to a well-lighted and elegant room where they welcomed us and told us what to expect. The eight of us paired off and went to our rooms to unpack. I was as excited as a child on Christmas. Velda Lee Walker was my roommate. (In the South, our philosophy is, why use one name when you can have three?)

Velda Lee was quiet at first, but after a couple of hours, we were chattering away, having a good time. It was going to be hard for me to fall asleep because this was the nicest room I had ever slept in. We were instructed to come down to the dining hall for dinner and orientation at 7:30 p.m.

On the tables was a sparkling array of dishes, nice glasses, and dinnerware. We were served little steaks, vegetables, and delicious bread. That was the first tender steak I ever had, so I savored every bite. When dessert came out, I was overcome with the beauty and elegance of it all. It was a quarter slice of cantaloupe with the skin still on it, and right in the middle was a scoop of heavenly vanilla ice cream. For me, that was the height of the evening. I was delighted and surprised about everything.

When we finished up, I felt a pleasant kind of full; I felt so content, I might have experienced a food coma. Velda Lee and I talked about a lot of things, including what tomorrow would bring. We finally fell asleep like contented babies.

The workshops were creative and stimulating. We were taught many skills and tricks of the trade. We learned page layout, how to optimize the use of photos, and to write interesting text to pull it all together. These skills would be an asset to any future career I was engaged in.

We got through the second day early enough to explore this area of the Ozarks. Being close to a big lake we pooled our money to pay for a boat and a handsome young college man to navigate it. He told us, for only $10 a person, he would teach us how to water ski. Only two of us took him up on it. That took me down to $5 from my original $20 with another two days to go.

The adventure was exhilarating. All the girls were flirting with the college guy but me. I felt very shy. Before the night was over, he asked me to go for a hamburger with him. It seemed to aggravate the other girls, but I enjoyed myself.

He was a nice young man and we talked about our plans for the future, things we wanted to do with our lives. I was especially interested in his college experience. I had always loved school but didn't think I would ever be able to go to college. He was a gentleman the whole time and delivered me back to my room safely. Velda Lee jumped on my bed and wanted to know every detail. I shared as much as I was comfortable with, and it was fun to have girly talk with her.

Our last day included half a day of workshops, then to the dining room for lunch, and closure to the experience. At the end, we were dismissed to go pack and get on our way home.

Velda Lee and I stood in our room saturated with warm memories and good feelings. It had been a truly lovely learning experience. While we were packing, Velda Lee was in a great mood and nostalgic. Sitting on the end of my bed, she said, "I want to tell you something. When we arrived here, the seven of us got together to discuss who would room with you. We all knew where you lived, and nobody wanted to room with someone from the south side of the tracks. We drew straws and I lost. *But* you have been so nice, smart, and creative, and we had such fun together, I really enjoyed being with you. It turned out great after all."

I sat there paralyzed. This couldn't be happening. A shock wave of shame and humiliation charged through my body. A knot rose to my throat, and I remember thinking, don't cry, don't cry. My heart shattered. Velda Lee thought she was giving me a magnanimous compliment. That she had sacrificed and stayed with me, the poor girl, but it wasn't as bad as she thought it would be. The shame was flooding over me like searing, liquid fire and I felt flawed just because I was poor. It made me sick to my stomach. The humiliation was complete and there was no way to escape it. Being poor was bad.

I didn't know what to do. I didn't want to tell her how badly she hurt my feelings. I didn't want to get mad because we would still be together two more days. So, I pretended everything was great, and choked out, "I really had fun too." That was true, I did have fun, and decided this sad experience shouldn't take that reality away from me. But it was as if I had been physically pushed back to the south side of the tracks where I belonged—and should know enough to stay there.

We got back to Midland, but I don't remember what happened on the way. We were dropped off at the school, and their mothers were there to meet them. I walked the mile home to 1210 Colorado Street where we now lived in Uncle Jay's three-room house. A small step up from the prairie.

For a short time, I felt the despair of it all as I laid on my bed trying to escape that awful moment with Velda Lee in my mind. I did not tell Momma or Ginger that part. They were so thrilled, and I wanted them to enjoy what they had done for me. It was pointless to stay in that pit of darkness. Instead, I picked up the pieces of my dignity and kept striving to change my life.

I eventually quit school in my senior year. But that is another story. And God has a neat way of pulling miracles out of such painful defeat. One of my daily affirmations became. "I will do what is possible and brave and trust God for the miracles."

LESSONS
- Humiliation is one of our strongest emotions. It is so painful; we will do almost anything not to experience it again.

- I learned the prejudice toward the poor, or people who are different in circumstance, is as real as racial prejudice.

- Being poor made me feel inferior as a human being.

- When society places you in your social position, it is difficult to move out of it.

- Generally, when people think you are inferior, they don't seem to think your feelings can be hurt. They can damage your soul.

- Velda Lee didn't mean to hurt me. She thought she was being a good person by staying in the room with me. I didn't want to carry ill feelings toward anyone. Another one of my daily affirmations is, "I forgive all who have harmed me in any way." I learned compassion.

- It taught me that being kind is a virtue, and I never, ever wanted to make anyone feel like that experience made me feel.

- In 1958, I created one affirmation for myself, because I was losing my confidence. I wrote, "I am confident and poised." That is how I began using affirmations. It has been key to my growth, helped me become a risk taker and to reach for higher aspirations than I thought possible. Affirmations trained my brain to be positive.

TWO QUESTIONS

1. Have you ever felt humiliation? Describe the incident.

2. How did you handle it?

GOD PLEASE USE ME FOR PURPOSES GREATER THAN MY OWN.
I LOVE & RESPECT MYSELF. I AM A WORTHY, CAPABLE, & VALUABLE WOMAN.
THRILLING PROSPECTS KEEP COMING MY WAY. I SEIZE THEM & DO THEM.
I AM PEACEFUL, RELAXED AND TRANQUIL. I AM CONFIDENT AND POISED. 🦋

I SLEEP 😴 SOUNDLY WITH A CLEAR AND PEACEFUL MIND. I AM FREE OF WORRY.
I SURRENDER TO GOD'S WILL IN MY LIFE & COURAGEOUSLY FOLLOW HIM.
I BELIEVE IN MYSELF AND THE VALUE OF MY MISSION. 🌴 I AM ANOINTED BY GOD.
I PASSIONATELY PURSUE MY PURPOSE. LIFE HAS NEW MEANING FOR ME NOW.
I BUILD A NEW, CONSTRUCTIVE LIFE WITH PURPOSE & LOVE AFTER WAYNE.
I AM BOLD AND COURAGEOUS. I ALLOW MYSELF TO GRIEVE WITH LOVE.
I LOVE AND RESPECT GOD WITH ALL MY HEART. I WORK JOYFULLY WITH MY
CHURCH AND CHARITY. I BEAR GOOD WILL TOWARD ALL I MEET.
I STAND FOR MY 5 CHILDREN & THEIIR GOOD. I MANAGE OUR RESOURCES WELL.
I FORGIVE ALL HAVE HARMED ME IN ANY WAY. I WISH FOR A LOVING, FORGIVING,
SWEET RELATIONSHIP WITH CINDY, BO, BRETT, PAUL, AND MARY ANN.
I TRUST MY ABILITIES AND EASILY REINVENT MYSELF FOR EACH PHASE OF MY LIFE.
I AM OPEN TO NEW & EXCITING OPPORTUNITIES. 🦋
I CREATE A DELIGHTFUL, HOME FOR MYSELF, LOCATED WHERE I AM HAPPY.
I LOVED FLIRTING WITH WAYNE AND BEING KIND, PATIENT AND GENTLE WITH HIM.
I LOVE 💜 AND CHERISH CINDY, JERRY & BRETT. I NO LONGER TAKE
RESPONSIBILITY FOR THEIR MOODS, DECISIONS OR ACTIONS. THEY ARE MY
CROWNING JOY AND ACHIEVEMENT.
I BELIEVE IN ALL 5 OF OUR CHILDREN, AND I AM PROUD OF WHO THEY ARE.
I CLAIM DARRELL, JANET, RENEE, ANNN, & DUANE AS MY OWN AND LOVE THEM.
I AM OPTIMISTIC 🖊 ABOUT LIFE AND ENJOY NEW CHALLENGES!
I KEEP A SLIM, TRIM, IN SHAPE BODY WITH A FLAT TUMMY...I EXERCISE REGULARLY
I RECOGNIZE WHEN I AM FULL, AND STOP EATING IMMEDIATELY!
I TAKE CHARGE OF MY LIFE AND MAKE A DIFFERENCE.
I LIVE MY LIFE WITH A SENSE OF DIGNITY. I KEEP ADJUSTING TO NEEDS.
I EMBRACE PROBLEMS AS POSITIVE OPPORTUNITIES. I STAY CONNECTED TO MY
FRIENDS. I AM BALANCED IN FAMILY, CHURCH, FRIENDS AND FUN.
I CONSISTENTLY WORK OM MY BOOK OF MEMOIRS TO HELP MYSELF AND OTHERS
UNDERSTAND THE LESSONS OF OUR LIVES. I LOVINGLY STAY CONNECTED TO PAUL
AND MARY ANN. I CHOOSE THE HIGH ROAD AND LIVE WITH GRACE.
I love you. You are safe with me. I will make you happy today.
I really care for you. You are worthy.
I listen to you and treat you kindly.
I'M A FREE, LOVING WOMAN!
I AM LOVED. I AM SAFE.
I AM ENOUGH!
I am an instrument of God's
will & love.
Orig. 1958   Last revised 5/29/22

I successfully complete the
story and lessons of my life
to help myself and others.
I AM GRATEFUL! I DO WHAT IS
POSSIBLE & BRAVE & TRUST
GOD FOR THE MIRACLES. 🦋

My positive affirmations have changed over the years to fit my life.

Sometimes, No Matter How Hard You Try, It Is Still Not A Match

I was 17 years old, walking down the aisle of the First Christian Church of Christ in Midland to marry Jack Richard Pasco. It was still a natural thing for a girl in the

Jack with our two sons Bo and Brett. We lived in Fenton, Michigan

South to marry at such a young age. However, I don't know if it was normal to marry someone I barely knew.

Jack was four years older than me, vibrant and fun. He was in the Air Force in Big Spring, Texas and was an extraordinary baseball player. We had a whirlwind courtship, with ignited chemistry. After only two months we were married. Hardly enough time to even know who we were. And certainly, we did not know who each other was.

Before I married, I had no idea what happened in the marriage bed. Mother came in while I was dressing for our honeymoon and tried to explain what would happen, but she gave up.

Me holding Jo's baby, Eddy.

She went out and told Ginger to explain it to me. After a few awkward words, Ginger left in frustration, and I still didn't have a clue. I went into that experience completely naïve. Fortunately, Jack was sensitive to the situation, and we started our life together. At this time, both my two sisters were married, and Jo already had a toddler named Eddy. About two months into our marriage, I visited Jo and played with Eddy. He was an adorable child and I loved him dearly. My heart felt so full when I held him. A short time later, I announced to Jack I wanted a baby.

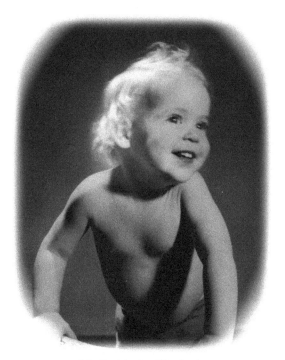

My first baby Cindy Jean

Eleven months later we had our baby girl, Cindy Jean Pasco. My heart broke open, releasing all the pent-up love within me. I was overwhelmed by this great rush of love and wept when she was laid on my heart. She was precious and joyful right from the beginning. It mystified me to love something so quickly and deeply. It was magical. Cindy was animated and happy. I felt like I had a little doll I could play with. I had no idea of the responsibility and gravity of having a child.

Fifteen months later, we had our first son, Charles Jerold Pasco. Cindy couldn't pronounce the word brother, so she called him Bo. The name stuck, and even today, in his 60s, he goes by Bo with close friends and family.

He was so sweet and happy. He was so innocent and pleasing. A very happy, smiling little boy. Bo just seemed happy to be alive. He was very easy to take care of. Waves of tears poured out because I wanted a boy so badly and now here he was!

Bo (Jerry) was born in 1960.

One year later, I was pregnant again, but very early on I knew something was wrong. Jack took me to the hospital, and things didn't look good. Jack left me in the hospital to go hunting; he left me to lose the child alone. This was a devastating blow I nearly couldn't climb-over. Neither of us had seen a good example of a healthy marriage. We were hurting each other pretty badly in our ignorance.

148

Brett Lynn was born in 1962.

A year later, in March, our second son, Brett Lynn Pasco, was born. He was a gentle, tender little baby boy and was content just to be home with his dad and Mom. My heart swelled to nearly bursting. He was a quiet-natured child. So here I was with three precious children that I loved with all my heart, but I could not create a stable home for them. The very thing I did not want my children to experience growing up as I had was happening. I was desperate.

Two years after Brett was born, I lost another baby when I was four months pregnant. This was devastating in such a strange way. I certainly did not want to bring another child into this failing marriage, so I thought I would be relieved after losing it. But because I had already felt movement, instead it took me years to mourn this tragedy. I didn't have much of a chance to be successful in creating a stable family life because Jack and I didn't have any idea how to stop our destructive ways with each other.

After 18 years of confusion, pain, anger, and disappointment, I told Jack I would be getting a divorce. I told him in advance to give him a chance to get on his feet financially. It wasn't my way to intentionally make him miserable, so I was respectful, still sleeping in the same bed. When the time came near, I found a small apartment near Oakland University, and soon thereafter we were divorced. It was a cold, heartless event. Not too long after that, Bo ran away to Houston, where Cindy lived.

A time after the divorce, I became aware that Jack was furnishing Brett with marijuana because he felt it was best if Brett used it at home. It was a long ways from

149

being legal. I was dumbfounded. A teenager wants what they want, not necessarily what is best for them. Brett said he chose not to live with me because he knew I would make sure he got help and went to school. I had been fighting an uphill battle.

I know many people have experienced divorce. It is replete with wide-open, gaping, pain. Pain so raw, it was like bile in my throat. The marriage was over, but the two corpses were still walking around. I had nightmares for years afterwards. I felt like a total failure and heartsick to hurt another person with the level of pain divorce causes. But the pain it caused our children was an even bigger wound. I tended to forget all the pain I had experienced in the 20 years of marriage. It took me a few years to understand that we just did not match. We didn't want the same things; our paths were not parallel.

I knew in my heart this was no one's fault. We were too young when we married. We were strangers. We were not in tune with each other spiritually, financially, emotionally nor did we share similar interests and values, what was important to each one of us. We were mostly just making each other unhappy. I am eternally grateful we had three wonderful children that we both love with our whole heart.

On numerous occasions, I tried to get Jack to help us build an amicable relationship so we could be civil to each other and be able to be in the same building together for our children–to be able to go to their special life events and those of our grandchildren. I tried writing a letter one last time about giving our children the gift of our civility with each other just a couple of years ago and he still couldn't do it after 45 years of being divorced and both remarried. I gave up hope after that.

Just this week, June 25, was my grandson, Jacob's, high school graduation party. He is Bo's son. It was attended mainly by family and just two or three of Jacob's buddies. I was the first guest to arrive, and Janet, Bo's wife, seated me on the patio off the grass since a broken hip has hindered my mobility. I was alone because my husband, Wayne, passed on July 18, 2021.

Jack and his wife were the second to arrive. His wife, Ellie, came over and politely greeted me. We exchanged pleasantries. But Jack walked past me to the furthest seating away and sat down. He didn't greet me or offer condolences. It is the same rude behavior I have experienced for over 45 years. I have allowed him to hurt me enough for any lifetime. The lack of kindness is palpable, and my heart doesn't want to be subjected to this treatment anymore. I have tried to keep the peace, but one person can't do it alone. This remains one of the saddest events of my life.

A part of me will always love Jack because he is basically a good man. He has been a significant part of my life and history. And mostly because he is the father of our children. Without him, I would not have Cindy, Bo, or Brett, whom I love with all my heart. They make my life worthwhile and make sense.

LESSONS

- I learned to be a "seeker." There were no self-help books or seminars at the time. I sought help from church leaders and textbooks to learn how to relate to each other.
- Be willing to change and seek positive resolutions.
- Be willing to get professional help. A relationship is worth the effort.
- Be willing to put aside my own pain so I can see the pain my children are experiencing.
- Important life events deserve time to unfold, not to be impetuously acted upon.
- Prideful grudges are hurtful and do not solve issues.
- Two months was not enough foundation to build a solid relationship upon.

Two Questions

1. If you have children, do you remember how you felt about first holding them?

2. What were some of your sweetest memories?

General Motors Was More Than Just a Job
It Was a Glorious, Life-Changing Event

Jack and I had all our belongings loaded in a trailer and drove away from Midland, on Highway I-20—again. We had moved back and forth to Midland because I got too homesick for my family when we were in Michigan, and he got homesick for his family when we lived in Texas. So here we went again. He felt he could get a better job in Michigan.

In between pregnancies, I had several inconsequential jobs, and none were what you would call career opportunities. Long story short, I applied at the GM Milford Proving Ground with more bravado than qualifications. I did not get the only job a woman could get, secretary, because I had none of the required skills.

Ralph B., the personnel manager at the time, said he really wanted to hire me, but I just didn't have the skills. I asked him to please tell me what I needed to get the job. Typing, shorthand, and experience were the secret ingredients to get in. I told him I would be back, and immediately signed up for typing and shorthand classes at Mott Adult High School in Flint.

As soon as these courses were under my belt, I got a job at the Office of Head Start. After about four months, rumors were going around that this office would be closing, so I immediately found a job in a small tool repair shop in Fenton. The experience was good, pay was poor, but this was not to be my last stop.

The time was right to return to see Mr. Ralph B. So, back to the Proving Ground I went with the assurance in my head that nothing should stop me from getting a job offer.

I told Mr. B I had done as he advised and gotten the proper training, plus over two years of experience. He hired me on the spot. That was in 1967 when women could aspire to be a teacher, a nurse, or a secretary. So, there I was in GM, but at entry level. Still, it paid more than I had ever earned before. At that low level the only way was up.

My job was to do secretarial work for ten engineers and answer the phone. The work was good, but I knew I needed more security to care for my children. I vowed they would never have to live as I had. Because Jack lacked good financial habits, it was not possible to count on him to be a stable provider. I had learned from my mother to never buy more than you could pay for with your next check. As such, going into debt or overspending my income was not my financial value.

Lying in bed one night, the thought bubbled up to my consciousness that if I wanted to support my kids, I needed to get an education. I already had taken two classes at Eastern Michigan University, so I enrolled for the next semester using the GM Tuition Refund Program. Until I was ready to declare a major, general required classes were predominant on my "educational dance card." It was imperative to learn what possibilities lay in this new environment. It was not yet a time when females were given equal opportunities.

It was my strategy to continuously seek more responsibility because that meant higher pay. There were many visits to Mr. B's office asking about jobs I thought I could do. Some of them were a little far out, like asking to apply for maintenance manager for the Chevrolet Building, but he would listen, then explain that women did not get those kinds of jobs there.

Eventually a position opened for secretary to the director of technical departments working for a man named Wayne Bonvallet. That was a step up. More and more, I looked for ways to keep my mind stimulated. He was forever plotting graphs on vehicle testing results. That really looked great and like something I could do.

I asked if I could do the graphs for him, but he didn't think I could. I told him the experience I had in my extensive science classes in college, but he still hesitated, to

153

which I replied, "If you really don't think I am smart enough, even having gone through four classes in calculus and differential equations, I will stop asking. But I believe I can do it. He let me try and later apologized because he thought I did a better job than he did! Meanwhile, I took two evening college classes each semester chipping-away at my Bachelor of Science degree.

An engineering manager friend heard of a job at the Technical Center in Warren, Michigan, in Mass Analysis. He asked me about my interest and recommended me. The job was to work with blueprints for the various car parts and calculate the mass of each different material. While I had the required mathematical skills, it soon became obvious to me that it did not require any interaction with other human beings. Before too long this became stifling and boring. My strong suit was working with and motivating people, getting them to work together as a team. But it was important to make good on this job first so the next opportunity could be pursued.

Sometime later, Wayne Bonvallet was transferred to the Tech Center to manage a new group called Value Engineering. They were to conduct seminars for

Wayne was a courageous and creative leader. When the department would not approve our training for Value Engineering as a group, he sent us one by one, until we all got trained.

about seventy people in teams of five multi-disciplines using value analysis to take unnecessary costs out of the products, while maintaining quality. It was an exciting new program going around GM, and Wayne said, after working with me, he thought I was the most qualified person for the job because of my creative skills and ability to motivate people, getting them to work together. He approached me to see if I would be interested in applying for the Value Analyst position. It included conducting the large seminars and being responsible for implementing the resulting cost advantages.

George Miakinin was the head of the department. Sitting in his office, I realized this was a big and important move for me. I had earned my BS degree in science and was qualified with heavy mathematics and science experience. However, George

My first non-secretary job. I felt like I broke through the ceiling.

had his doubts because a woman had never done that job.

I knew George's daughter was about to graduate with a business degree and I told him, "George, I sincerely hope someone will give your daughter a chance to prove herself capable of a job she is intellectually and educationally prepared for." I asked him to take a chance on me because I believed, with all my heart, I could do the job. George said he would get back with me.

I prayed that if this was God's will, He would bless me with the opportunity. The next day, George hired me. We would report all Value Engineering activities directly to the heads of all the major departments such as, the Plants, Purchasing,

Engineering, and Financial. This job would give me excellent and widespread visibility as a female trying to break through the glass ceiling holding women back.

There were to be three presenters of the technical problem solving of Value Analysis, and Wayne chose two outstanding engineers to present the function analysis and other parts of the discipline. We became a well-oiled machine. My specialties were motivation, stimulating creativity, effective habits and attitudes, and building a safe place for ideas to flourish. Ron and Pat did the hard-core technical parts, and it was a perfect match. We loved working together.

One of my cousins, Joe Riley, was a *real* character. He is Larry Kennser's older brother. Because he is such a funny man, I created a whole series of humorous stories around him. When people laugh, they are more open to information and change. This was a great way for the teams to take risks and stretch beyond their comfort zones through these great stories. Joe Riley became famous. Many people didn't believe he was real, but he was and just as far-out as my stories about him. It became a non-threatening way to make important points that the people would remember. The GM people loved to participate in our seminars and hear more of Joe Riley's capers. Joe Riley also was in his glory with his fame.

These were magical times at General Motors,

L – R Ron, me, Pat behind me, Herb, and Wayne formed the Chevrolet espri de corp team. It was a magical time in all our careers.

and I was getting to use my gifts of creativity, working with people, and making a difference. It was like a "movement" with tsunami wave proportions. Our contributions were robust and many of the projects were implemented, saving GM substantial unnecessary costs.

Many people played a key role in mentoring me. Wayne being a major one. I worked for him twice in my career and even though I had mostly great leaders, Wayne and I were unusually synergistic together. We had a beautiful and trusted friendship that turned into a most radiant love for each other. When he came to the Tech Center he was in the process of a divorce, and I was divorced, but didn't make it public because some men think they need to help women out when they are divorced. I didn't want the hassle. I did not think I would ever marry again.

Our friendship blossomed into romance, and I was completely smitten by Wayne's gentlemanly ways, intelligence, and his tender nature. Wedding bells rang on Friday, June 13, 1980.

This meant we could no longer work in the same department. That really hurt us both, but we understood. Wayne told me that as an engineering manager, he could take a job anywhere, and since I loved the work in Value Engineering, I could stay there, and he would go elsewhere. That was one of the most unselfish acts I had ever witnessed.

His integrity and devotion were impeccable. After he left, it was difficult to work without each other because together we were more. Before too long, I was pursued by an executive in Fisher Body named Frank F. He said he had written up a job posting for a high-level position to create and head up a Value Engineering department there. He was also a great mentor, and almost gave me carte blanch for what was needed to get a new Fisher Body department off the ground.

Right away Frank gave me two outstanding, hard-working engineers, Darrell C., and Gordon A., who, along with me would be the three presenters. Harold P. plus two college graduates in training, were to be our support crew—another high-powered team who became known throughout GM.

I facilitated a lot of meetings for executives at this point in my career.

Everybody was making huge contributions. My meteor was blazing across the sky, which culminated in my being promoted to Unclassified Executive. My career went from entry level secretary to executive. I had earned a BS in science and an MA in business.

Later Wayne and I both earned another Master of Science, this time in psychology. Wayne, in his gentle way, told me he did not want to pursue any more degrees. We could always pursue learning, but he didn't want to be committed to classrooms for life.

Wayne had thirty-one years with General Motors and retired at fifty-seven. I had twenty years with GM but resigned at forty-seven. We did not want to work apart anymore, so we started our own consulting business. We yearned for the synergy and fun as working partners. That part of our lives was another thrilling journey.

Few women were in the executive level at that time, so I felt grateful for all those who took a chance on me and helped me grow to become who I am today. It was a wonderful and fulfilling career journey and it was far from over. I am truly grateful for the blessings this afforded me to care for my children better. I also learned to mentor and help others along the way as it takes more than one. Many other changes were riding along as well. My life was heading to an unexpected mountain-top experience with dizzying heights toward the stars. Life is good in so many ways. And God is good. This was a life changing experience and led me to more success.

LESSONS

- When you help enough other people get what they want, you will get what you want.
- There is enough success to go around. Be generous with your praise and promotion of others.
- If you give with your whole heart, it will come back to you.
- When you pursue life with passion, determination and doing what it takes, others will carry you on their shoulders.
- Find out what is required and meet the requirements. Don't expect to get something for nothing.

- Believe in yourself. Confidence is golden. The first answer many people give is "no" because it keeps them safe in their comfort zone. Be persistent. Assume you haven't yet told them enough to get a "yes."
- Say "yes," then be creative and figure out how to do it.
- Be alert to ordinary opportunities.
- Sacrifice. Be willing to give more than is required. Be more than a "miserable minimums person." Be a "maximum force."
- Have fun. Treat people fairly and with respect.
- Don't let a little success go to your head. Be authentic.
- Make people feel better about themselves after an encounter with you. They should never walk away from you feeling diminished by you.

<u>Two Questions</u>

1. How do you think people feel after they have had an encounter with you? Share an example.

2. Do you think they feel better about themselves? Inspired? Important? Doubtful? Less than? Even depressed?

The Opal in a Blizzard

Jackie and I got into my car and left the Proving Ground to eat lunch in the quaint town of Milford, Michigan. Jackie was a different kind of girl. She was a small, dainty woman, but cussed like a sailor, and had a hot temper that would thaw out the February we were in. The day was frigid and gray with blizzard warnings. I was proud of my new white little Opal because it was the first car I had ever bought on my very own. I made a real effort to keep it looking good.

About a month earlier there was a black strip hanging down from the doors by the front seats. I carefully pulled both strips out. It looked better and didn't seem to pose any problems without them.

After lunch, I told Jackie I wanted to take my little Opal through the car wash to get the salt from the roads washed off. I paid the kid and started through the car wash. As soon as the water turned on and hit my Opal, the gates of Noah's flood poured into my car windows. Jackie was screeching and a-cussing. We couldn't get out. The water was pouring in like streams, pooling in our seats. We had to lift ourselves above the seats to keep our coats semi-dry. The water also gathered on the floorboards. It was a disastrous mess.

When we pulled back into the Proving Ground, I told Jackie we needed to leave the doors slightly ajar to let it dry out before going home. I forgot about the blizzard. While working the rest of the afternoon, the blizzard came in full force, blew both doors wide open and filled my little Opal with snow. Security came in to find the owner of the car and let me know they shut the doors. But the car was still full of snow. It was the coldest ride home I ever had.

That was not the end of my mishappen experiences with that little Opal. One day, that same winter, after picking up my daughter, Cindy, from Campfire Girls after school, there was a lot of accumulated snow on our back-country roads. The roads were treacherous and were not plowed as often as they needed to be. We were humming along on the straight section of the road, then came to a 90-degree turn. There stood a small pine tree directly in front of us. As I tried to negotiate the turn, the little Opal went out of control, straddled that pine tree, and climbed, slowly bending the poor thing over, and preventing my back wheels from touching the ground. I gunned it and got us off the tree, and slowly crept the rest of the way home.

When my husband, Jack, got home, he burst through the door and announced, "Someone ran up the pine tree at the end of the road. I could see the tracks." Cindy excitedly chimed in, "Mom did it; that was Mom!" Busted. That Opal was becoming the bane of my existence.

Four months later, an orange light started blinking on my instrument panel. I had no idea what it was for, so I just ignored it. It kept lighting up every time I drove. I got used to not really seeing it anymore. Usually, things seemed to happen to that car in the cold weather except when the fan belt broke one hot summer day and I drove it home not knowing what else to do. The Opal over heated, but it seemed to be okay. Now this pesky orange kept lighting up. Then I learned why.

The orange light was the engine light warning. This was the second bad winter for that little Opal. It was a doozy of a winter. One particularly wicked day, I started the car, and it blew up! A blast went off so loud it sounded like a shotgun under the hood. The poor thing shook, stumbled, and came to a full stop. It was finished. It was graveyard dead.

A wrecker came to drag it to the garage, and the damage was staggering. It had wrecked the whole engine, and they said the whole engine was damaged and had to be replaced. The opal was only worth the price of scrap without an engine. The cost of the engine work would be $500, in 1967 dollars. I googled this and found that would be the equivalent of $4,200 today. I had repaired the weather strips and the fan belt, and finally chose to put in a new engine so I could at least trade the car in for a new vehicle. It was a bitter way to learn some very essentials of life.

LESSONS

- I was in denial about responsibility for the car.
- Product maintenance is a fact of life when you own something. The longer it is ignored, the more it will cost, and it could be disastrous.
- I learned I needed to get out of my fantasy world and get into the realities of life. Things break, things wear out.
- I learned about wisdom and not to react rashly from Proverbs and took it to heart.
- *Think* before acting blindly. The orange light meant something. The black strips had a purpose to keep the cold air out.
- There is no such thing as a "maintenance fairy."

Two Questions

1. When have you ignored an important job that caused a bigger problem?

2. What did you learn from this? Did you become more conscious?

A Woman-Child is Missing

My daughter, Cindy, did not come home from work that Friday night. I called all of her friends, and no one knew where she was. My heart sank. I felt a creeping darkness in my heart. The sense of loss weighed heavily on my spirit and deepened as I tried to find clues to where she might be.

After two days of searching, we went to the police. They were of little help since she was an adult at age 18. The days ticked by, but we heard nothing. The shadow of darkness shrouded my whole world, and I could no longer function. I was drowning in my tears and haunted by my fears. My girl was missing, and all sorts of demons came out to taunt and disturb my mind. Was she even still alive? The idea that she was taken by human traffickers was a disturbing possibility. The intensity of my grief was ferocious, and my grief spun out of control. My first born was missing and I could not protect her.

Cindy Jean Pasco

Photo that was used in the flint journal.

I could barely get out of bed. I could not make sense of any of it. One day, when I did get out of bed, I fell to the floor in a crumpled heap of agony, weeping uncontrollability. When the tears dried up, and there was nothing but emptiness, I felt a stirring within me. "You have two sons here. They need you. Come back." I felt a

165

vague peace and got up and started functioning as a mom for my boys Jerry, 16, and Brett, 14.

It suddenly occurred to me to go to *The Flint Journal* and talked to columnist Alan MacLeese to see if he would put something in the paper for her to see and maybe come home. We hired a private detective who tracked down some of her friends and questioned them. He knew the right questions to ask, and one friend told him that she and Cindy had been in a bar, and two guys came up to them. They were from Texas, as are all of my relatives, so they got into a deep conversation. They were going back to Houston, and she went with them. That was the last we knew.

The following article, written by Mr. MacLeese, explains the incident very well. My copy of it is so yellowed and tattered, I have typed it below.

A Woman-Child is Missing

The matter has been reported to the proper authorities, although our proper authorities cannot devote time to hunting women-children who are 18 and therefore responsible and therefore not hunted.

Statistics and facts are taken by the proper authorities. Cindy Jean Pasco. Age 18. Height 5-feet-7. Weight 135. Her hair brown, eyes hazel. Parents Jack and Sidney Pasco, 1191 Gage, Holly Twp. Last seen July in a bar called The Town Pump on South Dort.

Some things aren't on the report. A mother's anguish, remorse, and soul-searching. You know the drill if you are a parent. Where did I go wrong, how did I fail? A father's fears that his daughter has met foul play, that she would not have vanished without a trace, that she would not have cut all ties willfully.

A woman-child is missing.

166

A mother, hoping against hope that her daughter is well, even traveling with men if that is the alternative to foul play, pens those lines:

> *"My child, my child*
> *Such tears of anguish trace my pain*
> *Where are you? Are you safe?*
> *Shall I see you once again?...*
>
> *In my mind's eye, I see your*
> *Sweet little freckled face*
> *Innocence and mirth etch their*
> *Smile creases of grace.*
> *Please come home, please come home.*

Cindy Jean, woman-child who is now able to drink at 18 because the law says she is able to drink responsibly at 18, went into the Town Pump to see a friend, Rene Stevens, a waitress there on July 5.

Mrs. Pasco said Rene later told her that two men – one in his 30s, the other in his 40s – had been trying to talk her (Rene) into traveling with them to Texas. Later, Rene told Mrs. Pasco, the men tried to get Cindy Jean to go with them.

The next thing Rene knew, they were gone, the two men and Cindy Jean. "I am from Texas–the Midland-Odessa area and I think it's possible that Rene is naïve enough to think she could have gone to Texas with these men without it becoming a sexual adventure. She has traveled with us to Texas on visits to my kinfolk there. She could have gone off with them."

Pasco doesn't think so. Jack Pasco doesn't believe his daughter even left Genesee County. Pasco, a test driver for General Motors in Milford since 1967, thinks his daughter has run into something she couldn't handle.

"She has been staying with a friend in Flint since she had an accident with her car," Pasco said. "She wanted to be nearer her job at the Small Mall on Dort. I don't think she took off on her own for several reasons. She apparently left with only the clothes on her back. She had clothes at the home in Flint and clothes at our home. She did not pick up a paycheck from The Vogue, nor did she make any attempt to get a considerable amount of money due from the insurance as a result of her accident. I don't think she has left the county," Pasco said. "And I have the feeling that something bad has happened to her. The police won't do anything, and it makes you wonder, does something bad definitely have to happen before they will do something?"

Mrs. Pasco rejects –does not want to think about- her husband's belief that something has happened to Cindy Jean. She is working on the theory that Cindy Jean indeed did go to Texas.

"Perhaps I'm not mature enough yet to think of violence being done to Cindy Jean," Mrs. Pasco said. "If she is off on her own or with someone, I think that Jack and I share part of the blame for Cindy Jean's uncertainties, her feeling unable to cope. She has been going through a difficult time. Her problems may have seemed serious to her. She had run up a considerable bill charging things at The Vogue where she is a salesperson. The accident bothered her, and she just barely scraped through graduating from high school in June. I know she had doubts as to whether her father loved her. I basically think that her problem is one that is cropping up all over these days. The children are no longer an integral, necessary part of the family. I grew up in a farm family in Texas and all of us children knew we were needed, to pick cotton *if nothing else. Nowadays, it seems like children have no goal, no baseline and they drift."*

A Woman-child is missing.

"Love gifts of handmade cards, and crumpled daisies
Offered with childish gladness.
Sunshine dancing in your hair,
Memories choke my heart with sadness..."

Mrs. Pasco had sent Cindy Jean's picture and information to Detroit papers and attempted to contact newspapers in Houston, where the two men who met Cindy Jean in the bar said they might go. Perhaps a news story about Cindy Jean's disappearance may not help us for Cindy Jean," said Mrs. Pasco. "But it could help others who have daughters and sons still growing. Runaways are one of our main social problems and one that we don't seem to be meeting," Mrs. Pasco said. Jack Pasco also sees a disturbing trend. "It seems, nowadays, if we have a problem and can't handle it, we just make a law to make that problem legal. Nobody seems to want to come to grips with our major social ills."

And meantime, a woman-child is missing, and she writes:
"My darling Cindy, forgive my ignorance,
My foolish awkward ways
For now, it is too late much too late.
I must give you up
To God's mercy and care
Not look back

In His strength only, courage share."

— Mother

Two months later, Mr. MacLeese wrote this piece as a follow up to his original article.

In Mid-July, I wrote a column about Cindy Jean Pasco, daughter of Mr. and Mrs. Jack (Sidney) Pasco. Cindy Jean, 18, had disappeared. She was last seen in a bar on Dort Hwy and had been in the company of two men who had asked her to go to Texas with them. I had written the column in hopes it might aid in the search for her. Well, the story has a happy ending. Mrs. Pasco wrote last week to inform me that Cindy Jean did indeed go to Texas, but she is no longer in the company of any strangers. She has moved in with Mrs. Pasco's relatives in the Midland-Odessa area.

I do not believe in coincidences. Jack and I prayed strongly and never stopped in our vigil. Our church family were all praying for us as well. Other things were happening. Through prayer and faith, I gained my daughter back she had truly panicked from all the events in her life, being in dept, wrecking her car and leaving her job. She went with the two men from the bar to our relatives in Texas. She was very fortunate they actually took her to my relatives. Paul, one of the guys, and she eventually started dating, and after several months he brought her back to me in Michigan, and after a period of time they married. Forty-six years later she has lived a meaningful and fruitful life. She is married to Darrell Christopher today who is a stellar man of value. She has had many successful enterprises, has four children and many grandchildren. Cindy, my second husband, Wayne, and I have created a 501(c)(3) charity through which we clothe and feed orphans, the elderly, and support education for people living in deep poverty.

We have built a Child Care Center in South Africa in the Bush to take care of orphans. We have recently completed a STEM Lab and Vocation Center to prepare

The HHTH team, - Wayne, Sidney, and Cindy.

Bush children to qualify for university, and skilled work, an opportunity they have never had before She has been and is leading a rewarding and fruitful life. Cindy is a beautiful daughter and is blessed with a compassionate and loving heart. I could not ask for better children.

Hennie (Director for luxury lodges in S. Africa), Sidney & Cindy giving Shangaan babies & women mosquito nets to shield them from malaria.

Out of my life's achievements, my children are my greatest achievement, and my most magnificent treasures.

LESSONS

- *Never give up*! I have always believed in my children.
- Lean on your faith and pray. Believe.
- It is never too late to create an extraordinary life.
- Give your blessings to your children.
- The first sign of trouble isn't the end of the story. Patience, patience, patience!
- It isn't over till it's over.
- *Stop* crushing children with control when they are older.
- I tried to control my children's lives so they would not experience the kind of struggles I had experienced as a child. They are *not* us, nor are they living in our situation.

Two Questions

1. Consider how you interacted with your children, describe how you tried to improve your interaction with them?

2. What difference do you see in them based on your changes?

Momma Never Saw the Movie "*Fried Green Tomatoes*" But She Knew What to do Anyway

Charlie Collier stood pensively in the middle of the room. Momma waited patiently, wondering why Charlie wanted to talk to her. Finally, he cleared his throat and said, "Sibyl, I love my Studebaker. It is the first new car I have ever owned, and I want to keep it as nice as possible. What I'd like to ask you is, would you please not let any of your grandchildren ride in it? Could you take them in your car if you want to take them somewhere, so they don't get sticky fingerprints all over my brand-new Studebaker?" It is as if he had sucked his breath in after his speech and never let it out again.

Momma had a fiery temper at this stage in her life, and she had not yet grown into a woman of calm wisdom and grace. Yet this day, she just quietly blinked those beautiful bright blue eyes, and slowly responded, "That is a reasonable request Charlie, so, yes I can do that for you." (Though she was clearly ticked off about it). Charlie finally exhaled his sucked in breath and the tenseness evaporated into thin air.

Charlie was Momma's third husband, and they had a very volatile relationship. Most of the time she kept Charlie off balance because he never really knew how she might react. So, this miracle took him by surprise. She had been married to our Daddy 20 years, and she was married to her second husband less than 24 hours. That was Bill. The first night after their wedding, she came back to where we had been living. We never really knew why. Whatever Bill did that night at his house, it made him single again. She had that one annulled.

Momma's agreement with Charlie about the Studebaker went into effect immediately, even though she wasn't really happy about it. But reasonable is reasonable, and she stuck by her word. Her response made Charlie nervous because he knew she was married to Daddy 20 years, but only because divorce was a huge stigma in those days. And given that she was only married to Bill less than 24 hours, she now knew where the front door was, and she didn't hesitate to use it. He knew he was "skating on thin ice."

Things seemed to settle down for a while, but just a while later, all thunder broke loose. Charlie worked as a photographer for an old guy who owned a studio in a little strip mall just off Wall Street, which was on her way home. This one day, she decided to go by and surprise Charlie, and they could go to dinner together. It would have to be her treat, as usual, as Charlie was chronically short of cash. But she was in a happy mood, and it seemed like a good idea.

Momma turned into the little mall and started down the line of cars parked in front of the stores. As she got closer to the photography studio, she spotted Charlie's new Studebaker. She couldn't believe her eyes! There Charlie was opening the passenger door to let his old boss's wife in the front seat. *Then*, he opened the back door to put in her two big, drooling Doberman pinschers, dripping and slobbering all over Charlie's brand-new Studebaker's back seat upholstery.

Well! Momma said she just plain saw fire-engine red. And she was now right behind Charlie's brand-new Studebaker. And even though she had never seen the movie, *Fried Green Tomatoes*, she knew what to do anyway. I guess Momma didn't like the angle or something. She backed up her great big old scarlet Lincoln and revved the engine like Mario Andretti at the Indianapolis 500.

By this time Charlie was at the driver's side and, to his horror, recognized her car. He frantically waved his arms shouting, "No, Sibyl! No! Don't do it!" Too late, Momma rammed that Lincoln into drive, jammed the pedal to the metal, screeching the smoking tires and made a full crash into the back of Charlie's brand-new Studebaker. She threw the car gear into reverse, burning rubber as she backed up and *bam!* She did it again!

The old boss's wife was screaming and crying, Charlie was yelling at the top of his lungs, and the dogs were wild-eyed, drooling and frantically barking their heads off. The chaos was at the top of the gauge. She sat there a minute, real quiet and peaceful then she backed up real slow as the metal untangled itself, and she drove calmly home, completely justified.

That is the way she told it to me, and like I said, Momma was the best storyteller in the world. To this day, I feel like I was there and witnessed the whole thing.

When she got to her little house, she pulled in her driveway, parked the Lincoln with a caved-in front end and went inside. She took all of Charlie's belongings and put them on the porch, and husband number three was gone. He never got to go back into her house again. When my momma is finished with something, she is plumb finished, there is no turning back for her. At least Charlie made it past the seven-year mark.

LESSONS
- We all have a limit as to how much we will take before the steel trap door of our heart slams shut. We ought not to push people past it. Particularly when it is the person you are supposed to love.
- Rage can cause anyone to lose control and it usually leads to disaster. Something bad can happen that will hurt people unintentionally.
- Justified anger can give us the impetus (force of energy) to do what we know we need to do, but we may be too weak of will at the time to do it.

Two Questions
1. Tell of a time you were able to get some kind of revenge for being treated poorly and made a fool of.

2. Describe your feelings right after the deed was done.

It Takes More Than One Disappointment to Make a Divorce

I was sitting in a courtroom reminiscing about what got Jack and I to this place. A sterile, heartless room with other people waiting in line to destroy a life with not much more than a signature. There is no help to bind the wounds, nor a fix-it-kit to start over again. That would require someone to care and willing to try again. It was over. Too many hurtful experiences. Too many unhealed wounds. Too many words that can't be taken back. Too many actions that can't be undone. Our marriage died a slow death.

It was heartbreaking to go through this hopeless process of a marriage that didn't have much of a chance to work from the beginning. We both tried very hard but, we simply did not know how to fix it. The day had come, and I was just going through the motions.

We had endured almost 20 years of hurt, confusion, and anger, each day experiencing a deeper misunderstanding of each other. And yes, there were many precious and good times. But the deep gashes in my heart were too many and outweighed the good. The major ones left me with devastating, searing scars.

Jack was very jealous and tried to keep me separated from my family and other relationships. I felt my only option was to stay at home, out of sight.

For the first seven years of our marriage, I thought he didn't like me. I remember early on asking him if he would take me to a movie. He refused. I ask if I could go with my older sister, and he refused again.

He said, "I am not going to take you to a movie, you are not going alone, and you can't go with your sister." Even though I was only 17 at the time, I knew that was an unreasonable position, but in the 1957 Southern culture, the man ruled the household whether or not it made any sense. I felt smothered, trapped. Locked in a pumpkin shell with no way out.

When he decided he wanted to move us from Texas, where he was in the Air Force, back to his hometown in Fenton, Michigan, we thought it would be a fresh start.

We were only two years into our marriage, our daughter, Cindy Jean had been born, and a year later I was pregnant with our son, Jerry.

Jack decided to send me ahead to Michigan to stay with his folks, Vi and Jess. The first thing I did was to find a church of my persuasion, the Fenton Church of Christ.

This gave me a church family who cared. I was isolated and felt totally alone in a culture that I didn't understand. Making friends was easy

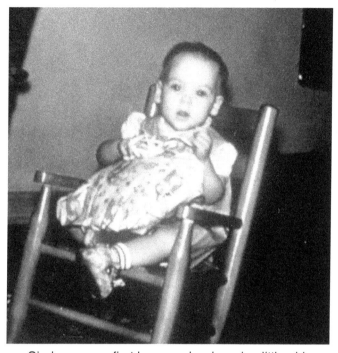

Cindy was our first born, and a charming little girl.

and helped me to feel a little acceptance. A couple of times the gal I used to work with called to check on us, but she eventually stopped. We were separated a couple of months while Jack mustered out of the Air Force. When he returned, we continued to live with his folks until Bo was born on March 3, 1960. This was a very difficult time. Things were not easy with two babies, but Mother and Ginger called me weekly to support and encourage me. Living with in-laws was hard on all of us. They readily accepted Cindy but not Bo.

We ended up on welfare which was a new low. We didn't have anything like

that in Texas at the time. It was a great humiliation for me. The whole situation was so stressful that when I nursed Bo, my stress made him throw up with such force he got sick.

Not too long after we moved out, I got pregnant again, but wasn't very far along when the baby miscarried. Jack took me to the hospital but left me there, losing the baby alone, while he went hunting. That was unbelievably hurtful and scary.

Bo was a high energy, busy little boy.

I nearly couldn't climb over this one, but life went on. The next day, Jack still wasn't there. I called Vi to ask when he would come to pick me up at the hospital. She said she didn't know how he could come pick me up because they were not going to lend him their car. The cruelty of this interaction was devastating, but it made me realize where some of Jack's resentments came from.

We moved back to Texas for a short time. Exactly two years after Bo was born, Brett was born on March 12, 1962. When Brett was a toddler, we moved back to Michigan.

My church life was my only positive outlet. In many ways it saved me. Otherwise, the environment was fairly hostile. I was 20

Brett was a calm and enchanting little boy.

when Bo was born, and 22 when Brett was born.

At about 25, I rededicated my life to God and was baptized as an adult. Jack went with me because it was evening and he drove me to the church. My exhilaration and hope were at the mountain peak, and I felt filled with the Holy Spirit. As soon as we got in the car to go home, Jack said he wanted to talk to me.

While I was in that spiritually high state, Jack told me that, during the time when he stayed in Texas and sent me ahead to Michigan, he had had an affair with the gal I worked with—the one that had been calling me. My world crashed to the ground. I couldn't hear over the loud roaring in my head. My "high" melted away into confusion and humiliation. I was in shock. My joy was ripped from my grasp. The out-of-control emotional spikes and lows were unstoppable. I went from inexpressible inspiration to unspeakably separate feelings of betrayal, raw embarrassment, and desperation. He chose that moment to tell me, I guess, hoping it would all be okay. The cruelty of it was staggering. The betrayal was bile in my throat.

I sought counselling with an elder in our church who was a wise, trusted, and compassionate man. Meanwhile, Jack's financial irresponsibility was getting us deeper and deeper in debt. The volatility of our personalities and our value differences clashed and created more fights.

If I questioned his spending, he escalated to screams and threats. I followed right along with him. Our differences were glaring and made life continuously miserable. Worry about the effect on my children plagued me. How could I take care of my children and provide them with even the bare essentials? I could not stand the harm our negative parenting was having on them. We both loved our children but didn't seem to know how to stop the rush of our raging destruction.

For a short period, Jack, and I both worked at the General Motors Proving Ground. He was a technician working on preparing to crash a car on the crash sled so results could be analyzed. At that time, I was a secretary. When I arrived at work this one day there was a buzz going on about someone who had tried to steal tires by cutting a hole in the fence to push them through to the outside. More detailed information kept coming in and finally, in the afternoon, a name was disclosed.

One of the rumor-bearers, Ralph, excitedly came up to me and asked if I knew that this guy, Jack Pasco, had tried to steal four tires. He had been caught, fired, and escorted off the grounds. I was horrified because I knew that was my husband. I backed away in shock, Ralph quickly put two and two together and realized Jack and I were married. He tried to apologize, but I just backed away, embarrassed to the core.

There were many times I was embarrassed when Jack yelled at me in public, but this was the ultimate. This dishonesty was excruciatingly hard to live through. I had to force myself to go to work each day with my head up and do my job, wondering if my job was in jeopardy. How would I take care of my children if I also lost my job?

After a time, the scandal died down, but my feelings were eroding fast. Dishonesty was certainly not my value. Jack's explanation was that he was taking the tires for a friend, who never owned up to being a part of the action. Something shifted inside me.

One evening, while taking my bath, I heard screaming from downstairs. Our main bedroom was the loft above our kitchen and living room. I jumped out of the tub, grabbed my robe, and rushed out to the railing and saw Jack two inches from Bo's face (he was about 14 or 15), screaming at the tops of his lungs, "Who do you think you are? Who do you think you are?"

The crescendo rose to fever pitch. "Who do you think you are?" Over and over again until Bo yelled out in wild defeat, "I am a nothing! I'm a nobody!" Bo slumped, broken, and defeated. I visibly saw the destruction of a soul. I knew on the spot I could not live in this atmosphere any longer. It was unspeakably painful to see my child emotionally ripped to shreds. The last straw had snapped. I could no longer tolerate this toxic existence.

Finally, it became clear to me that our monies had to be separated to ensure that the house payment and utility bills would get paid regularly. I feared we would lose our home. This was a nightmare worse than I remembered from my youth. The unrelenting stress, dishonesty, financial pressures, the screaming, and the psychological and emotional pain became unbelievably overwhelming.

We brought out the worst in each other. It was tragic, particularly for our children. We were never able to reach peace with each other even though we both had remarried. When the children were nineteen, seventeen, and fifteen, the marriage was torn asunder. Cindy was married and living in Houston; Bo left home to live with Cindy, and there was no unity or security for Brett. Divorce seemed to be my only path to stay sane.

Now, after seeking input from a trusted friend and my pastor, I have reached a new perspective on this. It will at least stop the shunning I am subjected to when Jack and I do happen to be at the same activity with our children. I will simply go to the children's activities at a different time. This is the side of my story, Jack has his.

LESSONS

- You cannot use reason with an unreasonable person.
- It takes more than one painful experience to break a marriage.
- My own Southern culture kept me from discovering how to end some of the destruction.
- If people aren't a match on values, spiritually, and interests, they can't force a relationship to survive that is headed for disaster.

- Betrayal is often too toxic to overcome.

- You cannot continuously hurt and demean another's soul and expect the person to love you no matter what. When parents are hurting each other, they are also hurting the children. When they are steeped in their own pain, they are blind to the pain they are causing their children.

- The leading causes of divorce are spousal abuse (physical or emotional), infidelity, financial difficulties, value differences, and dishonesty.

- A lack of communication skills makes it almost impossible to resolve differences or design alternatives for resolution.

- Just wanting things to be fair doesn't mean they will be fair.

- There isn't much hope to stop the devastating pain of a failed marriage when there has been betrayal, destructive behavior, financial inequities, conflicting values, and tearing down instead of building up. Not many marriages could survive it.

Two Questions

1. If you have experienced divorce, what were some of the reasons?

2. Knowing what you know now, how might it have been saved? Or could it have been?

The Volcano Phase of My Life Journey
Passions Have Led Me On Wondrous Adventures

The jet wheels hit the tarmac and screeched slightly, as if groaning under the weight of the passengers and luggage. At least ten of us geologists joined a volunteer expedition through the sponsor organization called the Journey. Dr. Richard Thorpe was our expedition leader. The volunteers came from all over the world. We were eager to deplane and travel by crude transportation to Poas, the active volcano in Costa Rica, Central America. It has erupted 40 times since 1828. It was 1974, and

Poas warning us of her powers to destroy.

the volcano was actively erupting. Our group was studying the patterns of eruptions and activity in the huge sulfur lake in the caldera (the depression formed when a volcano erupts and collapses). We pitched camp in the cloud forest above the crater and commenced studying the beautiful expanse of nature, complete with a romantic lagoon. The descent down into the caldera was 1,500 feet. We would descend that in the morning, study the volcanic fumaroles (an opening through which gases emerge) in the sulfur lake, and note the environment surrounding the lake. At the end of the day, we'd climb out, racing the darkness enfolding us. There was an air of irritation in the lake, and it reminded me of the beloved Costa Rican myth about the friendship of a girl and the Rualdo bird.

The Rualdo bird displaying its exotic colors.

Once, long ago, Poas volcano became disgruntled and threatened the lives of the local Shaman's tribe. Poas' great fury would not be abated. The Shaman went down into the caldera and asked Poas what he and his tribe could do to satiate its anger. To his horror, the volcano demanded the Shaman's daughter sacrificed for the tribe's "salvation." The Shaman ordered his daughter to be captured and thrown into the lake of fire.

Though she begged with her whole heart, her father would not yield to her frantic cries for mercy. Moments before she was to be thrown into the yawning mouth of the fiery pit, a Rualdo bird flew deep into the crater, pleading with the spirit of the volcano to exchange its song for the girl's life.

The Rualdo bird sang with all its might, and its beautiful song caused Poas to weep, flooding the crater, creating what is now known as the Boto Lagoon. The girl and the Rualdo bird became friends. And if you listen carefully, you can still hear the Rualdo's beautiful serenade for his beloved friend wafting through the air in the lagoon.

Meanwhile, back in 1974 with the Journey geological team, Poas' untamable temper was creating quite a bit of excitement. A crew of us went down into the caldera to set up a four-man tent. Our expedition leader, Dr. Richard Thorpe, professor from the Open University in England, planned to take a four-person team back down the next day for a 24-hour observation of the activity. Just as we got the tent set up, the earth began to shake, and loud hissing noises spewed out of the fiery lake.

Richard told us to leave everything, we had to get out of the caldera! We scrambled up the 1,500 feet to the rim. Just as we got to the top, Poas belched out great quantities of scree, small rocks broken from larger ones during prior volcanic activity, straight up into the air. The hot eruption sprayed them out in a steady stream, blackening the sky. People could see the eruption all the way into San Jose, about 30 miles away. We scrambled for our shelter, which wasn't much to escape the hot ash. It pelted us badly for about an hour and then settled down. Scree is only about one quarter inch in diameter, they cooled down enough so that they were warm but did not burn us badly.

After a bit of supper, we were weary from the climb in and out of the caldera and all the excitement of the activity, we dragged ourselves to our tents and fell into a fitful sleep. Then the fireworks started. Booming and sounds of exploding boulders pierced the quiet. It was almost like Dante's hell, with red hot boulders, called bombs, shooting into the sky and pounding back down onto the caldera floor. We had no clue what would happen next. It was pitch black and dangerous, making it untenable to evacuate. Fortunately, our camp was on the side of the volcano and the boulders fell back down into the caldera. There was a lot of praying going on in our tents that night. The activity finally settled down and once again sleep fell over us.

All the knowledge that had just been in a book, came alive as if by magic.

The next day, Dr. Thorpe asked me if I wanted to climb back into the caldera to assess the damage. I said yes, and down back in we went. Everything had changed. It looked like a scene from *Stars Wars*.

There were bombs, laying all around from being spewed out as molten plastic that solidified into huge rocks as they cooled. The sulfur lake was down seven feet. Then we found bits of the tent we had set up shrunk down to a one foot-square rag. That level of destruction made it chilling to realize what we had missed.

"Could this thing torch off again?" I asked Richard (Thorpe). When he indicated that it could, I told him, "In that case, I am going to give you my best version of a Southern parting: "Bhaa, honey, bhaa!" Geologists are a fearless, hardy group. What seems dangerous to normal people doesn't to them. We made it out safely and completed the organization of our data collection, content to add to the body of knowledge that would help future scientists who would continue to explore Poas, its Rualdo bird myth and his friend. We participated in several other adventurous expeditions in which the experience of the greatness of God filled me with wonder.

<u>LESSONS</u>

- I learned a lot from my studies in college, but it burst into living color in the field. Everything was vivid and real. All the puzzle pieces fit together. Geology was my major for my BS degree.

- Working with geologists from several countries brought a wealth of knowledge and understanding to the work we were doing.

- Our part added important data to understanding volcanic activity.

  This was important information for countries that experience disasters and could save future lives.

- There is deep fulfillment to know I had helped future generations.

- I learned one person can make a difference in our world.

<u>TWO QUESTIONS</u>

1. Have you ever been involved in helping make the condition of the world better? (e.g. cleaning up debris on a beach, saving an endangered species?) Briefly describe it.

   2. How did that make you feel?

Mexico's *Volcan de Fuego*: Volcano of Fire

The year was late 1976. Cindy was 18, living in Houston, Texas, and preparing to marry. Bo was nearly 17 and went to live in Houston with Cindy to get away from the destruction Jack and I were creating. Bo is a survivor, always a strong young man and I knew he was capable of adapting. Brett was nearly 15 years old and unsure what his future held. I was preparing to move out of our home and into an apartment with plans to start a divorce. My life was rapidly changing, but I decided to stay in our home until Cindy married. I was in emotional chaos because I knew I couldn't stay in the marriage yet felt desperate to finish my Mothering role with Brett.

L-R Donald Miler, photographer, Dr. Richard Thorpe, Dr. Ian Gibson between me and Richard.

We were forming human chains to help us climb through the rough terrain.

I needed to be alone to consider my uncertain future. Our last year's volcano team leaders decided to go to Mexico with a new international team to assault the Volcano of Fire, also known as Volcan de Colima, located in a wild area in Mexico with very dense vegetation, and almost no people other than a group of banditos hiding in an isolated corner of the world.

Even animals hid from sight leaving an eerie feeling of something watching us, but we could not see them. We were engulfed in a foreboding isolation.

The expedition was another 5-week educational leave and maybe that would give me enough time apart from Jack to consider my options.

Observing the lava flow which sounded like millions of pieces of glass crashing together and breaking.

Dr. Richard Thorpe and Dr. Ian Gibson lead our team. My friend, Nina Navarro came along to write an article for Mariah Magazine focusing on the two active volcanoes in the area and tell the story about our international team of volunteers. Donald Miller was our official photographer.

Colima was alive with fiery activity. Being out in the wonder of God's nature lit my own internal fire and refreshed my outlook. The remoteness and the absence of people gave me a calm, and welcome peace. The sense of freedom and being at one with the dramatic environment was as intoxicating as the finest wine. A new wild and mysterious adventure, charged with danger, awaited us. Our quest was to study the volcanic ash layers, map lava flows, and collect samples for further study on both Colima and Nevado Volcanos, and I was up for the challenge.

Upon arrival, our group walked into the magnificent Mexican wilderness and started the ascent to Colima through the tangled overgrown brush that viciously thwarted our push forward. The climate and environment could only be measured in extremes, sweltering hot in the desert during the day and frigid cold at night. The climbs were rugged and grueling requiring a system of hand over hand pulling each other up to the slope.

Don, a volunteer and I fought the tangled brush all the way to the bare zone. We were rewarded for our efforts with the awesome display of Colima. Richard and Ian determined that we should climb back down to cross over to the other side of the lava flow. Together the forceful volcanic gases spewed, and the fiery rocks pushed the lava flow forward, which cooled as it gouged out a valley in its wake and cooled. What sounded like huge jet engines combined with the shocking sounds of solid hot rocks bursting as they crashed together and shattered, reminded me of a Steven Spielberg, end-of-the-world-as-we-know-it movie. Having had enough excitement for one day, we ended our explorations and returned to our camp set up in a wooded area, which offered some protection from the heat of the day and the glacial cold of the night.

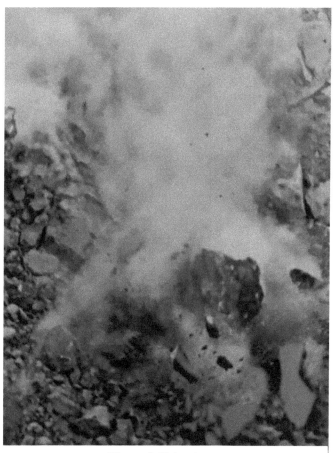

The solidifying lava.

Each day of this 5-week venture was full, preparing to get to Colima. We gathered supplies, water, found a truck large enough for our team and all supplies and equipment. Then we created our base camp site, organized the tent for the

191

scientific information we would be gathering and samples of rocks we collected. We set up our mess tent and kitchen for our meals. All this had to be done before dark he first day in the field. We gathered in the mess tent each night to discuss our findings for the day.

The lava was solidifying and cutting through the crevis from the hot gasses that were pushing it forwards.

We started each day by climbing either Colima or Nevado de Colima Volcanos to do our work. Two days before leaving, we climbed Colima to assess the advancement of the lava flow. I climbed as high as possible to observe it. As I made my ascent, I accidently stepped off onto a huge bed of loose scree. My foot disappeared and I started to struggle, which separated me from solid ground even more. I felt my heart and mind quickly jump from anxiety to full-out grisly fear.

My body was moving toward the lava flow, and I couldn't stop my descent. Ian yelled at me to lay down and be still. I tried, but I continued to slowly slide down toward the valley of fire. As I looked at the red-hot rocks and gases below me, I was seized by the thought of never seeing my children again. I would not get to see them grow up and become the magical people they were meant to be. My eyes, filled with

The team that saved me when I fell into the skree.

tears, fixated on that inferno thinking *this is it*, I tried to make my peace in one last desperate prayer when I suddenly felt a hand grab my hand. I turned my face to see that our team had formed a human chain and was pulling me out. My relief and gratefulness were indescribable. Together, they did something one person could not have done alone. Their fast thinking and determination saved my life.

These were just a few of the volcanos I had explored, but this last one gave me serious reservations. I lay still and quiet in my tent and could not sleep. I loved my adventuresome life, but I reluctantly admitted the excitement did not justify the risk for my children. I reflected on this dilemma for the remainder of the expedition.

It became clear to me I could not play games with my life because my life belonged to my children. They deserved my time more to have a mother around. By the time we all boarded our flights for home, I knew the only resolution was to resign from the chasing-live-volcanos business and prayed for ways to express my passions in areas that would not compromise my children's future. There was a little sadness, but I trusted God to guide me with His wisdom to lead a full life without putting myself in danger.

LESSONS

- God's beautiful world is full of adventure and wonder.
- Every adventure teaches me deep lessons about my life and the life around me.
- When we humans form bonds we can achieve more than any one person could achieve alone.
- My priorities need to be kept in order. God was not through with me yet. I still had years to do what he put me on this earth to do.
- I would soon discover that all of life was leading me to the noble purpose He had planned for me. This was truly being alive!

Two Questions

1. Share one of your life adventures.

2. How did it change you?

Introduction to Additional Adventures in My Life

In the years between 1976 and 1980, I lived alone and went on many adventures in my life. The ones I present here were international trips to Africa through an educational company called Educational Expeditions International. These expeditions were led by Professors from the host country and volunteer scientists came from different parts of the world. I took educational leaves of absence and joined the team. In this case, Geologist, Dr. Igor Loupakine, from the University of Nairobi along with three other geology professors were our leaders. I went on two consecutive missions with these leaders.

I had stopped going on active volcano expeditions because of my children, but still did vulcanology work. On this expedition, we were taking measurements by simulating seismic activity to determine the length of travel for a seismic wave in sand, vs rock, dry vs wet conditions, and other experiments to add to the body of knowledge about volcanos. We were far into the wilderness of East Africa. Everything was extreme. The terrain, animals, remoteness of location, weather, huge insects, and snakes was an exotic caldron of our living conditions.

Because the expeditions had a measure of risk, the volunteers signed a release of responsibility form and the professors took turns lecturing us on how to stay safe in the vegetation, around animals, and the drastic changes in weather. It was amazing and certainly educational. We learned animal behavior and many things about the people, their customs, and superstitions, their ancestral spirituality and how to act appropriately around them to not offend their beliefs.

I was still at General Motors, advancing in my career, and going to college. The education was essential to me, and these educational leaves were helpful in that arena. I was close to earning my B.S. with honors in Geology, with plans to go on for a master's degree in business. A promotion with more responsibility and more money was imminent.

Life was rich, exciting, and full of promise. I was free and learning all about a new way of being in my changed world. I remember the feelings of being thrilled like I was seeing with wide open eyes, and ears unafraid to hear.

I had finally climbed out of a lifetime of poverty and could handle my own finances. At last, I felt in a position to take care of my children. My career was secure with a bright future on the horizon. I had faith in my destiny and was pursuing it. It was a glorious moment in time.

Suguta, The Valley of Death, and Other Great Adventures

It was 1976, and the Suguta territory in Kenya, Africa was called the Valley of Death for good reason. Suguta is a harsh, wild, unexplored, and hostile land. Somewhat like our Badlands in North Dakota. It is an extreme desert where water is scarce.

The native porters assured us they knew where water could be found. They hadn't found water yet, and our supply was getting low. Not only had they lied about knowing where water could be found, they were taking our water because they had not brought their own as they had promised. Had we known the truth, we could have planned to get additional water brought to our base camp.

I had joined this international group of geologists to explore this uncharted wilderness. There were 10 of us geologists from different parts of the world—England, Australia, the United States, and Africa.

Maasai warrior appeared out of the bush. A boy only becomes a man by killing a lion, they become fearless.

The University of Nairobi headed this map-making expedition. Our mission was to explore and chart the area and to bring back samples and descriptions of the

After a night under the stars, we broke camp.

terrain. Suguta is in Kenya's Northern Frontier, near the great Rift Valley. It was Maasai country. The Maasai consider themselves lion hunters. They are a tall, elegant people with great pride. The practice of lion hunting has bred a fearlessness in their culture, and they feel sorry for all others who are not Maasai as they believe they have the best way of life.

A male Maasai must kill a lion to prove his worth as a warrior making him as confident and fierce as the lion. The women are elegant and at one with the earth. They wandered in and out of our camps to bargain for trades and observe our goings-on.

We started our trek with donkeys laden with food, water, and equipment. The temperature was constantly over 100 degrees, stifling in its intensity. The desert floor was covered with basalt and magna rocks, rendering it impossible to set our feet on solid ground. It was devoid of any vegetation.

At night we would search for a butte or high ground to set up camp. Carrying our packs over the rugged terrain in the oppressive heat, with a shortage of water was taking its toll on our energies. The nights offered little relief from the sweltering heat, and our water dipped to dangerously low levels. We were in search of the Suguta Lake, and just when we thought we would spot it over every rocky, ill-gained ridge, there was yet another barren ridge.

We took inventory and realized we only had enough water to make it out and back to our Base Camp where, Babu, one of our expedition leaders, awaited us, but not enough to go any further.

We had collected many samples, written descriptions of the terrain and mapped the areas we explored. We felt like we had gotten close to the unexplored lake area, but it was too dangerous to go on.

We were all suffering from dehydration that quickly put us in a desperate situation. The next team would get the joy of finding Suguta

We used mules to transport our goods.

Lake armed with our information after having cleared the way. They would have better knowledge of the supplies needed. We turned back, scaling the rocks, climbing back over ridge after ridge, almost floating in our semi-conscious brains. I could see the endless expanse of desert and rocks that could not be wished away. It took every fiber in my body to carry me forward.

Babu had stayed at base camp to be prepared for our walk back out. The sun and the heat beat down on me in merciless, silent misery and hammered away on my energy and resistance.

Finally, when I thought I couldn't take another weary step, I heard the weak sound of Babu's horn beeping in the distance. Suddenly it felt like magic from the legendary Wizard Merlin's hand was transforming my energy. Dehydration had us in its deadly grip, and yet that faint *beep, beep, beep* called to us much like the enchanted sirens called to Ulysses in *The Iliad*. We sucked in new energy and hope.

The horn got louder and clearer, giving us a direction to aim for while we

Almost in a semi-conscious daze we followed Babbu's horn to walk out of the wilderness. We were in an unexplored bare, hostile, and unforgiving land where no one walked before.

struggled against the disorientation and confusion dehydration causes. I finally walked out into a beautiful oasis, where Babu had set up a feast of east African pineapples, melons, mangos, cheeses, cold cuts, and the miracle of water! By this time, I was barely conscious, but I had forced myself to persevere. I felt a sliver of pride after drinking some water. We had done it! We had accomplished most of our goals with what we had to work with.

Our ride out of the uncivilized and unforgiving desert to our base camp was an unconscious dream. I fell into such a deep sleep that the trip was lost on me. Though the base camp was only 90 miles away, the roads were so treacherous that it took half the night to get back. After our sleep, we were revived and ravenously hungry. The leader of the Suguta Valley explorers, Edmund, announced that the cook crew were preparing a feast in our honor. The table was ladened with roasted goat, their version of sweet potatoes, veggies of all sorts, and fruits. I thought I might be able to eat some goat because I was so starved. It smelled heavenly. But *no*—I couldn't get past the strange taste. I ate everything but the poor little goat.

Suguta was a thrilling adventure shared with wonderful people. My heart was full. Such an experience is the lifeblood of my soul.

Philosopher, author, Joseph Campbell penned the phrase, "Follow your bliss" to become your highest self. He urged people to discover what they are passionate about and pursue it with their whole heart. It is transcendent, and when you find and engage in your passion, time stands still, you get lost in the thing.

One could also use the phrase, "Follow your passion," or "Follow your heart." My favorite one is the family motto I saw on a wall in a preserved plantation in Charleston, South Carolina, "Follow your star." This is the one I adopted for my family's motto. Campbell wrote many books with profound thoughts to stir our minds. I am struck by his wisdom when he writes, "The cave you fear to enter holds the treasure you seek."

His heavy-weighted philosophy spoke to the heart beating within me, and I began to follow my star the rest of my life. It led me into many deep and mysterious caves, yet the principle yielded to me its treasure of beauty, fulfillment, challenge, and enlightenment, leading ultimately to a joyful life. Suguta is but one example. Following are others.

LESSONS

- I learned so much about the Maasai, very unique people.

- I learned how to survive in a hostile environment.

- Just because people are different than we are doesn't mean they are less capable.

- The Maasai taught us a lot about the environment.

- The Maasai are a radiant role model for confidence and fearlessness.

- It was an education to see how their traditional ways form a high self-esteem that is natural and not easily shaken.

- The hope created by a beeping horn was an amazing lesson. Just knowing someone was out there and cared about us made all the difference.

- I learned the strength and courage I needed for the final leg. Believe you can go beyond what you thought you could. Be involved in life.

Two Questions

1. What are some of the passions you have in your life now?

2. Have you noticed they change as life changes? What other dreams do you have that can feed your spirit?

A Brilliant Blanket of Psychedelic Flamingos

Thousands of flamingos gather on lake Nakuru.

After the rigors of Suguta Valley, the valley of death, we restored ourselves and explored more of East Africa. On Safari to the Serengeti plains, we witnessed exotic animal life, such as The Rift Valley, replete with lakes and escarpments teaming with countless species of wildlife.

At Lake Nakuru, an explosion of pink flamingos was attracted to its shining shores.

In the Maasai language, Serengeti means "endless plains", and the place lives up to its name. It nourishes my soul to see such wonders.

The innermost part of my being is changed from the many moments of living my passion for adventure. I am in awe of what life offers us if we dare to enter our cave of fear and claim the treasure hidden behind it. Most of the things we humans fear or worry about never happen. The fear is an illusion that blocks us from what we could be.

This king of the jungle did not appreciate us disturbing his mating ritual.

Total Eclipse of the Sun

In1974 the total solar eclipse was the longest eclipse of the following 200 years. The ideal location from which to watch it was the sparkling shores of Lake Turkana. Our expedition team happened to be in the area. We headed for the crocodile-infested waters of the shining Lake Turkana. We got settled into our spot and enjoyed the cool proximity to the innocent-looking lake. We were living the thrill of being present at the very best site in the world to observe this phenomenon.

How could we let this moment pass us by?

Babu and I chose a semi-safe distance from the water's edge to wait for the magical moments. We looked through film, which protected our eyes. As the moon worked its way across the sun, there was a palpable hush as night creatures started making their noises and appearances, and daytime animals went to bed in their dens and holes. It felt eerie and a little scary, like watching a horror movie when the music gets suspenseful, people look wide-eyed and terrified for the monster who will jump out and scare them half to death. The eclipse was an awesome unfolding.

The medicine men also taught the tribal people to look through a filter. One exhilarating moment after another took our breath away, and etched the experience into our hearts, minds, and souls.

When the sun came back out, we felt somehow altered. We learned from our leaders that we could play in the lake if we all held on to each other so the crocodiles could not grab anyone of us and pull us down for a death roll. We ventured in and splashed around with childlike joy, a fitting end to this adventure.

Me viewing the eclipse through film.

The Thunderous Wonder of Thompson Falls

Wherever we found ourselves, we were surrounded by dramatic scenery, exotic animals in the wild, and unique plant life. Africa is called the Dark Continent because

The magnificent Thompson falls.

of the natural wildness that still throbs and breathes excitement. Its environment is still mostly raw, harsh, and untamed.

The animals, plants, and people are often just as wild as the topography, and full of mystery. When we arrived at Thompson Falls (now renamed Nyahururu) in Kenya, the drama continued to unfurl into even more breathless wonders.

To get the maximum experience, I climbed as close to the bottom of the falls as I could. I wanted to feel the thundering heartbeat of that great falls in my soul as it plunged 243 feet to the rising water level below. It was one of those moments when my whole body experienced the power of God's might amongst His creation. It was a tough climb down, but it paid off with intimate connection as I leaned back against the trembling wall of rock, felt the violent spray of water striking my face, and bathed in an experience that I would remember for a lifetime. I was reminded of the Mayo Angelou quote, "Life is not measured by the number of breaths we take but by the moments that take our breath away."

Climbing down to get to the base of the falls.

Sometimes we just have to let life shock us through all our senses. That

Felt the tremendous power of the water crashing to the bottom of the falls.

may require more from us than the ordinary to have the privilege of an extraordinary outcome.

Next, we stormed the silvery shores of the Indian Ocean. Floating around on the high-salt-content water made us feel almost as if we could defy gravity. After we stepped out of the salty waves, which were crashing on shore at our feet, Debbie, my tent partner and I showered off the salt under an outdoor shower.

We had an invigorating and luxurious break in our routine.

207

Everything was different in this wild and untamed world. The common became extraordinary.

Debbie and I taking a dip in the Indian ocean.

LESSONS

- I learned how to endure hardship with prayers and the positive belief of knowing we could do it.
- Be prepared for an endless adventure.
- It is important to keep moving forward and to believe that I can do what needs to be done.
- We must pace ourselves in life.
- We must keep the wolf of fear away, otherwise it will steal our hopes and dreams.
- Follow your passion.

- Opportunities pass. Grab them while they are within your grasp.
- Energize your life with breath taking moments.
- Give your heart something to remember.
- Breathe in that special moment. Capture it so you can imprint it in your heart, mind, and soul and you will never forget it. These experiences can become part of your life's treasures.

<u>Two Questions</u>

1. What have you ventured to do that truly brought you fully and consciously awake?

2. What is something you would love to try? Would you dare to start your Bucket List?

Our Hearts Will Go On

I laid my head gently on his chest so I could hear his heart. He was already spiritually separated and had closed his beautiful sky-blue eyes. It would not be much longer. I felt him shift ever so slightly and looked up into his eyes that still had their sparkle. He held me tenderly to his heart and spoke the last words he would ever utter, "Sidney, I love you with all my heart."

Cuddling in joyful love right up to the ultimate transformation.

After that moment, my precious husband of 41 years, Wayne Albert Bonvallet, passed through, the veil where I could not yet follow. A lifetime of love and devotion flooded my heart. At the same time, the pain was so enormous, it consumed me like a monstrous ocean wave crashing over me, depriving me of oxygen. Wayne was my one true love, the soul of my soul. We completed each other.

Now he was gone from me physically. Watching his spirit ebb into the unknown took my breath away. In his last words he gave me the priceless gift of those last sweet familiar, words that were so common, yet ours alone. We exchanged them as our sacred vows one last time.

I believe we will find each other in that other world beyond. Wayne always promised me he would be waiting just inside the pearly gates, sitting on his golden folding chair, the first to welcome me to eternity with him.

The song written by James Horner and Will Jennings, sung so eloquently by Celine Dion speaks of the feelings we shared, talked about, and wrote each other about throughout our marriage.

My Heart Will Go On

Every night in my dreams I see you, I feel you

That is how I know you go on

Far across the distance and spaces between us

You have come to show you go on

Near, far, wherever you are, I believe that the heart does go on

Once more, you open the door, and you're here in my heart

And my heart will go on and on

Love can touch us one time: And last for a lifetime

And never let go 'til we're gone

Love was when I loved you, one true time I'd hold to

In my life, we'll always go on

You're here, there's nothing I fear.

And I know that my heart will go on

We'll stay forever this way; You are safe in my heart and

My heart will go on and on.

Wayne and I gave our hearts to each other forever.

In a memorial service at Kenwood Church, July 21, 2021, after Wayne's passing, we celebrated his life, which was a life so well worth living. He was an inexplicably good and honorable man. As the service ended, the last gentle hug was given, the last condolence softly spoken, the last tender look of empathy, I went to our home, our place of refuge, but he was not there. Though other people were there to comfort me, he was not. We had shared our marriage bed for over 41 years. I closed my bedroom door.

When I turned, I fell headlong into a bottomless pit of emptiness. There was nothing to break my fall. I was plummeting down into the dark night of the soul. I desperately groped for something to hold onto. Everything was surreal, as if the world were far away and I could not touch it. Plunging into the emotional abyss of blackness, I was hurdled into the stark realization that I would never see Wayne again on this

earthly plane. He was a kerosene lantern that had gone out, his brilliant beam of light splashed against the glass, twinkled, then was extinguished from my sight.

I was left to wander around in a wilderness of gripping pain. Once, I was loved and held. I heard tender words of adoration and felt a familiar touch. I had a willing receptacle for my love. I could

Wayne, my consort, the one I was most in harmony with was gone. His absence was huge.

touch my Wayne, then in a blink, he was gone. "Oh, Wayne, Wayne, how can I live on this earth without you?" I called out. I wandered around in this harsh desert of the heart for over two months—lost and without sustenance. Slowly, with the kindness of our children, my family, our church family, and our loyal friends, my heart began to awaken and sense that God was not through with me. There was more.

Wayne and I gave our hearts to each other forever. We surrendered to the intimacy and vulnerability that takes so much courage and risk to create. Through our offerings of pure, unguarded love, we gave from hearts in a way that made us feel secure and safe. We had nothing to fear.

We talked about our relationship nearly every day and did not avoid issues when they appeared. For example, one of our winters we drove our 5th wheel to Charleston, South Carolina where Wayne's son lived.   We decided to go to a ballet performed under the arms of the Angel Oak, a 1,400- year-old live oak tree. We couldn't find it and Wayne wasn't stopping to ask for help. I hate to be late and was getting frustrated. We argued and arrived very upset with each other. As the performance unfolded in beauty and grace our mood shifted and we went back to the 5th wheel to bed, but there was uneasiness. The next morning, I got up before Wayne and set the table for breakfast. Even though the glasses were plastic, and the plates were corelle, the setting was beautiful. I was still tense from the night before, yet I did not want it to spoil our day and remained silent. Wayne appeared at the stairs and came down to the kitchen like a man on a mission. He sat at the table and asked me to sit across from him. He took his plate and turned it upside down and said, "This is me," Then took my plate and put it on top of his and covered 85% of his plate declaring, "this is you and we overlap by being in harmony more than 85% of the time." Shockingly he swiftly pushed them apart exploding the whole setting. Glasses, plates, and dinnerware tumbled to the floor as he said, "Something happened last night to destroy that, and we are not going to do anything else until we work this out and understand each other. I believe, as a child, I was so affected by the fighting in our home that I was seeking peace at any price and that would only cause resentment. He said he did most of the driving so he felt unjustly criticized, which he got an overabundance of in his home as a child. After much discussion, we committed to truthfully share our feelings without attacking each other but to seek clearer understanding between us.

At his brother Jimmy's wedding.

We were thrilled to be married, loved to wake up to each other and never tired of seeing each other's face and proclaiming our undying love. We spoke of our deepest needs and intimate feelings with each other. We felt totally safe with each other.

We were in almost constant physical contact, holding hands. We looked into each other's inner life and found the other one looking back. We knew each other.

At a glass blowing factory in the French country- side. Enthralled with the magic that drew us together.

Both of us had been married before. We had worked on our individual selves and knew what we did and did not want. We hoped we had learned from our failed attempts in our former relationships. We knew how we wanted to treat ourselves and others. We had made our mistakes and didn't want to bring poor communication or behavior into our marriage. We made commitments, we learned and worked together to create what we wanted from our union. We were on a sacred journey; a mission to develop the highest version of our relationship. Each day contained a new adventure, a new level of discovery.

Wayne and I attended a couples intimacy seminar in New York for three days. We were accustomed to making eye contact, so when they instructed each couple to pull our chairs face to face and make eye contact, it was no big deal until they added the instruction to continue to hold that contact until we discovered the real person we were facing. After several minutes, I began to see the hurt boy inside Wayne and tears came into my eyes. Then I saw the tenderest look cross his face. He told me later that was when he felt he got a glimpse into my soul. and he was shaken to his core.

We shared our greatest needs and promised to give those gifts to the other. We walked into the center of each other's heart and shared those mystical secrets of love. We created a soulful life that liberated us both. We made it emotionally safe to surrender and to divulge our deepest fears and desires. We became a haven of trust and cherished each other.

I don't think I can adequately share the intensity with which we experienced our life, but I will try to show with pictures, our letters, adventures, and discoveries how we fell deeper and deeper in love. We evolved into something so beautiful and unique that I can scarcely hold it in my grasp. The "us" became bigger than ourselves.

Learning to appreciate each other's skills and capabilities.

I think we can get an idea of how much we have loved someone by the intensity and depth of the pain we feel when we lose them.

We were devoted to each other. We strove for the other's happiness. We had each other's greatest good at heart.. I simply could not be happy if Wayne wasn't happy.

Over the years I worked for Wayne, we became trusted friends. We discovered we read the same kinds of books, we shared common interests and matching values. We loved God, our children adventure, nature, intellectual pursuits, theater, and learning. We treasured spirituality, honesty, integrity, and financial values. He was an extraordinary leader and mentored his employees with an excellent blend of teaching and hands-on learning. His patience kept the work from being intimidating and he worked out problems with us. He was safe to be around, which was striking to me. His even disposition manifested in his calm and the way he approached life ever so softly with wonder.

Eventually, I divorced and transferred to the GM Tech Center in Warren, Michigan. After a couple of years, Wayne was sent to the Tech Center as well, and I worked for him again as a Value Analyst.

Our relationship was like a slow burning fire. Finally, one day he asked me for a date. I had to think about it. His divorce was not yet final. I told him I do not date married men I was not a "backstreet kind of gal," to be hidden out of sight, and he would need to take me somewhere public. Our first date was at the Fisher Theater in downtown Detroit to see *Fiddler on the Roof.* We were dressed to the "nines," and magic danced in the air. Since we already knew each other so well our courtship was breathtaking. Our emerging feelings eclipsed anything either of us had ever felt before. The respect, tenderness, and emotional safety we felt for each other grew into adoration.

In our transformation we seemed to glow from the inside out. When we made eye contact, electric energy flowed between us, and we saw oceans of desire, kindness, and caring in a deep pool of inexpressible love. It was a depth of closeness that neither one of us had ever experienced before.

I vividly remember the night Wayne first declared his love for me. I was attending night college, and he had driven me to my class. The evening was beautiful. A gentle breeze wafted through the night. The moonroof was open, and he reached up to feel the flow of night air. As if discovering it that very moment himself, he said in wonder, "I love you, Sidney." On June 13, 1980, we were united into a lifetime of

Up until this moment in time, our happiest time was our wedding day.

L – R, Mary Ann, her sons Colin and Mike, Wayne, Paul and his two sons Joey and Paul Pierre.

magical, tender love. Our wedding ceremony was uncomplicated with special details. I made my dress and embroidered tiny red roses on the entire dress. We invited sixty of our closest people, and I started down the aisle to the soft music of my friend's daughter singing. Suddenly, I realized the profound life decision I would be making, and I froze midway to the alter. I could not lift my foot to take the next step. Wayne saw the paralysis and walked up the aisle to claim me. He gently took my hand and lead me to the alter to make our promises.

We were fluid and generous with our affection and found it joyful to express ourselves openly. We made lists of how we wanted to include our children and adventures we wanted to experience together—a bucket list of what we wanted to experience in our relationship.

Wayne was a very romantic man. We fulfilled our dreams for love, companionship, and care for each other's children. We embraced each other's world. It was our greatest wish to

L – R Bo, My brother Kayo, Cindy, and Brett. Joys of my life.

create a safe haven and a spiritual center for our children, one filled with love and acceptance. We did not try to parent each other's children, but rather to love, accept, respect, and help them whenever we could. We achieved a minimal measure of what this could have been, but we knew we could not force them.

We grew into helpmates that cared as much for the other's joy as we did for our own. We visited our children no matter where they lived, and we visited our families in Texas and Washington state. We travelled the world, backpacked, and often went camping. Our careers proved to be exciting, and our own businesses, successful, and we helped each other be more than we could have been alone. To develop our marital relationship, we attended many couple's seminars that grew us individually and as a couple. When we hit a situation that needed resolving, we went away for a few days to work on the problem, which almost always proved to be a communication glitch.

Wayne and I in middle row, his twin Duane and his wife are in front of us. One of many couples' enhancement seminars we attended.

We would stubbornly stick with it until we knew we had heard each other's thoughts, wishes and fears. Crooked communication can trigger a couple's pride and defensiveness. In these get-aways, we remembered we were on the same team.

Early in our marriage, Wayne's youngest daughter, Mary Ann, was planning her wedding. Wayne received an invitation to her wedding, but I did not. His ex-wife told their daughter that if I came to the wedding she wouldn't. Angered by this turn of events, Wayne was going to call his daughter to tell her he would not come. I couldn't see him not walking her down the aisle. It was too important and, hopefully, a once-in-a-lifetime thing. "You do not want to miss that," I told him. Once there he discovered that the plan was for him to dance the mother-father dance with his ex-wife. He felt manipulated and exploited, but he danced to keep the peace.

Wayne walking his daughter Mary Ann down the aisle.

When he got home, he told me all about it and we discussed it for several hours. We shared our disappointments and concerns about the potential trend of him attending all his children's functions without me.

At an appropriate time, he called all three children, one at a time, to let them know that we came as a pair. If Sidney wasn't welcome, they should not invite him. His children are good and loving, so it was swiftly worked out. His middle child, Jeanna, called a couple of days later to say, she understood, and to apologize. It never happened again.

When Wayne made the calls to his kids afterwards, he did so with firmness, love, and respect. Watching him navigate such a sensitive issue I learned a lot about Wayne's integrity, loyalty, courage, and fairness while also striving to be fair to us and to his children.

Another difficult problem we worked on uncovered our childhood spiritual wounds. I felt caught up in my workaholism, and Wayne in his criticism and we found ourselves growing apart. We wanted to find out why and how we could get back on a positive course. We knew we were each hiding in our defense mechanisms and creating distance. We were in a destructive loop.

We committed to staying with the conversation until we discovered why we didn't feel safe. Wayne explained that I was working so much that he couldn't get my attention. He was nearly 70 years old and didn't want to live life feeling unloved and unwanted. What I heard instead was, "You are working too much, I can't get your attention, and I am not going to live this way." I had already felt heavily criticized, and now I thought he was threatening to leave. This triggered my feelings of worthlessness and abandonment from a daddy who left us often, staying away for months at a time drinking and womanizing.

I got very upset, shut down, went to our bedroom, and curled up like a wounded bird. Previously, I had told Wayne that I could be more rational when we had a disagreement if he could give me a little time to process things without disturbing me. He did not follow me into the bedroom. As I lay there crying, I could tell my pride was pushing me to stubbornly defend my behavior and not take accountability. I asked myself, "Sidney, what do you want? What do you really want?"

I finally admitted to myself, "I want Wayne, no matter what." It was very difficult to swallow my pride, get up off the bed and go out to tell him that without trying to win the argument. Finally, my body carried me back into the living room. I sat at his feet and laid my head on his chest and told him, "I want you, that's it."

As we talked, I explained how his threat made me feel abandoned and unworthy. He was shocked that I thought he was going to leave. He wanted to resolve this if it took all night. "I said I did not want to live my life like this," he repeated," without your attention and affection. And when you chose work over me, I felt unloved and unwanted like when I was a child, and my mother did not express her love to me in any form."

We immediately took several days off and secluded ourselves in a quiet campground with our fifth wheel to bring ourselves back to a safe place. We had triggered each other's deepest pain, which allowed us to discover our core childhood wounds and commit to changing our threatening behavior.

A quiet campground in Wyoming to work out an issue we were having.

Ultimately, we realized we could gift each other the love and security we didn't receive as children. Our issues all started with a lack of clear communication, which triggered our pride and defensiveness. Then the battle shifted from fighting together against the problem to fighting each other. What I heard was not what he said. We both heard through our fears and not through reality. Realizing this was a seminal moment.

Wayne and I had a written purpose for our lives. Part of it was to build a center of love, safety, and comfort for us and our families. We respected and loved each other's children and our grandchildren. They enriched our lives, and we were thrilled to create relationships with all of them. Wayne really cherished being able to teach our grandchildren how to fix things. As the boys got older, he could especially help them understand how to work on cars and keep them running.

Wayne loved to teach our grandchildren how to do things. Here, Mike and Colin, want to see what their dad Duane and Wayne are fixing.

It was important to us to take care of emotional things as they came up and not create regrets or resentments which could fester and grow like a consuming cancer in our relationship. We strove to let the joy and thrill for life with each other breathe and grow.

Besides writing each other love letters, we kept a love and appreciation journal on our kitchen counter that we each used to record moments when a burst of love created feelings of joy and gratitude. We vowed never, ever to be stingy with our expressions of love. The practice taught us that we could trust each other and make it emotionally safe to share our inner-most feelings without fear of judgement or exploitation. The journal was not for complaints or scolding. Early in our marriage, Wayne promised me we would never have financial problems because he simply would never let it happen. We found that we were both of the same mind about financial matters. Neither of us wanted to be in debt and did not overspend our budget. Our values were in alignment. He mentioned in one of his love letters that we never once had a disagreement about handling our money. We have hundreds of love letters from each other over our 41 years of marriage in the form of cards, letters, and journal entries, and they are priceless to me. I now read a few every night. It soothes my spirit, and I feel his energy around me when I read his precious words. Though I feel an unrelenting pain in my heart with his absence, I thank God daily for what we shared. My heart is exceptionally grateful for the many gifts of love he so generously showered upon me. It was a daily thrill for us to wake up to each other every morning for over 41 years. Life with Wayne never got old or mundane.

Wayne wanted to read the Bible out loud to me in his last few days.

One of the most essential ingredients, one that superseded all else in our marriage was the spiritual enrichment we shared. We loved sitting next to each other in church. Peace enveloped us. We found one of the deepest of intimacies was to pray together. We poured out the yearnings of our souls when we joined together to seek God's counsel and His will for our life. We also read the Bible together and discovered a deeper, more profound level of closeness. I grew up in a church that encouraged knowing the scriptures. I had read through the whole Bible several times. Wayne asked me to read it to him and we would discuss what it meant to our lives in the present which made the words come alive in our daily actions. It had such a calming and purposeful impact on every aspect of our lives, and it braided us together even closer.

225

When hospice caregivers came to help Wayne, he knew what that meant and told me he wanted to read the Bible out loud to me. This gave him great comfort. He was making peace with his last worldly connections.

There were many priceless times together. One night, Wayne and I were lying in bed talking about what we each might be doing to negatively impact our relationship. I mentioned that we knew what I needed to change really well: I was a workaholic, driven, and controlling. "But we don't know what you might be doing, Wayne. What do you think you might be doing that could be causing a negative impact on us?" He lay there with the covers up to his chin and his fingers on top of the covers, lightly tapping on his chest. He looked up at the top of our canopy bed, circled his eyes around the room as if he might find the answer etched on the ceiling somewhere. Then he rolled back my way, making eye contact. Serious as sin, he said, "Would you give me a hint?" I nearly fell off the bed laughing. How can you be angry at that kind of response?

Sometimes, we just have to see the humor in our behavior and not take everything so seriously. We just left that question alone for the moment. He had dodged a bullet, and he deserved to feel that little victory.

There were so many ways Wayne expressed his feelings for me, and it always touched my heart. Right after the year 2000 rolled in, he made a sign and hung it on one of the crossbars of our canopy bed. It simply reads, "Together Forever." It now hangs on my bedroom blinds in my apartment, so I can still look at it in my new surroundings. We looked at that sign every night and engaged in our pillow talk. Then after many years we were lying there and looking at that sign. He had added two hearts pierced through with an arrow. He took a breath and said, "Do you see that?" I asked, "What?" He looked at our sign. "Look at what it says, do you see it? Read it out loud", I obediently read, "Together Forever!" "No, look closer", he urged. Finally, he read it out loud. "It says, 'To Get Her Forever'. And that's what I did!" He was so proud of himself for discovering a deeper meaning in his sign. It melted my heart.

What an adventure! What a ride! We knew what we had and spoke to each other about our love story every day with awe and gratitude.

Walking with a Chitah in South Africa. It was being healed so they could send him back into the wild.

Versita, my dear friend, said to me one day, "I love to hear your and Wayne's love story. I am looking to find my Boaz someday." I was filled with gratitude and wonder because the story of Ruth and Boaz is one of the greatest love stories of all time. And their story was part of our wedding vows.

The Story of Ruth and Boaz

The Book of Ruth in the Old Testament tells us the ancient love story. Naomi was married to Elimelek, and they had two sons, Mahlon and Kilion. A famine came upon the land, and they fled Bethlehem to Moab to find work. The sons married

Moabite women, Orpah and Ruth. Naomi's husband and two sons died. Without the men, Naomi was unprotected in this foreign land, had no income so she decided to return to Bethlehem.

Orpah and Ruth wanted to return with her. Naomi told them to go back to their families. Orpah took her advice, but Ruth clung to Naomi and cried, "Entreat me not to leave you. Where you go, I will go and where you stay, I will stay. Your people shall be my people and your God my God." Moved by her loyalty, Naomi let her come with her to Bethlehem, and they arrived penniless at the beginning of barley-harvesting. Naomi had a kinsman of great wealth from Elimelek's side whose name was Boaz. Ruth said to Naomi, "Let me go to the fields and pick up the leftover grain behind anyone in whose eyes I find favor." She was a beautiful woman, and she was working in the fields of Boaz, who asked the overseer "Who does that young woman belong to?" The overseer replied, "She is a Moabite woman who came back with Naomi. She gleaned in the field all day except for a short rest."

Boaz said to Ruth," Do not go glean in another field. I have told the men not to lay a hand on you."

"Why have I found favor in your eyes?," Ruth asked. Boaz tenderly answered, "I have been told what you have done for Naomi, your mother-in-law. When she sat down with the harvesters, he offered her roasted grain. She ate some but saved some for Naomi.

Boaz gave orders to his men, "Let her gather among the sheaves and don't scold her. Pull out even more of the choice stalks for her to pick up." Naomi asked her where she worked, and Ruth told her in the field of Boaz. "That kind man is one of our guardian-kinsmen," Naomi replied, "his kindness knows no end." A guardian-kinsman is a rescuer. If they choose to, the guardian can buy land from kin who are poor and must sell their land, and marry the undefended woman, if she is of marrying age. He must carry on the name of the deceased husband.

228

One day, Naomi told Ruth, "Go to Boaz at the threshing floor, lay at his feet, and ask him to redeem you." Ruth did as Naomi advised, laid ay Boaz's feet and asked him to redeem her. Boaz was honorable and assured her, "Do not be afraid. All the townsmen know that you are a woman of noble character. I promise I will grant your request. But there is a closer Kinsman than me and he has first rights. If he wants to redeem you, let him. If he doesn't, as sure as the Lord lives, I will do it."

Before Ruth left, Boaz gave her six measures of barley for Naomi so she would not go back empty-handed and so Ruth would know his honorable intentions. Ruth reported these things to Naomi, who said, "Boaz will not rest until the matter is settled today."

Boaz went to the city gate where he met the guardian redeemer and told him he was first in line to buy Ruth's land. The redeemer was interested, but when he found out he had to take Naomi and marry Ruth and carry on her first husband's name, he refused. Boaz happily took Ruth as his beloved wife. Wayne was my "Boaz." I had worked for him, and he saw that I was a hard worker creative, intelligent, and capable of much more than most women were given the opportunity to do at GM at the time.

He was devoted and wanted to protect me. He wanted me to succeed in GM. This letter that he wrote to me in 1979 is one of my precious possessions:

My Dearest Sidney,

I love you from the depth of my soul. But loving you is only a part of my feelings for you. I want to always protect you—to be a dependable safe place for you. When you hurt yourself or feel sickly, I want to make it all better for you and exchange winks☺.

I am so completely connected to you. When you experience joy or sadness, I feel the joy and the sadness. It is as if we have one feeling to share and both experience that common feeling; we're both aware of the same experience, but between us we are having only one and the same experience. I think we have entered into each other's minds and souls. I will never leave; you're where I belong.

I love you Sidney, and then some, Wayne

Wayne mentored me. In essence, he had the workers drop extra sheeves for me to glean. He believed in me. I was able to have a glowing career because he skillfully brought out potential in me. Like Boaz, Wayne was a well-respected man, with a reputation of honor and kindness. Though I had come from poverty, he saw that I had gotten an education under great duress, and he saw my possibilities. We were trusted friends and saw the good in each other. He was a man of integrity and strength of character. He was financially sound, and we shared values. Wayne and I married in 1980 and said the vows Ruth said to Naomi: "Where you go, I will go, where you stay, I will stay. Your people shall be my people and your God, my God."

And We lived happily ever after.

In Austria, another exciting adventure.

LESSONS

- Be generous in your many expressions of love with your mate. Say it, hear it, feel it, make eye contact, and find each other's soul.
- Demonstrate it with many hugs and kisses and give them your attention.
- *Do not be stingy*. Be fearless in demonstrating love to each other.
- We can fall in love over and over again, with the same person at a deeper level, to infinity. What a glorious treasure. Guard it with all your might.
- Always, always take the time to work out issues while they are small.
- Keep your love pure and clean without building up resentments or regrets.

- Create an emotionally safe zone whenever you are together.

- Commit to each other's good. Never, ever hurt each other intentionally. *Be kind.*

- There is no room for pride in your relationship. Be brave enough to push through your pride to be honest and true.

- If you need to apologize, *apologize.* Forgive quickly and easily. If the ice needs to be broken, be the first to break it. Be courageous. Speak your truth. Strive for common ground. Seek adventure and expose each other to new experiences. Explore! *Have fun.* Forgive each other. Clean the slate and start fresh.

- Develop and maintain a strong spiritual connection between you and your mate that puts God at the center of your love universe. Practice your faith.

- See the humor in our humanity. Don't take everything so seriously.

- Express yourself. Ask for what you want in your relationship.

- Talk about your relationship. Nurture it, honor it.

- In the end many things that demand our attention will go away, and if you have taken care of your relationship, it will take care of you in your final chapter together. _And there will be joy_.

Two Questions

1. In looking at some of the many things Wayne and I did to improve our marriage, what might you be willing to try to improve your relationship?

2. Could you suspend your pride and look at how to come together?
Or would you rather be "right than happy?" You choose.

Singing "Stay Young and Beautiful" for a couples' class we were
teaching.

Our life was interwoven with fun and joy, letting our inner children out to play. And the super-responsible side motivated us to take care of each other. The urge to walk on the edge took us on many exotic and great adventures. Life was rich, fun, and romantic. We created it as we went along.

Sidney and Wayne's Purpose for Our Lives

Original 1981- Revised 5 times as of 2013

Our Covenant: We are bonded to each other through eternity, we vow to be vulnerable, honest, and safe and will not allow pride to stand between us.

We will love and serve God, emulate Christ in character and deed, follow where He leads us, courageously, without question. We will use our combined gifts of intuition, clear thinking, leadership, intelligence, creativity, and humor to liberate ourselves and others from pain to discover the magnificence within all of us. We will partner to create a loving and safe center in our home for ourselves, our children, and friends. To love without limit, live passionately with integrity, serenity, and compassion. We will act as healing Facilitators and Visionaries to bring Hope, Enlightenment, and Freedom. We will not shrink back from our passion or the life to which God calls us.

I, Sidney, commit to write the story of my life to honor Wayne, and my children, and to run our charity, Helping Hands Touching Hearts, as long as I am physically able to make a difference with my life.

"We will do what is possible and brave and Trust God for the Miracles."

By Polk

Remember what I said earlier?

"Those who have no goals will be *used* by those who do have goals."

Dearest Wayne:

It's hard to believe we've had two whole years together. What two years it has been! We live in a dream world... what an extraordinary life we "live." I can hope for all things beautiful in a relationship. I can have romantic love. I can dream and not be disappointed. How much I look forward to the rest of our lives. Thank you for the best two years of my life so far. I am aflame with love for you. My heart swells at the sensitivity we share. I feel inspired. You have pulled me to heights unimagined. I shall dwell with you all the days of my life.

My family loved Wayne for how he treated me, and he loved them.

I cherish you, Wayne, Sidney

Sidney,

My most special moment was when I took you out to dinner and offered you the engagement ring, and you said YES! We connected and we were on our way.

Another time was when we did the follow up with Dr. Brown after breast cancer surgery and he announced you were cancer free.

Love, Wayne

Dear Wayne,

You opened my youthful heart and spread it full of joy and love. I still feel the freshness and the mystery of it all. You are

My favorite photo from the many cruises we hosted.

my truest love—my hero—my friend and my soul mate. I do feel like a "winner" having won you. You are my life's best prize. Thank you for the elegant dinner and our beautiful bathroom to-be. I love you even more today if it is possible.

Sidney, 2005

Dearest Sidney,

You still make my heart "♥" go thump, thump! The more I discover about you the more I appreciate and love you, the more enthusiasm I anticipate the future with. The best thing that can happen to me is to live all the remaining days of my life with you, to wake up each morning and face the day with you. You are the sunshine in my mornings. I want to share my special place with you. Please come in whenever you wish. You are welcome. Sidney - I want you forever - I love you forever - I am yours forever.

With Heartfelt Love,

Wayne

My Dearest Husband,   December 30, 1983

I love you more than anything in the world. When I walked out to my car under the carport and didn't have to scrape the windows, I was "touched." Remember, the leader of the couples seminar said, "feeling touched happens when someone does a kind act <u>unexpectedly</u>. You treat me like a special person. You treat me like a lady. You make me feel like a very special, loved person. Our life is romantic, it is "straight," it is caring, it is exciting, interesting, reliable. I am in love with our life together. Today will be filled with loving, warm thoughts. The future looks "expected." We are <u>FOREVER!</u>

I love you Wayne, Sidney

Never forgetting where I came from and where you took me with your devotion. srb

My Soul Mate,

I know I have loved you since the beginning of creation; God created us for each other. If I have lived before in other lives, I had to come back until I found you. Now I am complete. I truly feel ONE with you. How unspeakably blessed I am to share love with you. I love you with every bit of me, my body, my mind, and my spirit. I am totally yours forever.

With inexpressible love, Wayne

October 15, 2010

Wayne –

This card so eloquently says how I feel about you being my soul Mate.

> You are everything
> I've ever wanted,
> And I am going to love you
> For the rest of my days.

I feel as though we've been together through eternity. It is exciting to know our souls will dwell together in grace and love. You are my heart of hearts You are the whisperings of love songs and vivid colors splashed in my mind.

I love you deeply, Sidney

Forbidden beach when we snuck on the shores of Lake Michigan and got chased away by police.

My Dearest Sidney,

What a wonderful beginning it was nine years ago. The joy and growth I have found with you was unforeseeable and is my greatest blessing.

I love you Sidney – I love everything about you. You bring me happiness, and you help me grow. Joined with you, I am more than I thought I could be. My one moment in time has been every moment since June 13, 1980. You are the harbor in my storms, you are the silver lining in my clouds. I cherish you Sidney – you are the most precious of all women.

I gladly recommit myself to you forever.

I love you dearly, Wayne

Wayne –

My entire life is enhanced because of you. Your love makes the sun brighter, the clouds prettier, the air sweeter. It makes joy more abundant and hope always alive. It thrills me that I grow <u>more</u> in love ♥ with you every day. And that we still find the beauty in each other.

You are my forever Valentine. You are the keeper of my heart.

I love you <u>Madly, Sidney</u>

My Dearest Sidney,

My fondest desire is to love and be loved by you. We are forever – And I joyfully re-dedicate myself to you. It is so special to have joined my life with yours. I am uplifted by you, my heart feels safe with you, my soul soars to unexpected heights beside yours.

Let us go yet another step together.

I love you with An Abundant Heart, Wayne

Our life reaches beyond ourselves to embrace the generations to come. srb

Wayne –

We've been gifted 21 years of loving, life challenges, support, growth, and soul-touching together. I grow ever more in love with you. I become more and more appreciative of you and what we have consciously built together. Only 29 more years till we renew our contract. 🥰

I never tire of our life together.

It refreshes and sustains me.

I love you forever, Sidney

Dearest Sidney,

I love you, my beautiful bride! You've been gone a whole hour now, and my heat breaks. I shall never live without you – I cherish each moment with you, Sidney.

You've probably completed the test by now and aced it of course. I am indeed proud of you, my love. You are a very special woman. Take good care of yourself for me and hurry home.

I am helplessly in Love with You,

Wayne

My Darling Wayne,

You do so much to enrich my life. You are always loving and respectful. You understand my needs and respond to them. You give me the opportunity to love you and live out my desires for romanticism. Life is so abundant for us. I often feel like a glutton for having so much. After many struggling years with feelings, spirituality and lack of material things, my life now floods me with ample supply. I love loving you, my dear husband.

Restaurant in Italy.

May our lives be long and constantly reveal new areas for expression and caring.

I love you Wayne, Sidney

Dearest Sidney,

I optimistically commit to working through each exercise with complete honesty, so we gain the fullest possible growth from them. I believe that coming together in genuine loving relationship is the fundamental objective of human life - and the relationship between spouses is the most important of all. From it springs confidence and energy to reach out to others. To this process, I am fully committed. To know and love myself, and to know and love Sidney more deeply is my highest priority, and my highest joy.

I Love You,

Wayne 4/22/1990

P.S. I will never give you cause to regret sharing your needs and vulnerability with me. I will protect all about you with tender caring.

Our love has never dimmed nor lost its bright luster. It shines like a beacon guiding us to eternity, where we will find our love once more. srb

The Magical Journey of the Empowerment Years

The room was once again fired up with mountain climbing energy, the music pounded to the wild beat of our hearts, and the group was ready to climb. The participants had worked their way to that special place of empowerment in which they were ready to conquer any obstacles or fears that stood in the way of their sacred journey to their peak...their Top!

Two of the three days of the seminar the group went through exercises, and sharing their life story, they had learned what had happened in their lives that had caused them to let go of that natural self-confidence and let fear block their primitive courage. Now was the day of truth. Fears were confronted, we all stretched outside our comfort zones, and stretched beyond our safe borders, and charged into uncharted waters. It felt new, exciting, dangerous, liberating, and thrilling. The participants came out feeling empowered.

Wayne, Cindy, and I had conducted these seminars for 14 years and trained thousands of people. Our richest reward was the deep and lasting friendships this created over the years. We formed groups of 5 with a Volunteer G.A. (Group Assistant). The G. A.'s were former participants, who came in to help other people reclaim their natural power.

Lives were changed, their living became more authentic, empowered and a sense of enrichment filled in the hollow spaces, and they reclaimed the power and spirit they were born to. Very exciting, and it was my mission in life. I felt called by God to do this work.

The process was so successful, my Mother, my siblings and my three children all went through the Empowerment concepts.

Photo of my Mother and siblings (L to R, youngest to oldest) Kayo, Me, Jo, Troy, Ginger and Mother. They went to the various phases, and it gave a richness to our family dynamics and ability to communicate with each other. My Mother was 81 when she went through what was called the Quest. She also went through Inner Child work, and finally the Strategic Life Assessment Process   Ginger also came to help as a G.A. and she was very good at guiding people through the process.

We worked mostly in Michigan, but also in a few other states, Texas and Indiana, then in Canada, and Mexico. Marco Nunez and Reginald Chapa individually conducted seminars all over Mexico.

I had met Marco while I was still in G.M. and we became instant friends and have had more than 40 years in a loyal and loving friendship. I know and love his entire family, his lovely wife Lupita, sons Alex and Alvaro. Marco's one daughter, Sidney Marina Nunez is my name's sake. She is now a grown woman, married and with two sons of her own. And his youngest daughter Cristiel lives in San Antonio near them.

Cristiel is very creative, and Cindy hires her to do creative computer work for her own business. Marco and I have been through the worst of times and the best of times with each other. No questions asked, we showed up for each other in many of life crisis in those 40+ years.

We have become part of each other's families. We are welcome into each other's world, and part of each other's soul. This kind of friendship only happens when you truly have known each other at the soul level and enjoy perfect trust. We are totally authentic with each other.

Marco and I at a later stage in our lives.

Working together through empowerment for so many years built this treasured friendship. The last crisis in my life was losing my beloved Wayne. I came home to Texas to get my life back together, but I couldn't talk to anyone. Marco kept calling me, but I was still in shock and in high anxiety and could not take calls. San Antonio is 5 hours from Midland. He told Cindy to let me know he would be here in 5 hours. He came, walked with me in silence, patiently followed my moods and responded when he thought I wanted it. He helped me get back on a sleep cycle since I was very sleep deprived. I still use his magical recording and get restful sleep. We just spent the days together following what was needed in our hearts. Lupita and Wayne always understood this friendship, it was no threat to their place in our lives.

Now, with the new challenge of cancer, Marco calls me every Friday to check on me, how the treatment is going and how I am doing mentally through it all. His dedication and loyalty give me great strength. I have learned the lessons well as you have read in previous chapters, to let people in to help me. We all need somebody sometime and Marco is my "Amigos para Siempre," friends for life.

Don showing kindness to Wayne prior to his passing.

Another deep and abiding friendship from empowerment is Don Burton who is also a lifelong friend. We have been through many of life's crisis together. Many times, if one of us can't sleep we might call one another to see if we are awake and can talk. He especially is helping me through my "Wayne grief" and sorting out process. He reminds me that it is a gift to a friend to let them help. He asked me, "Please don't rob me of this gift." I know he is right because I know how it has made me feel to help others. It is a true honor. His calls give me so much comfort and consolation. His encouraging voice steadies me. So many little diamonds he sprinkles along my path.

Through Empowerment so many deep friendships have been created, and there is a circle that continues to check on me to assure I am OK. Sheila Ricks often calls to check on me even though she has moved to Arizona. Mike and Cathy McCarthy call, bring flowers, come take me to dinner, and we have great visits.

Patty Watters accompanies me to the Oncologist, Kerry and Neil Taylor, Donna Marie, Jane Johnson, and Linda Linder stay in contact, come over to visit and we lunch. Lisa Wicker has always regularly called me, and we keep up as well as Janie and Bobby Bellairs. Karen Sanford, texts, calls, comes by. Our Board of Trustees Alan Salomon, Dr. David Brownstein, Mike and Cathy McCarthy, Jeanette Abraham, Clark Sanford, and Todd Lackie have been constant in their support.. I feel very much cared for by all of them. It is hard to place the great value for their presence in my life, but it is huge. I could not have done as well as I have with my loss of Wayne without them. And there are so many others that it is difficult to name them all. But each one is a treasure. I feel God has so richly blessed me with just the right people I need in my life.

Because of the unique nature of the empowerment process, it creates the depth of trust in just three days that lasts a lift time. I am forever grateful for these special people in my life. I do not feel that I *have* to wander this planet alone. We travel this journey together to discover how to get the best life has to give us, even when it is hard.

LESSONS

We have probably all had experiences that have both negatively or positivity affected our lives. Which in turn affected how we react to life. Whether it is with courage or fear. Confidence or with doubt. And we may not consciously know the origin.

- To relook at our life, we can change the script now that we are an adult.
- Learning the truth about ourselves is a brave thing to do.
- We can choose our outcomes as we step into the future.
- Armed with the truth clears our path.
- My Mother, siblings, and children honored me by doing the work I so believe in.
- Friendships can go to a level of trusts that lasts a lifetime.
- Living at the soul level with other human beings is indescribably fulfilling.
- The value of trust.

THE TWO QUESTIONS

1. When have you experienced an extraordinary close and trusting friendship. Describe it.

2. How has it affected the quality of your life?

Our Noble Purpose: Helping Hands Touching Hearts

It was 2006, Cindy and I were planning an exotic vacation for ourselves and our husbands and chose Egypt. However, soon into the planning process, we changed our minds because the country was experiencing a lot of civil unrest which broke out into violence. We decided to change destinations, but still wanted to use our time-share rentals. We investigated several options and settled on South Africa. Which had endless exciting activities to make it an ideal choice.

A water hole that attracts the wild elephants. They are majestic and stature.
Our guide Janco, found a tunnel that was an observation site and patiently waited to get that perfect shot. Cindy, Darrell, Wayne, and I were literally awestruck. The air was charged with an inexplainable energy.

We finally narrowed it down to Hazy View, South Africa. It was close to Kruger National Park, which is world renowned for millions of acres of wild animal habitat. Seeing the majestic elephants proved to satisfy our call of the wild. Cindy and I sewed

These photos show a tiny sample of the life in the bush. From the camouflaged zebras to the brilliance of the yellow saddleback stork, seeing these animals matched our most vivid imagination. In the photo of me under the elephant the handlers assured me it was safe.

150 school bags, filled them with school supplies and purchased 150 mosquito nets. We packed our safari clothes and flew across the Atlantic to step foot on the Dark

Continent of Africa. I had been to Kenya and Tanzania in the 1970s, so I knew we were in for a great adventure.

These photos show a tiny sample of the life in the bush. From the camouflaged zebras to the brilliance of the yellow saddleback stork, seeing these animals matched our most vivid imagination.

I trembled as the massive elephant towered above me and stood in awe of the fierce lion as he patiently stalked a wounded wildebeest. It captured my heart just as it had so many years ago.

The bush was much like the wild Texas prairie that raised me into its harsh reality as a child. Next, was the life of the people who lived in the wild of Africa in the village of Massingir Velho, Mozambique. It seemed like we had stepped back into time when life was primitive.

We witnessed an entire population of souls who lived in extreme poverty. The marvel was that the children smiled as if all was well in their world. They were sitting in the shade of a huge tree. When they saw our Land Rover coming, they jumped to their feet to dance and sing their welcome-to-the-village" song. We passed out mosquito nets, then announced we would pass out school bags filled with supplies.

The children excitingly ran to the schoolhouse where they would each receive a school bag.

The little *gazelles* ran to their one-room schoolhouse. Cindy and I were so touched, we quickly decided to adopt this village and committed to bring them all shoes when we returned. That was when we thought there were only 350 people in the village! We found out the next day there were actually 1,400 villagers. God has a sense of humor, for He knew if we gave our word we would carry through, no matter what. I lay crying in my bed that night wondering how we could possibly buy 1,400 pairs of shoes because we would be using all our own money.

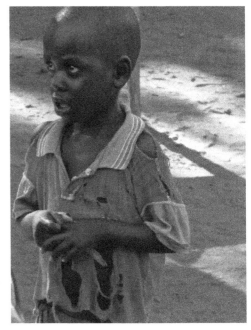

This little guy's shirt was hanging by threads.

We went back the next day and saw this little guy in the photo. He inspired us to accept the challenge to not only get 1,400 pairs

Here we are distributing 1,400 pairs of shoes to the whole tribe.

of shoes but to clothe the tribe as well. When we got back to the States, we immediately started fund-raising and conducting shoe and clothing drives. Our church, Kenwood Church of Christ, in Livonia, MI, joined our effort. It took us a year, but we finally knew we had reached our goals.

The whole village stood in line for hours to be sure they got a pair of shoes.

God is always good, and He is faithful. We had enough shoes and clothes for everybody. In the photo on the prior page is my grandson, Richard, Cindy, Wayne,

Our
board
of
Trustees:

257

and me. It was a miraculous occasion, and we were humbled to give to those who had no way of returning the favor. It was given from the love in our hearts for these precious people. Their gratitude was overwhelming.

They stood out in that hot African sun very patiently until their turn came. The following year we decided to apply for the 501(c)(3) so we could be tax exempt, do fund-raisers, and be able to operate on a much larger budget. We also created our Board of Trustees who volunteer their services. Cindy, Wayne, and I volunteered our effort and time as officers.

Helping Hands Touching Hearts' mission is to:
Empower impoverished people beyond survival through Sustainability in Education,
Food, Health, and Hope.

We received our 501(c)(3) status on September 9, 2010. Cindy, Wayne, and I bore most of the expenses until that time. This enabled us to do higher level fund-raising, which meant we could help more.

With the help of our many supporters, Helping Hands Touching Hearts (HHTH) was able to make a difference in the many villages in which we worked. After three years in Massingir Velho, the villagers were moved into towns because a fence that protected the village was taken down to allow the animals more room. It was a migration route for elephants, so the people had to move to houses built for them by the government. And the village of Massingir Velho was no

Hennie was a great supporter of HHTH.

258

more. A friend, Hennie Van der Colf, approached us to consider serving the Venda villages in South Africa. HHTH has worked with six villages there for 12 years. In that effort, we have made a sizable impact on the tribal people, doing many projects that help the whole area.

The farmers farmed with mule power.

We have consistently fed 60 orphans in South Africa and 60 orphans and 20 starving elders in Victoria Falls, Zimbabwe.

HHTH helped several people in small entrepreneurial endeavors to farm gardens, start chicken businesses, and taught many ladies to sew on a pedal sewing machine as many do not have electricity.

Most villagers live in mud rondevals, or huts. We lived with a family for a month while we worked in the area. The people know how important education is for their children so as part of our mission, we helped supply schools with brightly colored tables and chairs and built a creche for the preschoolers.

We partnered with Gilbert Mbedzi, Fethani High School principal, to provide copy and laminating machines, filing cabinets, and made it possible for the students to have a graduation

Typical village dwelling. They lived in mud huts.

ceremony. Orphans are cared for with food, clothing, and toiletries. The first time we took them bars of soap, they cheered and started stamping their feet and clapping. They were grateful for a bar of soap because they usually wash only with water. Cindy and I sewed for the children.

She cried because she never had a new dress.

The girl in the photo is crying because she had never had a new dress. Kai and Shana Schutte sponsor 29 orphans with regular food distribution, clothes, shoes, and school supplies.

We have several friends who sponsor one or more orphans. HHTH has had wells drilled for a shanty town project, built a childcare center, created a farm coalition, among other projects. Food means everything to these orphans. The boy in the photo with Janco below, can't believe he is getting a three-month supply of food. He cried. He won't have to worry about food for several months. Hunger is a constantly looming threat for these orphan children.

HHTH had a well done in a small shanty town settlement.

Janco teaches leadership classes, which are a special privilege for the Fethani seniors. Then they get to have recreation at the Avelani lodge and enjoy the rare treat of eating a meal there and swimming.

Janco distributing a three-month supply
of their basic foods to orphans.

HHTH has built a Children's Care Center for the community. It has become a place for the orphans to come in from the bush to get help. It is well known in the six-village area. Because HHTH has done so much for the people here, other charities come in and help the community as well. The Care Center now has a playground, thanks to Alexandra Simenco. There is a separate kitchen, pantry, and office. The playground is so essential to the children because there is no other place like it in all the villages, and children everywhere, no matter their circumstances, want to play.

The children have found immeasurable joy
playing on the playground.

Team training for seniors of Fethani High
School as a reward for good performance.

This lady was dying of cancer, and I asked her, "What is your greatest wish?" She replied, "I want some pretty clothes so I can feel beautiful." Cindy and I quickly sewed her three outfits, and she trembled with gratitude. They are used to having so little that they find it truly amazing that they can wish for something so extravagant. They certainly do not have an entitlement mentality.

Gail Welsh and her husband Ralph have been donating new clothing from their uniform store for years. In 2019, when they decided to

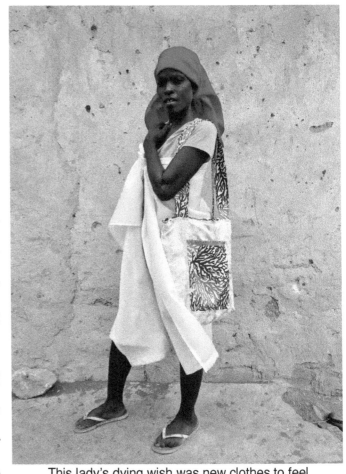

This lady's dying wish was new clothes to feel beautiful.

retire, they gifted HHTH with over 6,000 new garments for our Venda villages. It was the most excitement the people have had in a long time. Countless families, especially orphans, were richly clothed with their generosity.

Gail and Ralph Welch's generous gift of over 6,000 garments.

Sidney with orphans who have come for help to the children's care center.

We are especially proud that our contributors helped to build a STEM and Vocational Lab in the bush. The only one in this whole six-village area. It has taken three years, but the building is finally completed. It is named after my brother and his wife: the Kayo and Martha Randolph STEM & Vocation Lab. They were the first ones to hit the $20,000. mark in contributions. Many people, especially our Board of Trustees, have helped us with a Smartboard, computers, microscopes, lab coats, and science kits for hands-on teaching. We already have students graduating from the STEM Lab and going on to university. This was not a possibility before because they had not taken the required classes to qualify. The children see

The children in their new lab coats.

the first graduates succeed and now believe they can succeed too. Because HHTH built the lab, the government provided the teachers to teach the classes. The work HHTH does is an initiative that gets help from the government just because the Lab

263

exists. The STEM and Vocation Lab is a phenomenon in the community and has created "umbutu," which translates to, "we are one." And the community are working

The new microscopes give them hands on experience with science.

together to promote the unity. We were able to get them six computers and five microscopes. More are badly needed, and I trust God to favor us with donations. The umbutu got the 30,000 bricks to build the Lab up the mountain where the school is located. The brick truck could only get them half of the way up. The community and students volunteered and got every single brick to the top of the mountain. One miracle after another has brought an amazing dream a reality. Lives have changed and opportunities have opened up to these students. Gilbert and Janco are our driving forces that make all this possible. Because of the Covid-19 pandemic, we were not able to go to South Africa for three years and have managed the project from the States. Gilbert and Janco drove it to completion.

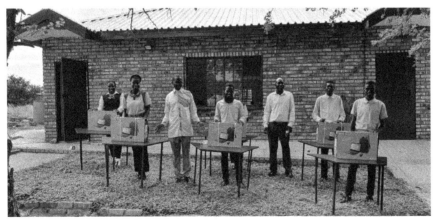

Six new computers make them competitive with other high schools.

Janco routinely makes the distributions of food to our many orphans and elders. He is a trusted and loyal worker on our behalf.

So much has been accomplished over

264

Umbutu, working together as one to get 30,000 bricks to the top of the mountain.

the 15 years HHTH has existed. It has left an indelible imprint on the people in Venda territory. It has been a labor of love for Cindy, Wayne, and me. Cindy is one of the most creative people I have ever seen in my life. She came up with so many ideas when we needed to overcome an obstacle and responded to the needs as they came up. Wayne was a physicist, and an outstanding problem solver. He took care of the technical side of our work. Their skills made everything come together and work.

I believe it is what God had prepared me for my whole life—from the personal experience of poverty and knowing what it is like to be hungry, to getting a good education, to my career in a large corporation which gave me the skills to understand how to run large-scale projects. We are humbled by all

Janco, our very capable guide, and representative for HHTH gets projects implemented. He speaks their language.

the help we got along the way from trusted friends, family, and our church.

<u>LESSONS</u>

- This was what I was *born and have lived for. My destiny.* This was the significant thing I was to do with my life. I was to become the answer to many people's prayers.

- It is inspiring and rewarding to help others discover possibilities for changing their lot in life and helping them accomplish them.

- So many people are willing to help us achieve a worthy goal.

- When we are living our passion, we can trust there will be others who want to join our cause.

- Believing and acting like it can be done will make it so.

- Dream big, you are not alone.

- Once you pursue an idea, it soon develops a life of its own.

- Trust in God to walk along with you.

<u>Two Questions</u>

1. Write about a time that you were inspired to do an unselfish act to help someone else.

2. How did they react to your help? How did you feel about having done it?

The Baboon Who Came for Cookies

Did You Ever Wonder What You Would Do? It had been a busy and exhausting day. Janco, our guide for our charity work in South Africa and Zimbabwe, had taken us to the Monde Village near Victoria Falls, Zimbabwe. We distributed food and other essentials to 60 orphans and discovered over 20 elderly people who were literally starving in their huts. We raced back into town to purchase 25 kg bags of mealie, cooking oil, sugar, tea, beans, salt, and other necessities to give to these dear people. We were both physically and emotionally drained, we needed to restore with a nap.

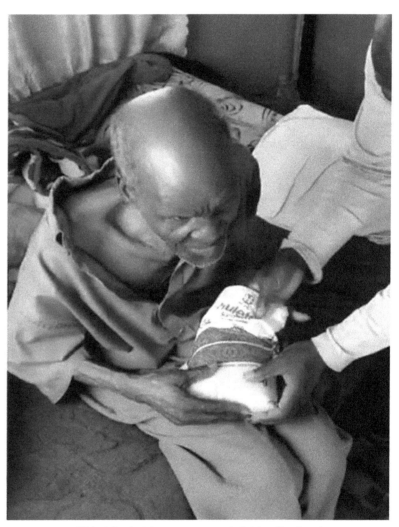

This blind elder was so grateful for the food.

Cindy, my daughter, claimed the sofa in the living room, and opened the canvased wall, making her spot like a porch. She could feel the perfect, gentle breeze and hear the mysterious African sounds. I retired to my bedroom on the second floor. Janco disappeared, and we were all set for the most delicious nap ever. I was in that zone that felt like hypnotism, with the lazy buzz of the insects humming in unison outside our chalet windows, lulling us into another dimension.

A Baboon has longer teeth than a lion. Scary.

Just before disappearing into REM sleep, I heard my daughter make a startled and scared sound, then she softly and cautiously called out, "M-o-mmm!" Even though she was nearly 60 years old she sounded like a little terrified three-year-old. I jumped out of my mosquito-netted bed and plunged down the stairs. Cindy had inched up on the sofa with her back against the wall.

Then I saw him. I froze in my tracks. Just less than five feet away from my child was a huge, silver-back baboon! My eyes darted all around me to find some sort of weapon to scare this ferocious and uninvited guest from our dwelling. Unaware of what I picked up, I began to beat on it, scream and make as much noise as I possibly could, stretching out my arms and making myself as big as possible, I advanced toward the baboon.

Cindy had pulled a small chair up on the sofa with her, made a threatening move, and slightly leaned forward. Mr. Baboon mincingly hissed and charged at her. I worked my way in between the baboon and her, then he just looked from one of us to the other, bared his teeth in warning, grabbed the cookies on the coffee table, and trotted off when *he* wanted to. In these towns, baboons are so used to being around humans, they don't fear them. As you can see, the baboon's teeth are bigger than a lion's.

This photo on the former page was taken two days prior to this incident when we drove through Kruger National Park. We learned that they have amazing strength and are capable of ripping a person apart. They are an awesome force.

As a mother, I sometimes thought if any of my children were in danger, I would gladly give my life to save them. But was never tested. This certainly taught me that a parent is genetically wired to do just that—sacrifice ourselves for our offspring. I am grateful that it wasn't necessary.

LESSONS

- In life threatening situations, there is no time to think things through. We act on the genetic impulses, our Amygdala - "fight or flight", we have as humans for survival.
- My child's life was more important to me than my own.
- And in life-threatening situations, our bodies supply enough adrenalin to fight or take flight, no matter how sleepy you might have been.
- Our primitive survival mechanism does work.

Two Questions

1. When have you been faced with a threatening situation in which you went into the "flight or fight" survival mode?

2. What happened?

Unbearable Pain

Wayne and I were in Texas for Christmas with my folks when the call came from his twin brother, Duane. What a horrible phone call for someone to have to make.

This photo was taken on Christmas Eve, two days earlier.

Wayne's oldest daughter, Jeanna, was almost 26, vibrant, intelligent, and beautiful. She was preparing to be a model. One horrendous act, December 26, 1983, and she was no more. Her husband shot her and then took his own life.

Her husband had been physically abusing her, putting her in the hospital at times, but she didn't tell us. She was trying to leave him, but he committed this violence before she could escape. Jeanna went back to their home that fateful day of December 26, 1983, not expecting him to be home. But he was and then the unspeakable happened. They got into a fight; he charged after her with his .22 rifle. Jeanna ran out the back door. Her husband shot her in the legs. She crumpled to the hard frozen ground. Jeanna lay there helpless and unable to move. She could hear him walking up to her and experienced the horror of him shooting her.

Wayne and I had to drive two days through an ice storm to get back to Michigan. He was devastated. The most horrible thing that could happen to a parent had happened. He wasn't able to protect his child. His pain was unbearable.

Jeanna was well-known and achieved in academics and music in high school. She went on to college with many promising opportunities.

L – R: Jeanna, Mary Ann, and Paul.

Wayne's three children were, and are, precious. Jeanna was the second oldest child and the oldest girl. All three were born in February. Paul was the first born, Jeanna next, and Mary Ann is the baby (middle in the photo above).

As we drove along to Michigan, the hurt would overwhelm Wayne and he would groan just trying to let the pain out, but there was no relief. He was so proud of all three of his children and it was still not believable that one was gone.

Jeanna and Mary Ann were unusually close and became confidants in their adult years. For such a bright light to be extinguished in such a violent way was a devastating impact on the family. Mary Ann's pain was acute, dropping to unfathomable depths. Witnessing this amount of pain, especially Wayne's, left me feeling helpless. And I am sure Jeanna's mother was lost in the grief of all griefs. How can you handle this level of despair? We could not imagine something like this happening. We could never be prepared for such tragedy.

When something hurtful happens to our children we, as parents, often see them like they were when they were little and helpless. We feel like we should have been there for them. Guilt haunts us.

Wayne's parents were overly practical people. They lived in Spokane; we lived in Michigan. They called to see if he wanted them to come to the funeral because they couldn't see how they could be of any help since the tragedy had already happened. Wayne was a very gentle and accommodating man. Even though it was plain he needed them to be here for him, he was about to tell them they didn't have to come so as not to inconvenience them. I signaled him to put them on hold and asked him what he really wanted. Did he want their support? With tears in his eyes, he shook his head yes. So, they came. And they should have come just because their son needed their support. But their signal to him was not a positive thing in this crisis. Another layer of hurt poured over him.

In the funeral home, on our way to the sanctuary Wayne started crying and

L – R: Jeanna, Wayne and Mary Ann.
Jeanna and Mary Ann were very close.

pulled me inside a private room. He needed to be comforted. While I was holding him, a friend opened the door to say he couldn't stay for the services, but he wanted Wayne to know he had been there. People have good intentions, but it is amazing how insensitive some people can be. That shut Wayne down.

Wayne and his first wife were both spiritual people and had instilled those values in their children. Jeanna lived in Traverse City. There is a huge iron cross in nearby Indian River with stairs leading up to it. People go to ascend to the cross and pray. I believe Mary Ann had gone up to visit Jeanna and took her to the cross so she could do this ritual. It is eerie how that was almost a premonition because this photo was taken in 1983, the year of her death. I believe Mary Ann tried to convince Jeanna not to go back to her house to get her belongings. She pleaded, "Just leave them. It is too dangerous," but Jeanna instead stepped into a nightmare.

There doesn't seem to be a "normal" after such an event. Wayne brought one of the huge plants home from the funeral and lovingly cared for it for over 20 years until it withered away. In the aftermath, Wayne would have days that were incredibly sad, and we would talk about Jeanna and his love for her. I would just hold him in my arms, sometimes soothing him, often with no spoken words. Some years later, when Wayne and I were on the board of a publication called *Integrity*, he wrote an article about his grief, finding a lot of relief in expressing his pain:

Jeanna climbing the stairs to the Iron Cross.

The Hurt

The natural order holds that parents give and nurture the lives of their children and that those children usually survive us.

When my daughter was murdered at the age of 25 the anguish of losing a wonderful daughter in the prime of life was made more horrifying by the insane taking of her life. My mind was twisted by the senselessness of this loss.

In a frantic attempt to avoid any other hurt I retreated into myself. I had been unspeakably hurt by the act of another person – not by disease, not by accident, but

273

by intent. I wanted to saw myself off from all humanity. I did not cry for three days. I would do nothing that might draw attention to myself. I sat quietly—I wanted to be left alone.

Healing Begins

But Sidney, that significant other who most beautifully reflects God's Love to me, patiently enfolded my hurt and fearful spirit. Few were her words and consistent was her support. She let God's Love, abundant in her, flow to me. She made His Love real to me.

If a kindred love had not been there with a genuine desire to help, to be an instrument of God's Love, I might have remained inside myself for safety. How important it was to have been comforted. But I was blessed by the true God-given Love of Sidney, and was able to emerge ever so slightly to test the world – would it strike me down again, or is there room for trust? Sidney had suffered the wounds with me – and somehow the burden was not quite as hard to endure.

Healing Continues

My willingness to trust was lifted – I allowed myself to cry even though it would attract others toward me. AND THEY CAME – those dear friends, relatives, and Christian family to whom I am bound in ways I cannot describe. They shared my pain. I did not hurt any less – but the burden that seemed beyond endurance was made more bearable. Those wonderful people, everyone a sinner like myself, imperfect in so many ways, were perfect instruments of His Peace. Jesus did not take away the hurt – but He did strengthen me that I could endure it.

Improved by Suffering

And my soul has been tempered a little more. From this tempering I have been more sensitive and responsive to hurt in others. My soul has been made a little more worthy a vessel of God's Grace. His Love flows more fully in me than before. And I still hurt from her loss – I suspect I shall always have this hurt – it does not seem to lessen. With His Love I have simply become more able to endure it.

If we do not allow His Love to flow into us, if we refuse the outstretched hand of our family and friends, we remain trapped in our miseries, to eventually die an embittered soul. Oh, how His Love strengthens me, allows me to see in tomorrow that the sun will shine again.

The Purpose of it All

And this is the purpose of Jeanna's dying – that those of us who loved her be further refined from suffering her loss – that we be made more humane, more Christ like.

And that's the meaning of SUFFERING, without it we should surely be lonely, destructive, and miserable creatures.

LESSONS

- An abusive person does not usually stop their aggressive behavior. They usually get emboldened and escalate to a higher level of abuse.
- They have a way of dismantling the victim's courage and self-esteem.
- The best action is to leave at the first hint of violence.
- The victim must not let the shame they feel for being abused paralyze them into staying.

THE TWO QUESTIONS

1. Have you ever experienced pain at such an intense level that, it felt unbearable? Describe it.

2. How would you find the courage to go on?

In Loving Memory of Jeanna

The Eternal Country of Love and Passion

Being that Wayne and I were so in love; Italy was an amazing choice for our honeymoon. What a perfect setting and atmosphere to start the most beautiful adventure of our life together. I had gone twice before marrying Wayne, so when he mentioned it for a possible honeymoon choice, I was thrilled. It is such a dramatic and romantic place, we never tired of it. Wayne and I felt such a riveting magnetic pull to experience all the wonders it had to offer that we returned seven times.

The rich history preserved as a witness to the past made it breathe and burst to life like no other place we've traveled. It had an eternal impact on our life together and we created unforgettable memories that added to the magic which sustained us.

Love under the Arch de Triumph in Rome.

On our last visit to Italy, like on our first, we were very much in love, and even more so than ever. Love was everywhere: in the air, around the corner, and in the city's ancient history. It was in the shadow of the Arc de Triumph.

Because we had been in Rome so often, we no longer hired guides. We knew what we wanted to do and see. In a moment of rash judgment, we decided to do as the Romans do and rented a motorcycle to tour Rome Italian style. This did not end up well, and I have the scar to prove it!

Weaving in and out of the monstrous Rome traffic, Wayne turned the wrong way, and quickly discovered that the accelerator would not shut down. He climbed the curb to a tiny park and my foot got caught between the motorcycle and a tree. The pain was of childbirth intensity. Then he yelled, "we need to jump off because the throttle is stuck." I was screaming from the pain in my foot but jumped anyway. Writhing in pain and holding my foot, my attention instantly left my

The motorcycle that cut my forehead and squashed my foot.

aching foot, and I grabbed my head. It was bleeding profusely and hurt more than my foot. The motorcycle had spun around, bucked up, banged me on my forehead, and I saw stars in the daylight. It was as if Charlie Chaplin was in town hopping from one disaster to the other.

Within an instant, police swarmed around us, not to see if we were hurt, but because they saw lots of foreign money for tickets. Their little emergency vehicle door yawned open, they put a huge bandage on my head, left me there, and took Wayne to the police station. Not sure where we were, I started ouching and limping forward to find our hotel. Exhausted and with the pain so intense, even my fingernails seemed to hurt. I still have some Roman dirt under one of my knuckles.

Struggling to open the hotel door, my first sight was of our friend Donna, lying on the stairs she had just fallen. She, my daughter, Cindy, and her husband Darrell were on the trip with us. This was our first week in Rome and already we had two casualties with five more weeks to go.

Wayne took me to the hospital when he got back to the hotel. The doctor did her magic. The x-ray of my foot revealed no broken bones just bruises, and I ended up with a huge bandage on my forehead which got covered up with a flower-print scarf. This was quite noticeable.

Woman assuring Donna she had not licked her ice cream cone.
We took it.

One guy even came up to me and asked, "Are you some kind of old hippie or something?" "Why, yes, yes I am," I crooned. He huffed off. Donna and I sat our wounded selves down on a windowsill nursing our boo-boos while a lady walked behind her husband carrying a melting ice cream cone. She had just told him that she didn't know why she even bought it because she wasn't hungry.

Donna piped up and said, "We will take it!" The lady stopped in her tracks then Donna had second thoughts and asked, "Are you sick? Have you licked it yet?" The ice cream lady assured Donna she was not and had not, so we got a big free Italian gelato. It was heavenly.

The bandage was my companion for most of the rest of the trip, but it was necessary to keep the wound clean. It was challenging to find scarves to match my ensembles of day-touring clothes and evening attire, with my big white bandage. People stared more with me wearing the naked bandage than they did when I hid it with the scarves. So, scarf

Roman pinched Cindy under his cape.

it was.

Can't let a little thing like a head wound spoil a perfectly good dream vacation.

As soon as we got into Rome, we were walking around to get into the joy of this special adventure. We happened to go past the Coliseum and ran into a handsome Roman Centurion decked out regally. Cindy wanted a photo, but she got more than she expected. While under the cover of his bright-red cloak, the naughty Centurium did the Roman thing. He pinched her boob and Cindy nearly

Taking my wounded forehead out for the evening.

jumped out of her skin. Well, we got that over with and went on our way.

The bus in which we toured all over Italy. Very European.

We rented a small bus that nicely accommodated all five of us, a sure thing for fun and friendship. Wayne was our driver and Darrell acted as navigator. The adventure had no limits. We were all very good friends and very compatible. We were like a traveling comedy show, especially with Donna's wild sense of humor. It was her first time to Italy, so she was in awe of the whole romantic experience.

Wayne and I had a favorite restaurant, Caesar's, located right in front of Trevi Fountain. Their fettuccini was to die for. Of course, Trevi Fountain is one of the most romantic spots in Rome. I saw the movie, *Three Coins in A Fountain*, and I was with my love. We just had to do the coin toss every time. But our hearts belonged to one person and one person only. We had found our true soul mate and didn't have to hope for it to happen "someday."

Wayne's romantic heart never cooled, and it thrilled me. There aren't adequate words to describe our life-long love affair of 42 years. Every day was exhilarating. We didn't need the

Wayne tossed in another coin, and we fell deeper in love.

actual song. We could hear that famous love song playing in our heads.

Next on tour was Pompeii and Mount Vesuvius. What an eerie and strange place to be. Standing 4,190 feet high, the famous violent eruption in 79 A.D. covered the people of the towns. Through the ions of time, the bodies decomposed, and archeologists discovered perfect casts of what used to be inhabitants. They were able to pour plaster into the cavities, resurrecting the mysterious history of life so long ago. Today we can see exact replicas of those citizens. The little that was preserved speaks of a vibrant life in two bustling cities of the ancient past.

After a glorious experience on the Amalfi coast, in Sorento and along the Mediterranean Sea our gang went on to Florence, which was the center of the Renaissance. The city invited us in, and then we lived it in wonder all the while we were there. It is famous for its leather gloves, the David, and Ponte Vecchio bridge, where a world of gold, diamonds, and pearls are transformed into magnificent pieces of jewelry.

Wayne bought me a beautiful gold, diamond, and pearl necklace there. My heart

Donna making a belt deal with a street vendor.

almost burst with joy. The stores looked like treasure chests full of exotic shining jewels. Donna was thrilled to learn how the bartering system worked, and she quickly became a true haggling Italian.

Wayne and I revisiting our most treasured memories.

She found a guy with a cart full of fine leather belts and bought herself a designer-looking belt. She came and got Cindy and me and rushed us back to the guy, who was overjoyed. When we finally made our selection, Donna took over as the chief barterer. When the guy told her how much, she said, "What price will you give us because there are two of them?" She held up two of her fingers and emphasized, "That's two." He gave a lower price. She said, "That's not good enough. I brought you two people and I need a finder's fee." He was sweating now. Finally, he hit his bottom. Donna commanded us, "Put the belts back and walk away." I whimpered, "But I... I...really..." She grabbed my hand and pulled me away. I whispered, "But Donna, I really want mine!" Again, she pulled me away. "Turn your back to him, he will call us back, trust me." We did as she ordered and walked away. After about five steps, he called out, "Alright, alright, I will give them to you for your price." So, Cindy and I bought two belts each from him to make it worth his while.

Wayne and I had to hug in the shadow of Michelangelo's mighty David. The city of Florence leaves a mark of beauty etched in the imagination. At the same time, we saw an entire selection of Valentino's red fashions. This breathtaking work of art can only be appreciated by being there.

St. Mark's Square is the place of the ugliest Cathedral.

We left Florence to head for Venice in a torrential downpour. Cindy and Darrell's room leaked like a sieve. In our room, the bathroom was so small, we had to sit on the toilet to shower as the water sprayed all over the tiny bathroom. We went to St. Mark's Square to see the cathedral that the city's rich patrons built if God would only stop the bubonic plague. It is known to be in the grotesque style of architecture.

A gondola boat ride is a must-do for Venice.

In the evening, restaurants had bands who dueled with each other, to the delight of their patrons. Wayne and I had come ready to dance in the glow of the moon and let the mood work its magic. Naturally, we found a gondola to glide us through the canals by the light of a full moon. The romanticism filled our hearts with joy. The evening culminated at a gorgeous restaurant tucked away in a little quaint neighborhood. It felt as if perfection was all around and guided us from one adventure to another. It was made complete by Donna's joyful reaction to all the wonders. Italy is a place that brings out the heart of romanticism and a place in which to vividly experience dramatic history.

LESSONS

- My first time in Italy opened my boundaries. I left the U.S. in the evening and in the morning arrived across the ocean in Europe. It was a revelation and a freedom.
- A place of such vivid life and history left its mark in my heart. I was forever changed.
- As couples, our lives can be refreshed and enlivened if you give in to the romanticism of such a place of beauty.
- Our lives can be renewed and made interesting to each other when we are willing to step out of our comfort zones. It adds mystique and interest to our lives.

Two Questions

1. What has been your favorite vacation?

2. What made it special for you?

The Sorrow of Sorrows

A young man is down. Pain and agony are no respecter of persons. Wayne's youngest daughter, Mary Ann, is married to Duane Horton, a high-powered sales manager for a Ford dealership. He is an accomplished and serious man, dedicated to his family, and financially astute.

Duane and Mary Ann with their first-born Michael

Mary Ann is a gifted cosmetologist with a joyful personality and a light-hearted sense of humor. They have two sons. Michael is five years older than his brother, Colin. Mike was born with a heart defect, which limited his ability to participate in the high energy most sports required. Very early in his young life, he developed a passion for hockey. But because of his heart condition, he could not play on the ice. He played on asphalt instead.

Mike was extremely well liked in his high school because he always loved helping his classmates. Mary Ann became an A-1 class Hockey Mom. She and Duane did not miss a game. The whole family supported his love of hockey.

One night as Wayne and I were driving home from dinner, I got a call from Mary Ann. She was distraught. She said she was sitting in the stands at Mike's Hockey game and Mike, 18 years old, had been skating hard. Suddenly, he fell to the asphalt.

Duane immediately hurdled over one seat row after another and jumped down into the rink. He got to Mike and cradled him in his arms. Then he noticed the blood trickling out of Mike's ear. Mary Ann kept saying, over and over, "This doesn't look good, this doesn't look good!" I can still hear her anguished words in my heart from time to time.

She was finally able to tell me the name of the rink where they were. Wayne made a quick turn in the direction towards them. Meanwhile, the ambulance had arrived, and Mary Ann told us which hospital they were taking him to. She was clearly fraught with fear. A dark dread washed over us. We were both praying as I called our pastor, Todd Lackie, who had beat us to the hospital. Todd is a true pastor who takes care of his flock and not only comes when any of us are in the hospital, but also when a close family member is hospitalized to comfort and help in any way he can.

R - L Big brother Michael Shelters his little brother Colin.

By the time we got there, Mike had succumbed to his injuries. That bright and shining light seemed to fade slowly, while at the same time the events of the evening had happened so fast, it was shocking. Colin, fourteen, also loved hockey, emulating the same passion Mike had experienced. I went outside with him and sat on the curb by the emergency entrance.

He was confused and angry. He asked how this could happen to his big brother. The same brother who went ahead of him in life and could show him the path. I just sat and listened to him without saying much. His anguish was as deep as the tumultuous black ocean and was as gut wrenching as any pain could be. They had been a close and loving family. The rawness of their pain seemed to suck all the oxygen out of the room and was a bottomless pit of confusion, emptiness and loss.

Wayne loved being an influence on all of our Grandchildren's lives.

Wayne and I were ourselves experiencing an overload of grief, for we so dearly loved Michael. But to witness Mary Ann, Duane and Colin's pain felt unbearable. To watch them go through the motions of planning the funeral was agonizing. It was like being in a nightmare that you can't awaken from.

Because Mike was so loved, it was the largest turnout for a funeral I had ever seen. The entire hockey team came dressed in suits to honor their friend. So many classmates came to pay respect to Mike, who had meant so much to them for all the help he had given them in one way or another—giving rides, helping them with homework, or loaning them money if they needed it. It felt like all of Grosse Ile, Michigan turned out to celebrate the life of this extraordinary young man.

Wayne and I had been fortunate enough to go on camping trips with his daughter and her family or go with them to their cabin in the northern woods. Those were very dear and loving times for us. Now we must live without his precious presence.

My prayer is that Mary Ann, Duane, and Colin always feel Mike's brilliant energy near them, loving them in the purest way. And that Mike be able to feel the unbridled love they send back across the great divide. I know they have already experienced his love in so many special ways.

Michael Horton was born on February 22,1991 and passed to eternal life on June 10, 2009.

His beautiful life left an everlasting mark.

LESSONS

- Such a loss as this is a bottomless pit of pain and the years can make it seem unending.
- Society responds to the loss of a sweet and kind person.

- No one close to the beloved will ever be the same.
- Sometimes people innocently say things that doesn't comfort the bereaved. It is OK not to say anything, just to be there to support.
- Nothing can prepare the family for a loss of this magnitude.
- There is comfort in knowing I will be able to recognize and love my loved ones when I go around the veil separating us.

Two Questions

1. How would you comfort someone who has lost a loved one?

2. How could you support beyond the funeral?

Across the Andes to the Epic Inca Trail

The snowcapped Andes were the backdrop for our Inca Trail
Spiritual Quest.

Eighteen or us women came to Cusco, Peru with a dream in our hearts. We gathered from different parts of the U.S., ready and open for a spiritual experience that would unfold through the mysteries located in the place of the Incas.

Most people think "Inca" is the name of the indigenous people who lived there. Back in history, Incas were the rulers of the Peruvian people. But now all the people are called Incas as if it is a generic term. The Spanish conquerors were convinced they had great quantities of gold and silver. But they found out the Inca's great wealth was not in precious metals, but in the art of their amazing weavings. The Spanish killed many of the Incas in an attempt to get them to reveal where their gold and silver was hidden. The conquistadores had horses and guns, and these gentle people were no match for them.

My circle of friends: top R to L Trisha, looking up at Mary P. on her L, Jane J. in front of Mary P, second row down I am on the far left in black hat holding Mary B's arm, Mary B., then Sandy with red hair, and in front of her is Janie B., in tan vest and hat. Rosa, our guide prior to the Inca Trail.

Cusco is the capital of Peru and stands at 11,152 feet in altitude. The first concern was how to avoid altitude sickness. The natives chew on cocoa leaves, but they taste very bitter. Most visitors prefer to drink it as tea or take altitude-sickness pills.

We were all vibrating with excitement for our adventure to begin. Rosa showed us around Cusco, taking us to interesting and delightful cultural sites and activities. We shopped for the unusual and lovely weavings. I found two unique runners and purchased one for me and Wayne, and one for Wayne's daughter, Mary Ann. They were very expensive, but the workmanship was unparalleled. We also bought cashmere sweaters, which I still wear today.

After the grueling flight, a day of rafting and picnicking was the perfect way to help us ease into this beautiful, easy-going culture. The next thing was to start enjoying the spiritual aspects of this

The Inca's real treasure was their weavings.

We each said our own special prayers.

293

enchanted land. Rosa took us to a sacred circle and had a shaman there to read our auras. First, we said our own private prayer in the circle for the upcoming trek. The energy was soothing and quieted us into a mellow acceptance creating a reflective mood free of the normally frenetic pace of our home environment, with all the demands on our attention.

The shaman read my aura and told Rosa that mine was a deep purple, which is the highest level of spirituality. He said he felt the peace

Shaman reading my aura.

and spiritual energy in me. For some time in my life, my emphasis was on developing myself spiritually. I relished learning the mysteries of that other world. I want to know God. We took every opportunity to tap into holy energy and express our hearts in prayer.

A lady in our group was having trouble with her adult son and wanted prayers for them both. Sharing our intimate concerns with trusted others

Jane listening to the voice of the rocks.

294

This would be a 2000-foot drop if you slip off the edge.

grew a common bond. Our next step was to do a little practice in the Andes. The next day, we would go to the Lightning Bolt, where we would experience the wisdom of these ancient peoples.

Mary P. shared encouraging Scripture with Cindy and the rest of our group to prepare us as we tested the temperament of the Inca Trail. It was getting more real.

The ancient people sculpted huge stones into a tongue-and-groove fit and then shaped it so that from the air it is a giant lightning bolt that crisscrosses for miles. Jane is listening to the energy of the past inviting her to leave whatever she wants to let go of, so she has complete freedom while trekking through the Andes. The highest and most dreaded station is Dead Woman's Pass at almost 14,000 feet in altitude. This day of exploration was getting us mentally and physically prepared for the days of trial ahead.

We thought it was going to be a "piece of cake," but *wow!* What a surprise we got when we were experiencing our trial run. Then Rosa told us we would experience the temperament of the trail just around the next bend. There is barely enough room to round the corner. That looks like a smile on my face, but it was naked terror. My nails were dug into the bolder. One slipped step and you would be a "cooked goose." When I inched myself to a wider spot on the trail, I felt like a real wimp.

295

A native woman came strolling up the trail with a baby on her back, a young boy and girl walking beside her, and singing as she spun wool. I thought, "Good grief, Sidney, get a grip! If she can climb with all that going on, you should be able to also since all you have to do is watch out for yourself." I scolded myself into being a little braver than I was currently demonstrating. We took a panoramic snapshot of tomorrow's Trek. Looking at it stood our hair on end. It was up and down, up and down, hugging the mountain, and rounding sharp curves. All along the path there were tiny settlements.

Woman spinning wool, singing with her two children on the Inca Trail

Cindy was having a lot of trouble with the rickety bridges, and you can see why. Janie was

The weight of our equipment was within strict limits.

struggling with the many rock steps because of her injured leg. The "rickety-ness" Cindy was hesitant about. It was very foreboding and for a few seconds she was paralyzed into a "no go" position.

It is a very long drop to the bottom. Finally, tearfully, Cindy and Janie decided they weren't physically prepared for the trail. They should stay at the base camp and welcome us when we returned. It was a hard decision, but it was best for them.

My blood hummed through my veins. This was one of my lifelong dreams—another bucket list item. It is a four-day trek one way. On a scale of one to six, the Inca Trail is a five. The El Camino Trail is probably a six. It was a formidable challenge. But right now, I didn't know enough to be afraid. I would soon learn this was not for whiners or sissies. We established a base camp and weighed our equipment because the porters would have to carry it across the Andes.

Lilly, our trail guide, was anxiously watching the weigh-ins as it would determine

This was the reality of the rickety bridges.
The trail was so ominous it paralyzed people in fear.

the number of porters required. The porters set up all the tents, and we spent our first night on the trail. What a cold night, indeed. There would be extreme fluctuations in temperature between the heat of the sun during the day and losing the heat to deep

As the porters took their much-needed rest the song of the flute drifted through the air.

space at night. This would prove to be a problem for some of our group as we got further down the trail.

But for now, we passed through the portal of the mystique of the Incas. We left a grounded world of realty for a different place in time. Bridges were scary and

The exotic scenery held us spellbound.

treacherous in contrast to the awe-inspiring beauty. But the intensity of the trail bared its hidden traps, which proved to be extremely difficult. Water, wind, sun, cold, thinning air, and rickety bridges hovered around every bend in the trail. That wasn't going to change. The question was, could we outlast the harshness of the conditions?

When it was time for the porters to rest their loads, it was a super treat for us because they would sit on a boulder, allowing the mountain to cradle their burdens, and play the flute. The melodious notes drifted on the wind currents, to the delight of our spirits. Our energy was refreshed. The trail was much more difficult than I initially thought, and the effort was beginning to take its toll on us. By the time we got to the next camp, we were cold, wet, and exhausted. Getting to relax inside a warm tent was a luxury. And the hot tea was soothing to our aching bodies. What I had learned in my years of geological expeditions and mountain-climbing was that the battle must be won in our minds first. We had to "see" ourselves making it. It was what kept me going through so many situations. And I knew each time I was about to hit a wall, my thinking had to strengthen and keep me focused on how I could make it, not how I might fail.

Our nighttime tea revived us.

While it was harder for me to climb down the trail, Jane J.'s heart hurt to climb up. A complementary pair, we decided to team up so we wouldn't be holding the others back. We would set small goals to keep progressing forward. We might set a goal to climb 20 or 30 feet to a bolder or a tree. One night we had to have a group meeting. Several gals had gotten cold and wet, and they didn't have enough dry clothes to get them through the next three days. Some were getting ill—it seemed like dysentery—and needed medical attention. Lilly arranged to get the sick ones out

Preparing for the last final descent to the Dead Woman's Pass

on donkeys. That whittled our numbers down to 11. It was brutal, and the weather was not going to be our friend. We had to wear our ponchos most of the time, but it did not get rid of the sense that we were wet all the time. This was only the second night on the trail, and we were probably going to lose five more ladies.

We were at the foot of Dead Woman's Pass (14,000 feet, named after the shape of the profile of the pass. It looked like a dead woman lying on top.) The Pass stood in defiance, mocking us with 1,000 more feet to conquer.

We woke the next morning, and the five ladies *did* have to go back. Dead Woman's Pass was the highest point on the trail. Jane J. and I committed to help each other make it to the end. Oxygen deprivation, combined with the steep path, slowed our pace considerably.

My legs were weakening from the downhill part of the trek, and Jane's chest continued to hurt during the uphill part, but we slowly advanced toward our goal. When our resolve weakened, we would pick out our short goal, then another,

We left momentous of our life on top to mark this spiritual experience.

doggedly bent on going upward and forward. I was awestruck. We were really in the Andes, rugged white-capped peaks above, green slopes with waterfalls around us, and the sun beaming through the snowy haze.

This was our longest, most demanding day. By now my legs felt like rubber and I was shaky. Lilly kept asking me to let her help me, and I kept refusing. We soldiered on and at last, we were standing on the peak of Dead Woman's Pass. I had brought photos of Wayne and my three cherished children. Janie had given me photos she wanted to leave at this sacred place. I prayed for health and happiness for all of them, dug a shallow hole, and buried the photos. It was extremely emotional for me.   All my hopes and dreams for my children went into that moment. If only they could see into my heart's intention, they could see the depth of my pure and mighty love for them. There was never a moment in their life that I did not love them. The truth is preserved there at Dead Woman's Pass. Though we each had our struggles, Jane and I made it to that peak feeling victorious. There was so much we tolerated and overcame. Jane has the

Jane and I surprised ourselves by making all the way to the top.

heart of a lioness. We took the moment to celebrate and then gird ourselves for the today's trail destination. We were getting more and more exhausted, but the trail required still more. Our slow pace was marching us into darkness. We were behind everyone else in our group, and knew we needed to make it to camp before nightfall. The pain in my thighs and calves made each step agony, and Jane's pain in her chest and shortness of breath was alarming.

302

Fortunately, we had head lanterns and could see the trail, but it was dangerous

My pride was my astounding lesion. It almost robbed me of the glory to achievee my goal.

to negotiate in the darkness. Suddenly, to our surprise, Lillian showed up with five porters carrying tents. One had a metal contraption on his back that looked like a chair. Lillian again said, "Sidney, please just let us help you." I balked again and said, "I absolutely will not be carried out!" Jane and I agreed we wanted to make it to camp with our group instead of camping by ourselves along the trail My legs were cramping so badly they were shaking. I could no longer command them to carry me forward. I was angry and disappointed in myself. Always, in trouble spots, I was able, by sheer force of will, to do what needed to be done. But this time, it wouldn't work. Tears of frustration overwhelmed me. My brain was racing to figure out what to do. It was not within me to give up. Lillian then said, "Sidney, please just let a porter get on each

The agonizing climb to the Gates of the Sun

side of you to help you walk." By this time, I was almost immobile. I said, "I can't, my pride won't let me!" Jane blurted out, "Well, mine will!" She got between two porters, and they took off! I stood there dumb-foundeed. I had said it out loud to God and the whole universe, "So this is what it's all about for me. This is why I am on this trail. All my life I had felt I could not depend on anyone. My dad's undependability had taught me that. I had to do it myself. My cursed pride.

Now I had the choice to either be stubborn or let someone help me so we could all reach the goal together. I put my arms around the porters and was slightly concerned how three of us could walk along the trail and not tumble off the side of the mountain. It was amazing how quickly we learned how to work together. I had a death grip on the inside porter. If he could stay on the mountain, I could too.

There was magic in that night. Lillian had us all turn off our headlights and look up at the stars. The Milky Way was vivid. We called out to the stars and watched their blinking splendor. What awe in God's magnificent works. We reached camp with shouts of joy from our group.

Porters set up a tent for Jane and me and brought us hot tea. We could feel our bodies reacting to the care. Sleep never felt so good.

Cindy coming up to the path making sure that we were OK.

The last day brought us to the Portal to the Gates of the Sun overlooking Machu Picchu. Jane and I tearfully embraced; thankful we had held on till the end. As I contemplate the climb now, there were challenges around each corner that we could not have expected. We were climbing the stairs to the lookout portal for the sunrise. Nothing was easily gained. Each advance had to be hard-won in a battle with the rough conditions. I set goals that were shortened by the quest against the cold and the thinning air. We were all going at our own pace.

I carried my precious Dr. Pepper to celebrate this moment.

The Window to the Sunrise was a big goal to reach. The victory of looking out across the Andes was another one of those breathtaking moments. I had to make this celebration special. It was the right moment for just the right thing. Dr. Pepper won out. I had carried that sucker throughout the whole adventure. It was now the day to break it out. The image of my 6-foot-5-inch grandpa drinking it gave me a special kind of pleasure. This day would be a gift for all the many experiences we had gone through to reach Machu Picchu. It is one of the best-preserved ruins in the world. Now was the time to hear about the exotic history and hidden mysteries. People came from all over the world to step back into ancient times. But first, one of the most beautiful and exciting surprises was coming toward us. My daughter, Cindy, and friend Janie were rushing towards us. We were all crying big-body boo-hoos. What a blissful reunion that was. It is a curiosity that humans cry when they hurt, and when they are overcome with joy.

There it was, the Lost City of the last of the Incas. The huge peak (center, just behind the ruins) is an imposing challenge to climb. Trisha and Mary P. did this unbelievable climb. That was not on my bucket list, thank goodness. Porters carried the Incas the whole way for their summer retreat, and they lived in luxury, provided with everything they could possibly desire. The guide really made the history come alive telling it to us right on the spot. It burst into living color, leaving a vivid picture in our minds, and spoke to us. Cindy and Janie got the whole lay of the land while we were on the trail. They found out a delightful secret. It took us four days to walk the

The Magnificent Machu Picchu

trail on foot. But! They found a helicopter that would get us back to our hotel in only two hours. You can guess what we did. My memory was way too fresh with all the obstacles of the Inca Trail. I was ready to be light, warm, and dry. Jane, Cindy, Janie, and I climbed on board in a New York minute.

Janie was ecstatic to be able to get out of Dodge quickly. And she declared, "It's a miracle!" that we could, with the snap of our fingers, change our exit time from

The trail was a real challenge to our character.

four days into two hours. And we were making a memorable trip back to Lima. What memories and soul-stirring experiences we had had! There was so much I had learned. So many important insights had enlightened me. I was going home with a full heart. And I was going to get to share it all with Wayne. He would always get so excited when I was happy, and he'd share in my joy with gusto. My spirt was saturated with new insights and possibilities. I felt like a feather floating through the air, free of all burdens. Most of us came back as wounded warriors, but we were overflowing with fulfillment and gratitude for what the adventure had done within us and for us. The glaring lesson about my pride changed me. I was different. I could free myself of this erroneous perspective. It was time to let this go. I am grateful for this experience and all that I learned. This was more than an adventure. I realized that the Inca Trail mostly taught me that difficult challenges are brought to us as gifts. To open us, to discover who we are and what we are made of.

The helicopter ride out was a real blessing. L to R: Me, Jane, Cindy and Janie.

LESSONS

- Seek the thing you need to learn about yourself to let it go as it no longer serves you.
- Check pride at the entrance of your challenge. It compromised my success, and someone could not get the gift of pleasure that comes from helping others.
- Don't give up at the first signs of difficulty. Trust in yourself.
- Set short term goals to overcome obstacles that could stop you.
- Follow your dreams and you will be rewarded. I like to say it differently: Follow your star. Endure short term discomfort to achieve your ultimate desire.
- Live in the present moment—take delight in what the universe is bringing to you.
- Believe in yourself—Trust the seeds of greatness that propel you forward.
- Let others help so everyone wins.

309

<u>Two Questions</u>

1. When were you involved in a very demanding task, and you had a flash of insight, like in my pride experience?

2. How did it change your perspective or change you?

There it was Again... My Star was Blinking at Me

It was 2013, and for the 15th year in a row, walking the 500-mile El Camino Trail in Spain has been on my bucket list. At age 73, how much longer would I even be able to do it? It was decision time—*either do it or take if off the list!*

My pen started to mark it off my list, but I couldn't do it. A knot swelled up in my throat and my chest tightened. What did that mean? Time was running out. I needed to train and get myself in shape to walk 500 miles. I decided to do it. After all, my star was guiding me, right?

By this point, I had been on many adventures and knew I had to be prepared. The first thing I did was to recruit my friend, Izabela Jaworska. She is a world competitive dancer who would not only have the strength but also the motivation and sticking power. She could go the distance, and we could make it together.

The first thing we did was to envision ourselves standing in the Courtyard of the Cathedral, in the town of Santiago de Compostela, Spain after having made the Pilgrimage. The Courtyard is believed to be the resting place of St. James the Apostle's bones, and people have been making the pilgrimage to his burial site ever since medieval times. We had to win the battle of our minds first, then we could win it on the trail. Once our heads were straight, we needed to check our health and start training for this challenging quest.

Dr. David Brownstein of The Center for Holistic Medicine in West Bloomfield, MI volunteered to be our official medical advisor while we were on the trail. He proved to be an invaluable resource when we got injured.

Dr. Brownstein kept us on track when we had health issues.

Isabel and I would start in the French Pyrenees, cross over to the Spanish Pyrenees and, essentially, walk across Spain in a trek that would amount to 850 kilometers, or 518.5 miles.

It would be like walking from Farmington Hills, Michigan to St. Louis, Missouri— a very daunting task for a soon-to-be 74-year-old woman. For the younger Izabela, not so much. When she got too far ahead of me, she would lean over on her walking stick till I almost got to her, then she would take off like a banshee down the trail again. Seems like I could never quite catch up to that "sweet thang." But I was determined to make it.

Izabela and I set aside 40 days and nights for the entire quest to symbolize Jesus being tested in the wilderness. We walked a total of 33 days, one day for every year of Jesus' life. We rested for three days and nights to acknowledge the length of time between Jesus' crucifixion and His resurrection. All of this added spiritual meaning to the quest we were on.

There are defining moments in life that set us on our journey to "follow our star." They are usually not marked by flashing bolts of light, or vicious claps of thunder. They are more often small and insignificant events. My friend, Lizzie, told me her moment came when she was in the first grade. Her mother was holding her hand, trying to get her out of the school, but little Lizzie had not hugged her friend, Johnny, goodbye yet. Her mother was pulling on her and insisted on leaving. But Lizzie yanked her hand away from her mother's and ran back to hug Johnny. She felt so powerful because she insisted on doing what her heart wanted her to do.

My daughter, Cindy, told me her moment was when we were closing our Empowerment Seminars, which we had been conducting for 14 years. The seminars were a power force for helping people overcome their fears and obstacles to become who they were destined to be. For many reasons, we were closing our doors, one of them being that I had burned out after so many years. Cindy said the seminars were so fulfilling for her. They had become her life, and now they were over. But then she got to thinking. She was not too old to follow other dreams. And that is what she did—she empowered herself to dream another dream.

For me, one of my most life-defining moments happened in 1949 when I was 9 years old. When we lived on the Texas prairie, in that unfinished house, and she had kept us out of school. We were out of food and butane. The frigid wind blew the winter inside the house and seemed to never leave. She reminded us, "we will not always be cold and hungry, this is only temporary.

I sat looking at her and wondered how long "temporary" might be. To this day, I think she was proclaiming this to convince herself as much as to hold us up. I know now she was desperate to give us hope. This experience taught me that hope can lift us up and carry us through. We could dream new dreams. And most things are temporary.

Izabella and I hiking the Spanish and French Pyrenees on our longest day.

At our campfire I learned that moment instilled into me that I could be bold and create a present not bound by the limits of the past, which turned out to be important to believe when tackling the El Camino Trail. We entered a 21-mile trek over part of the French and Spanish Pyrenees mountain ranges, Izabela, and I were on the hardest day of our entire quest. It was tough going. Many people have lost their lives getting caught in unexpected storms in the Pyrenees.

I could feel my body losing energy. My legs had turned to jelly; they would no longer follow my brain's commands. I called out to Izabela, "I'm going down!", before I collapsed to the ground. She ran to me, with her backpack on, circling me like a nervous Taco Bell Chihuahua, frantically yelling, "I will help you… I can carry you!"

"You little squirt", I said, "you cannot carry me. That isn't going to happen; you are a tiny, 5'4" munchkin, and I am 5'9 1/2" tall Texan!"

I insisted she leave me and go ahead for help. She didn't want to leave me. "In Poland we are taught to help our elders.", she told me.

"In Texas we are taught that God helps those who help themselves.", I replied. Now, go on...git!" I told her not to worry, and I scooted up to rest against a huge boulder. Two gals from Australia came upon me and decided to stay with me till help came.

My Spanish rescuer made it all the way to the red running board before I slipped from his arms.

Soon, a bright red Hummer came crashing through the woods and pulled up as close to me as they could. One of the three gorgeous young rescuers exploded from the Hummer, rapidly questioning me in Spanish. I couldn't understand a word he was saying.

Finally, he used the word "cortisone," and I realized he was trying to find out if I had had a heart attack. I looked at him and said, "Why, no! Honey, I just needed a hamburger! I was out of fuel."

He then yanked me to my feet to an upright position, I felt his body shift, and thought, "Oh no! He is going to try to lift me!". I instantly yelled, "No, No, No!". Too late, he already had me up in his arms. "Oomph... heavy woman!", he grunted. He got me to the red Hummer and opened the door but dropped me on the running board. His two buddies were laughing their hind ends off as the gallant young man cringed and loaded up.

Turns out we had almost made it to our first night's shelter only a half mile away

- a noble conclusion for our first day on the trail.

On the El Camino, the Albergues are dormitory-stye rooms of 15 or more bunk beds. Hikers must get there by about 4:00 p.m. to get a bed. Since we were rescued, though, they had designated bunk beds

Fortunately, we got a bed because I was injured.

for us, along with a meal. Once we settled in the server brought in a huge bowl of pasta with big puffs of bread. We dove in and ate every bite. Feeling overly full, we were shocked to realize the pasta was just the appetizer. Soon, staring at me was half a fish, eyeball and all. By the way the server looked at us and stood over us, we figured we needed to eat that *big* plate of food too or something bad might happen. Eyeball and all, though, that wasn't going to happen!

We walked through the enchanted woods where wild horses lived, and over rock-covered land where you couldn't walk on solid ground. We climbed up mountains, across meadows, resplendent with poppies and wildflowers, across dry, hot mesas, and through the wind, rain, and heat. There were many wonders along the way. Pretty soon all of us pilgrims became the "walking wounded", suffering from blisters and cuts – that is everybody, except Izabela.

While I was patching up one blister after another by sewing up the burst skin, Izabela found one tiny blister on her right little toe. She dubbed us the "blister sisters."

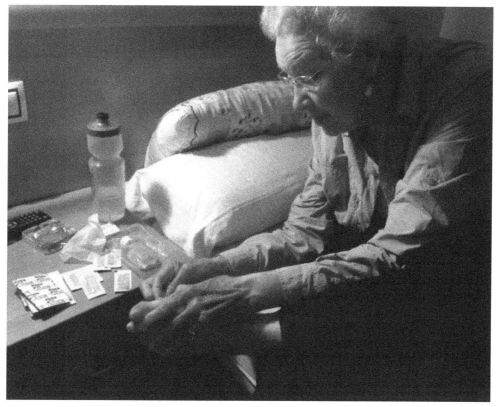

Izabela only got one blister on her little toe! Mine were more plentiful and getting worse. But we soldiered on.

There was so much pain along the way and yet there was also inexpressible magic too: places to experience spiritual wonder, the marvel of nature, with luxurious fields of poppies, crosses where we could meditate and feel peace, a labyrinth to walk through and feel serenity and oneness with God. And Izabela, how could this girl jump like that despite all the pain and misery? She was a phenomenal bundle of energy, like the ever-ready Energizer Bunny.

Fields of beautiful, colorful poppies covered the landscape. Izabela couldn't resist playing amongst them.

Since we were walking and not driving, we could take things in at a natural pace. We walked by thirteenth-century cathedrals and valiant white horses in people's backyards. In the village, we walked into little cafés for a delicious sandwich or discovered a MacDonald's to get a taste of

Often the trail was so rugged we could not walk on flatground.

318

American hamburgers and French fries. We saw thrilling snapshots of ancient memories as we walked past the last standing Castle of the Knights Templar. We learned such interesting things—such as how the Knights Templar were there to protect the pilgrims. People have been walking the El Camino or The Way for 1,400 years. As an early banking system, the pilgrims deposited money with Castles of the Knights Templar and drew on it to fund their pilgrimage. Each ancient cathedral had a dramatic story. The Trail was rough and sometimes there wasn't a flat place to put our feet. When it rained, our boots collected so much mud, we could barely lift our feet.

We were marching forward with the silent metal pilgrims.

Each day was a new adventure. One day we came upon Shamus, a good Irish singer who sang us "Danny Boy" early one morning. It carried on waves of melancholy through the air.

We joined the metal Pilgrims on their ancient journey across a mountain, anchored down with the windmills gathering their energy from the wind. Their blades

I left my rocks of love for Wayne and my children on this mountain of many dreams.

mourned as they relentlessly turned in their circles. It was a fitting place to catch our breath.

At the end of the El Camino stands a famous cross where pilgrims have brought stones representing afflictions we carry or people we want to bless. Throughout the centuries pilgrims have laid them at the foot of the cross, creating a small mountain of burdens released into God's care. It was a sacred moment for me, to release a heavy pain in my heart and leave it there alongside a massive pile of human suffering, knowing I did not have to carry it any longer. Its groaning would no longer echo in my heart. It had found its resting place.

Each night our passports had to be stamped for legitimacy.

Along the trail, pilgrims had to get their passports stamped at each place we spent the night. We then presented these to the correct authorities to verify we did walk the whole 500 miles, after which we were awarded an official certificate of completion.

The "icing on the cake" after finishing the El Camino was my precious, devoted, and loving husband waiting for me back home with a sweet love card that read:

The last marker. Only 17 more kilometers to go!

June 24, 2014

My Dearest Sidney,

You're coming home today; the moment I've dreamed of ever since you left for El Camino. I am incomplete without you, and my only purpose is to rejoin you. You did it! You walked over 500 miles on the same path of the Apostle James. You can't believe how proud I am of you. To wake up every morning knowing you must walk another 17 miles today. WHEW!!! You define the words "commitment" and "determination." Sweetheart, you got what it takes—and more. In your absence I got to know the true meaning of desperate loneliness. I DON'T WANT TO EVER LIVE WITHOUT YOU! Without you, my life is meaningless. And with you, it is fulfilling beyond measure. WELCOME HOME SWEETHEART.

I LOVE YOU MADLY,

Your Wayne

Victory at the finish line.

Izabela and I earned the sweet reward of making it to the finish line.

It just so happened that there was a St. Francis of Assisi monastery in Santiago. They award certificates only once every 100 years to pilgrims who complete the El Camino Trail. Izabela and I received that one too.

It was a life-changing spiritual journey. Though we felt very weak at the end of the trail, over time we were able to realize the internal strength it gave us to face obstacles in life.

LESSONS

- Endurance is as much in the head as it is in the body.
- Keep your eye on the goal instead of on the many roadblocks.
- I received deep spiritual fulfillment.
- Most people want to help us when we need it.
- A worthy goal is worth what it takes to achieve it.
- To achieve a worthy goal, never quit. Be a finisher.
- The pain will eventually heal and go away; the memories will stay with us forever.
- We can choose what we focus on - either the impossible odds, or the prize to be gained.

Two Questions

1. When have you completed some challenge that was so tough, that it took everything you had in you to get through it?

2. How did you feel about yourself after accomplishing the challenge?

You Can Do Whatever You Believe You Can. Climb Your Mountain

The year was 1976, my legs felt rubbery, out of control as I pumped the stationary bike up an impossible incline, gasping for oxygen. Dr. Stranski, Professor at Oakland University, had gotten so invested in the training processes he had designed for me, squatted below me as I pumped with all my might, he yelled, "Don't you give up now. Keep going! You can do it! Ride! Ride!"

My heart was pounding, my legs were on fire, and my hands hurt from gripping on the handlebars. Then cheers rang out in the lab as I pushed myself to the summit. I had reached the top of the mountain in training for the ultimate goal of climbing to the real top of Mount Kilimanjaro. This was no small challenge. Kilimanjaro is the tallest free-standing mountain in the world. It is a dormant volcano, which hosts the remnants of a shrinking glacier on top. It is a mountain of phenomenal extremes with six climate zones climbers pass through: the Cultivation Zone, the Forest Zone, (known to locals as the Green Gloom

Sidney off to Kenya and the Mountain Top.

of the Rainforest), Moorland Zone, Alpine Desert Zone, and Arctic Summit Zone. Standing at 19,341 feet in altitude, the challenge was to climb it without additional oxygen. I had done exhaustive research on the climb and trained a year for this challenge. Part of the training was to get up to running six miles a day. My son Brett ran with me one day, but he left me in the dust because I was too slow for him.

The next thing I knew, I was back in Africa and dizzy with the thrill of it. My soul felt at home and at rest here. Our five weeks rediscovering Africa were coming to an end. We had camped all over East Africa to study the environment, culture, and

The pilot dropped us off at the nearest air strip inside Kenya. He couldn't fly at night.

animals of Kenya. This included the Serengeti Plain, the Ngorongoro Crater, The Great Escarpment, Thompson Falls, and Lake Turkana. Five of our team were on our way to climb the mighty Kilimanjaro. We needed to get from Kenya to Tanzania to meet our mountain. We ended up bribing a pilot to fly us as far as he could without instruments. He dropped us at a little air strip closer to Tanzania, but still in Kenya. We hitchhiked awhile, but it was getting dark and dangerous. Finally, we heard the rattling of a vehicle and the blasting of music from a local truck racing towards us.

The guy sitting in the shotgun seat was banging on his door yelling, "Ride is coming, ride is coming!" Like magic, people came out of the bush to get a ride. We did too. For a price, they gave us a ride to the regular bus for the Tanzanian border.

Because we were hitchhiking, we took any type of transportation we could get.

Just as we got there, darkness descended on us like a heavy cloak. We boarded the bus for Tanzania border. The bus driver left the bus because he had a girlfriend there. When we got out of our seats a guy rose from his seat and said, "Do not get off the bus. It is too dangerous." We asked why. He gravely replied, "You see the sign and the buildings? Look closely. All those holes, they are bullet shots. The border guards will shoot you."

"We are not getting off the bus," I said, and we settled in for the night. The next morning, we grabbed our belongings and left the sanctuary of the bus. I had a borrowed army duffle bag, while the others had suitcases. We struggled down the dirt road for the Tanzanian border post. Every once in a while, I had to stop and sit on my duffle bag for a few minutes before I could get my second wind to go on. By the time we got to the border, the guards there were laughing at my struggle. They were not friendly to my four companions.

The guards searched them and took their money. They did not search me or take my money because I had entertained them. After that, I was the only one with money and paid for stuff we all needed until we found our hotel and the money was running thin.

That night I lent a girl one of my evening gowns, and we dressed up for a formal

Girl to whom I lent one of my gowns.

dinner in the hotel where Ernest Hemingway wrote, *The Snows of Kilimanjaro*. The ambiance immersed us in its exotic history. We were transformed to a by-gone era and wondered what it would have been like for Ernest Hemingway, who clearly must have been inspired in this exotic place. After dinner, we all sat around a warm fire and talked about our adventure that would begin at dawn in the morning. We retired early to get a good night's sleep. But sleep wasn't in the cards for us that night. The air was taut with fear and excitement, which pumped adrenaline through our bodies, making it almost impossible to get our eyes to obediently close. Finally, the dawn arrived and quietly poured through our windows. The guides including our head guide Siara, and porters gathered and made ready for the climb. Exhilaration mounted to a

Porters and guides sang us songs to set the tone for our climbing adventure.

peak and flooded us with nervous energy.

Our guides and all the lodge staff came out to sing and clap us off to our adventure. Little did I know how quickly we would need the energy and the hope in that song. Besides our team of five, ten others joined us for the climb. We started out in the Cultivation Zone, which was easy at first. The weather was ideal, and nothing threatened this stage of our ascent.

The fertile Cultivation zone.   In the green gloom darkness swallowed the light.

Our five folks optimistically attacked the climb with vigor. The guides and porters kept telling us, "poli, poli," which meant, "slowly, slowly." They wanted us to climb at a sustainable pace so we could acclimate to the swiftly changing altitudes. The climb would take us three days up and two and a half days down.

After a hard push forward, many scratches, and much exhaustion, we reached the Green Gloom of the Rainforest. We needed to pass through this zone to get into proper position for the trek and climb the next day. As soon as we got beyond the strobes of sunlight, on the edge, the Green Gloom transformed into a damp, forboding veil of blackened green. It was so dense, the darkness sprung to life with frightful shadows that tormented me while we were passing through this forrest of fear.

We emerged out of the pit of darkness (since there was so much vegetation) and trudged our way through part of the Heather-Moorland zone. The cold began to fill the air, the vegetation was getting sparce, and the air was quickly thinning. We were at 12,000 feet. The pressure in my head felt immense, and my eyes were straining in their sockets. It was painful. Nothing was comfortable, and I was quickly

Oxygen deprivation was frightening.

losing my motivation. At 15,000 feet, ten of our party were having doubts—they wanted to quit. Our skin turned purple from the lack of oxygen. By then, my eyes felt like they would pop out of my head from the pressure. Alttitude sickness threatened to get violent, and we all wanted to throw up from the oxygen deprivation and anxiety. It was not a pretty picture.

I kept repeating over and over, "I can breathe, I can breathe, I can breathe," which helped me make it through the night. It was a real panicky feeling to realize. I was trying to suck in oxygen, but I couldn't get enough to fill up my lungs. Knowing to control my thoughts and not panic was essential for the ability to carry on. At this point, the ten who wanted to quit the climb left with a guide to climb back down to oxygen and civilization. The climb sure wasn't for the faint hearted. At 4:00 a.m., Jim, Jeff and I were shaken from our slumber and told to get dressed. It was time for our rondevous with the sunrise, which rose above the clouds of Mt. Kilimanjaro. What a mystical experience. We climbed through the silence of the pre-dawn. All was still and quiet. We wanted to feel the sacredness of the moments to come. Through the little slivers of light, I could hear my mother's gentle voice. Her whispers skipped

Mother's firm and determined voice came to me from the prairie to the sunrise above the clouds.

across the clouds and reached my heart to remind me of her promise, which came as little sunbeams of light sparkling beneath the morning clouds, "We do not belong here." I remember her saying, "This is not our lot in life. We were not born to this. We will all get off of this prairie. We will all create good and worthy lives." Little slivers of light showed us where the sunbeams would come from and the bottom of the clouds announced their presence. Then the sun burst above the clouds and radiantly illluminated the darkness of the night. I was in awe. We revelled in this take-your-breath-away moment.

When our hearts and souls calmed down, we refocused our attention to "what next." We still had the ascent of the final two zones to conquer, but by this point I knew I would make it to the top. My mother often told us with great conviction,

We made it to the Alpine Dessert. I am in the foreground recovering with hot tea.

"You can do anything you set your mind to do." I knew I must not fail myself. I had to "make it off the prairie and into a worthy life." It was the moment in time to do as our British friends suggest: "stay calm and carry on." We tackled the Alpine Desert and ran out of any vegetation above the frost line. Even though it was barren, our guide, Siara, danced with glee to celebrate getting that far.

For the rest of us, our breathing was a real impediment to joining Siara's dance. Struggling for oxygen held me in a barely controlled-panic mode. The desert was an airless, barren wasteland. A landscape straight out of a Mr. Spock and Captain Kirk episode of *Star Trek*.

When we made it this far, Siara danced triumphantly.

I concentrated on putting one foot in front of the other. The biting cold stiffened my joints, and my extremities were burning from the frigid wind. I gritted my teeth, keeping my mind on what I needed to do, not on the extreme discomfort screaming inside my body. Yet we stood on the edge of the world for a timeless moment. We were aiming for Uhuru Peak, the peak of freedom.

As we climbed, frigid temperatures combined with the altitude to make it difficult to breathe. It felt like my lungs would freeze if I deeply breathed in that harsh, raw air. We were not to the Uhuru peak yet, and I felt like I would fall asleep walking from the oxygen starvation. It was affecting my thinking as well. I couldn't let any doubts enter my mind or think thoughts of failure. "Just keep walking forward," I told myself, "keep my eyes on the prize." It was very difficult to think rationally.

Jim, Jeff and I made it to the clouds of the Artic Summit

Our group was down to Jim, Jeff, and me. All the others had dropped off. We were too near—I could not conceive of quitting now. The pain and cold were unspeakable. I had learned endurance at so many points in my life. I trusted it would push me over the finish line this time with the Artic Summit in sight. Jeff and I were headed for Uhuru at the top of the world, not looking back. At that point, my breathing was laborious, hollow, and jaggedly rasping for any ounce of air to be had. Though my eyes could barely stay open and my mind was playing tricks on me, I desperately repeated over and over, "Sidney, breathe, walk, breathe, walk. Keep going forward. Keep going, Stay awake. Breathe, walk, go forward. Siara kept urging Jeff, Jim and

On the top there is the remains of the glacier and the dormant volcano.

me on. If we could just hold out a little longer, maybe we could make it. The prize was in sight. Siara whistled and pointed forward. "Only a few more feet! Come, you

On top of the world!

can do it!"

This was much like Babu honking his horn in the Suguta wilderness adventure, giving us just enough energy to hang on and push ourselves to the finish line. If Siara thought we could do it, then surely we could. And then it happened. We saw Uhuru Peak within 50 feet. The battle had to be won in my head first. My crazed mind shouted, "We can do it! Just a few more feet. We are in sight of victory!" Jeff and I fell on the markers and flags, and Jim was right behind us. Jeff and I grabbed each other for a victory hug. "Sidney," he told me, " you have a lot of balls." Awkward, but I accepted it as a compliment.

We saw joy, tasted it and experienced the cost and reward of the mammoth thrill of *being on the top!* It is something no one can diminish or take from me. So many peope along my path believed in me. For those earth angels in my life, I am

On a clear day you can see the magnificant Kilomanjaro.

truly grateful. We must pay it forward to people in our lives as well. Finally, almost unnoticed, I had a complete sense of well-being and peace. I believed in me too. That was a powerful moment. We stood at the foot of the glacier and felt alive with the universe.

We had made it to the top of Kilimanjaro!

Discovering and marrying the love of my life.

As I reflect on my life, all the experiences that got me here taught me lessons so important to life, opened me to insights, and expanded my enlightenment. Each time, I stepped into a new way of being, a new world of wonder and insight refreshed my enegy. My life had been renewed with different colors. New horizons opened up to me. Music played a deeper harmony. The air was different. There was more, and I could see further into the next step. Yes, we had made it to the top of that majestic mountain, and I realized it was also the story of making it to the top of my mountain of life. It has been a thrill to see what only those who dare to take the path less-traveled see. To have experienced passion, and to have used the gifts God gave me has enriched my life. The sounds of music have been absorbed deeply within my soul. God plants that seed of greatness within each of us, and we are expected to find it, live it, and intimately know fulfilment. I have known great love to last my lifetime.

I have born three wonderful children, who have given meaning to my life and shown me the glory of motherhood. I revel in the pride and joy I have in them. I did

The joys I have experienced in motherhood

not give up or waste. Many big dreams became my reality. I have known pain. God taught me how to live through it and receive the lessons pain came to teach me. I have made many mistakes, my greatest lessons came from my biggest errors I have risked and I have fallen. Out of the rubble of disappointment, God has shown me hope. It is a life that ultimately led me to great joy, and my destiny.

My siblings and I all got off the prairie, and discovered a great big wide and wonderful world. I had the great pleasure to discuss these wonderful things with my wise and wonderful Mother and to witness her pride in her part as our way out of poverty. This was particularly fulfilling and Mother saw all her children succeed. That was her reward for the batte she fought.

God sent me many wise messengers along the way, and I paid attention to those voices of wisdom because He was sending me enlightenment. As I look back on my life in these last few chapters, all these experiences and lessons have enriched my life. They have had their place in growing me up. They have shown me the way to better choices, which moved me in the direction for doing God's will. This all has led to a rich peace within me. It has been an amazing journey and it is not yet over for me. Ahh, the great mystery of "now what?"

LESSONS

- This Mt. Kilimanjaro story is a culmination of the many lessons life has taught me as described in prevous chapters.
- I learned not to give up.
- Pain will diminish and disappear, but the vivid lessons and illuminations will last forever.
- Experiencing greatness has very few equals. Do something extraordinary!

- Overcoming many obstacles on the way to doing something unusual has given me a lot of confidence and has strengthened my courage to try great things.
- Climbing Kilimanjaro enhanced my personal life and my career.
- I learned to trust and believe in myself. I learned to trust others.

Two Questions

1. What unusual and difficult adventures have you experienced?

2. What did it teach you? How did it make you stronger or more confident?

Acknowledgements

There are so many people who have woven in and out of my life that I need to acknowledge. I cannot put them all in, but you know who you are. For what you brought into my life, at the right time and under the most opportune circumstances, you were there. If you are not named, just know you touched my life.

My Mother, Sibyl Randolph, my mentor, wise guide, hero, and earthly security. She never left me or forsook me. She gave me hope at the lowest pits in my life. She kept her promises, and I could trust her word. When despair seemed to darken my path, she adamantly assured me I would achieve my dreams.  She was so convincing that all five of us children believed her. Mother was determined and never ever gave up; she was courageous and defied the odds against her. Through all the heartbreaking falls, she managed to get back on her feet and keep going. She was my most treasured role model.

My beloved husband and soulmate was my hero. With Wayne beside me, I felt  strong, courageous, and pressed forward when I needed that extra push. I was emboldened to attack any challenge. He was ready to do anything to help me achieve a dream. Wayne championed me in so many ways; I felt totally loved by him. He stabilized my life. I could unequivocally count on him and, I learned from him, for the first time, to trust men. We were co-travelers on this earth, totally devoted to each other's good and happiness. We were a team. This gave me a deep confidence, which was a gift beyond measure.

Cindy Christopher, my daughter, has been intertwined in my life since 1958. She and her brothers, Bo and Brett, have been the joy of my life. She and I simultaneously decided we should adopt a large village of Shannghan people. Along with Wayne, the three of us created our 501 C 3 charity Helping Hands Touching Hearts, that has been in existence for over 15  years. Cindy is incredibly creative, compassionate, and hard working. She has been key in the success of our Empowerment business and our HHTH Charity.

Liz Kearns traveled many roads with me, lightened my load and gave form to  my endeavors. Liz didn't just talk a good game; she took my book and went through it line by line, page after page and corrected all typos and the grammar and offered many great suggestions. Liz is a successfully published author and shared her knowledge with me in my quest to finish my book. She has been a sparkling inspiration. Liz has a gift of stimulating creativity with whoever she is with. She introduced me to my editor, Maureen Dunphy. Liz has offered me so many insights and comforting faith.

Patty Watters has been my loyal friend for at least 30 years. She always shows up just when I most need her. We seem to know just when we  need each other. Going through the current uncertain journey of cancer, Patty is walking that difficult path with me. This gives me great hope and comfort. When we don't have to bear life's burdens along, the journey is not as fearful. She gives me strength. With a friend like Patty, I could fight any battle.

Maureen Dunphy, my editor, has stimulated me to dig deeper and search harder to find the jewels of interest for my readers. From the moment I met Maureen, I knew I was in very capable and creative hands. She taught me so much about writing and getting to the treasures in an experience, how to dig it up, polish it till it sparkled and present it in its most glorious form. Her questions motivated me to stay with the gold while it was mined. I felt transformed by her guidance.

Ken Rose is my new friend, and earth angel. We live in the same neighborhood. One day while out walking, I had my head down praying for someone to come along and help me get to the hospital for tests. Just as I raised my head, Ken zoomed up

to me on his bicycle and jumped off. With his *heart killer* smile he said, "Sidney, how are you? It has been a while since we have talked. What have you been doing? Tell me exactly what you need. How can I help you?" I stared at him like the apparition he was. Here he was, the angel I had just prayed for!

Not only that, but he is also an extremely intelligent angel as well: Ken has helped me countless hours with the program to write my book. God sends us who we need. And I surely needed Ken. He has a gift for caring for elderly people. Ken had the ability to create trust and safety in our friendship quicker than anyone I have ever known.

Leeaigh Marie Flynn Combs has helped in book organization, making copies of all texts, imbedding photos, and tying them to the captions, and solving many computer issues. She also carries my middle name, Flynn, and is very special to me. Her systematic and attention to detail has made my book better. And I had the

privilege of working with her for many hours.

Leeaigh is kindhearted, and her greatest ambition is to be a mother.

McCollough Blessing, lives in Tennessee with her husband and two young boys with a third one on the way. She was very thorough and detailed in bringing my script to life. McCullough was careful to grasp my intent to capture the impact in my southern culture even in the difference in our languaging.

Alex Nunez, the son of my friend Marco Nunez, has helped me organize all the chapters, formatting the document, and solved computer problems for me, so I can prepare for publishing. Alex is finishing his Master's in Biology, integrating it to his previous Psychology and behavior field in order to continue his studies. He has been of invaluable help to me, lightened my burden, and dissolved much anxiety about technical details.

Kayo Randolph, my younger brother, and his wife, Martha, were the first patrons to donate over $20,000 toward building the STEM & Vocational Lab. Therefore, it is named in their honor. Kayo and Martha have been supporting my efforts and encouraging me for many years. Kayo and I are the last two of our family of origin. Even though Kayo is younger, he has been a large inspiration in my life. He is joyful, and I have observed how he has always found the opportunities in his life and put them to use. It was a valuable lesson to me. There are opportunities all around us, but we must search them out to improve our lot in life.

Printed in the USA
CPSIA information can be obtained
at www.ICGtesting.com
CBHW041411010824
12550CB00003B/5

9 798218 976125